THROUGH FIRE, SHOT AND SHELL

Soldiers' Stories from the Trenches to the Desert

THROUGH FIRE, SHOT AND SHELL

Soldiers' Stories from the Trenches to the Desert

ROMY WYETH

First published 2018

Copyright © Romy Wyeth 2018

Every effort to identify the author, photographer, artist of copyright holder has been made and, where successful, appropriate permission has been sought and acknowledgements made. If we have included anything for which you are the copyright holder and your permission has not been obtained, we apologise.

The right of Romy Wyeth to be identified as the author of this work has been asserted in accordance with the Copyright, Designs & Patents Act 1988.

All rights reserved. No part of this book may be reproduced, stored in a retrieval system, or transmitted in any form or by any means, electronic, electrostatic, magnetic tape, mechanical, photocopying, recording or otherwise, without the written permission of the copyright holder.

Published under licence by Brown Dog Books and
The Self-Publishing Partnership, 7 Green Park Station, Bath BA1 1JB

www.selfpublishingpartnership.co.uk

ISBN: 978-1-78545-364-9

Cover design by Kevin Rylands
Internal design by Andrew Easton
Front cover photo by Romy Wyeth, Megiddo looking onto the Plain of Jezreel, Israel

Printed and bound by CPI Group (UK) Ltd, Croydon, CR0 4YY

FOREWORD

Through Fire, Shot and Shell is the third book in a trilogy that began with *Over the Hills and Far Away* and continued with *Over the Hills and O'er the Main*. This book of soldiers' stories takes us from the trenches of France and Flanders, to the training camps of Salisbury Plain then onto the Normandy beaches and beyond, to the stifling deserts of the Middle East, to Mesopotamia, Abyssinia, Palestine and Egypt. Finally, to one soldier's baptism of fire on the streets of Northern Ireland, to Berlin during the Cold War and to the inhospitable Falkland Islands.

The search for great stories often leads in unexpected directions, when some seemingly insignificant detail turns into something quite extraordinary. This time, researching Palestine became a detective story, the tale of two remarkable men, allies in wartime and on opposite sides in the final days of the British Mandate. Simultaneously, while looking at the role of the Palestine Police Force, I inadvertently uncovered a little-known episode in the history of the Holy Land during WW II.

For me one of the most difficult tasks with writing is to find a title for a book- it is either blindingly obvious or I am desperately seeking inspiration. I have found past titles from Shakespeare, Churchill and the Bible. It was when watching an old episode of 'Sharpe' that the traditional song 'Over the Hills and Far Away' clicked. 'Over the Hills and O'er the Main' contained several stories relating to the sea so was a natural successor. This time John Tam's verses from 'Sharpe's Company' provided an identity for this collection of military tales.

'Through smoke and fire and shot and shell,
And to the very walls of hell,
But we shall stand and we shall stay
Over the Hills and Far Away'.

As always, I am indebted to the people who have trusted me with their stories. To David Belchamber and Martin Higgins who gave me access to their father's diaries; to Alec Saunt for allowing me to use his comprehensively researched and fascinating history of the BEF; to Peter Butler, Duncan Boyd, John Bosley and David North for sharing their sometimes harrowing military experiences; to David Delius for finding me Lionel Roebuck's written account of D Day and contacting him and his family for permission to use it; and, finally, to Brian Marshall who has once again, and very patiently, rescued indistinct photos from oblivion.

Romy Wyeth
September 2018
Through Fire, Shot and Shell

CONTENTS

Chapter 1	The Contemptible Little Army Alex Saunt	1914 -1918	9
Chapter 2	The Australian Invasion	Salisbury Plain WW 1, 1916	46
Chapter 3	The Long Road Home Douglas Belchamber	Mesopotamia 1918-1919	55
Chapter 4	Mazra'a Internment Camp Michael Higgins	Palestine, 1942	99
Chapter 5	With The 2nd East York's on D Day Lionel Roebuck	1944	176
Chapter 6	Post War National Service Peter Butler	Egypt 1946 -1949	203
Chapter 7	Insurgency in the Holy Land John Bosley	Palestine 1946 -1947	214
Chapter 8	AWOL in the Canal Zone Duncan Boyd	1952	231
Chapter 9	Taking the Queen's Shilling David North	1983 -1989	243

CHAPTER 1

The Contemptible Little Army 1914 -1918
Alex Saunt

The story of the expansion and development of THE BRITISH EXPEDITIONARY FORCE (BEF) 1914-1918 and how the Contemptible Little Army became a huge, effective machine.

BEF AND THE START
The conception: In 1904 King Edward, having decided our pretty frosty relationship with France should be improved, went to Paris with the Queen. As they were driven through the streets their reception was, well rather quiet. But they went to the theatre that evening and afterwards went backstage to meet the cast. There the King exercised his charm, particularly on the young ladies, which strangely enough, was favourably reported. The next day they went to the races which again drew a favourable response. Out of this successful visit the Entente Cordiale was born.

Army staff talks with the French started in 1906 and by 1911 had resulted in a plan, but not a treaty, to send the BEF to the area of Mauburg and Le Cateau to extend the French line westwards should a war with Germany break out.

Its strength and days after mobilisation to arrive were not stated. Previously the War Office had had plans to send a BEF, consisting of six Infantry Divisions and one of Cavalry, to possible trouble spots which included the North West Frontier of India, South Africa and Canada.

Secretary of State Haldane's reform of the Army started in 1908. He chose two military advisors, one of whom was Haig, clearly already a marked man. Haig was very well connected, a cavalryman from the Scottish Whisky family who had been to University which was unusual then for an Army officer.

Haldane reorganised the Army into two distinctive entities: A Regular Element geared to produce the Expeditionary Force and to police the Empire, and a part-time Territorial Force, for Home Defence, to expand and support the Army, and to take the field itself after six months Post Mobilisation Training.

He had a census of horses and motor vehicles taken for requisitioning. 30,000 horses went with the BEF. By 1917 there were 436,000 horses and mules with the BEF, only about 50,000 of these with the cavalry, the vast majority pulling guns or wagons. In August 1914 the Army Service Corps had 507 vehicles, by 1918 the BEF had 22,000 trucks, not counting the tractors for the Heavy Artillery.

THE EXPANSION OF THE BEF

In 1914 the Regular Army after mobilisation numbered 460,000, add the Territorial Force of 240,000, and it could field 700,000 compared to the Germans 4.5 million. They had conscription and further training resulting in an enormous pool of trained men. Their other advantage was that they had only one thing to think about - Continental Warfare, whereas that had been our last consideration, policing the Empire coming first.

On Deployment the BEF had four Infantry Divisions and one of Cavalry, a total of about 100,000 men and 30,000 Horses. In 1917 it would have about 1.7 million men.

An Infantry Division had 18,000 men; 12,000 Infantry in 12 Battalions in three Brigades each of four Battalions. It had 24 machine guns and 76 guns plus Engineers and Medicals. A Pioneer Battalion, which could act as fighting Infantry, would be added, but its Cavalry Squadron and Cyclist Company would soon be withdrawn. Corps would later have a Cyclist Battalion.

A Cavalry Division had 9,000 men, 10,000 horses, 24 machine guns, 24 guns and supporting troops.

These four Infantry Divisions, organised into two Corps, one commanded by Haig, had increased by Christmas 1914 to 12, by the Somme to 53, and later to about 63.

Of these Infantry Divisions:
    13 were Regulars

About 19 from the Territorial Force
30 from the New Armies.

Plus, from the Empire:

Two from India, four from Canada, five from Australia, one from New Zealand, but only a brigade from South Africa, as they were also deployed on their continent. The Indian ones were withdrawn in 1915 and some of the British Divisions were sent to, or brought back at various times from Italy, Gallipoli, Salonika, Palestine, or Mesopotamia.

EMPIRE DIVISIONS

The Official History states in Volume 4, 1918, on page 515 'On the whole the leading of the Canadian and Australian officers and NCOs was superior to that of the British regimental cadres, and no doubt for the reason that they had been selected for their practical experience and power over men and not for theoretical proficiency and general education'.

Elsewhere it is stated 'During 3rd Ypres, the Canadians were not qualitatively 'better' than their Imperial or Australian counterparts except in one crucial respect: they understood that if artillery power defined operational success or failure then it was roads and rail that defined that firepower.'

Australia never had conscription, but Canada and New Zealand almost certainly introduced it in 1918, after immense arguments.

EARLY DAYS

The retreat from Mons to the Marne and the battle there were followed by the Allied Advance to the Aisne and the start of trench warfare there, in which the BEF was involved until early October 1914 when it was transferred by train to Flanders in order to simplify its communications to the Channel Ports.

The BEF was formed into two Armies by the end of 1914, one commanded by Haig, and into 5 Armies for most of the War. Haig took command of the BEF in late 1915 from Sir John French who joked as he left his headquarters in St Omer that his knighthood would be 'Lord Sent Homer!'

The instruction from the War Office to the BEF's Commanders should be stressed, that their chief job was to co-operate with the French. Thus, it was the French who decided where and when the Somme would be fought including zero hour, all against Haig's preference.

THROUGH FIRE, SHOT AND SHELL

The Somme

THE THREE TYPES OF BRITISH INFANTRY DIVISIONS
First The Regulars
On mobilisation about 40% were Reservists. Of these 13 Divisions eight were formed from troops stationed in Britain, and five from Empire Garrisons as soon as Territorials could replace them, then add the 63rd (Royal Naval) Division formed from Royal Marines and surplus sailors, and the Guards Division which was formed in 1915, the same year as the Welsh Guards came into being.

SECONDLY, THE TERRITORIAL FORCE, PART TIME SOLDIERS
Pre-war it had 14 Infantry Divisions and 14 Yeomanry Brigades, but it was under strength and under trained. The Territorial Force men were not liable for foreign service, unless they volunteered, or were volunteered… They were deployed in 1915.

FINALLY, NEW ARMY DIVISIONS

Kitchener, realising that the Army would need massive expansion, decided to raise new Divisions, instead of relying on expanding the Territorial Force. In January 1915 500,000 volunteers had been formed into 30 Divisions. There were immense problems equipping and training them. There were initially no officers, NCOs nor instructors, let alone weapons. But they were deployed before the Somme.

PALS

The PALS Battalions were part of the New Army, the difference between them and the other New Army Battalions was that they were raised, clothed an equipped by corporations of large cities and were composed of men from a particular area or profession. This allowed them to serve with their friends - as examples: The Stockbrokers Battalion became the 10th Royal Fusiliers, and the North Eastern Railway Battalion became the 17th Northumberland Fusiliers. In one Brigade its four Battalions were known as 'The Hull Commercials', 'The Hull Tradesmen', 'The Hull Sportsmen' and for want of a better name 'The Hull T'others.'

The War Office, which could not provide for all the volunteers, was delighted with this arrangement, which contributed 38% of the New Armies.

CONSCRIPTION

Was introduced in January 1916, however, of the 5.7 million men who served in the Army, almost half were volunteers rather than conscripts.

THE WELSH

Lloyd George wished to raise a Welsh Army Corps, but the numbers and Kitchener did not allow this. Instead there was the 38th (Welsh) Division which was shattered at Mametz Wood early in the Somme.

THE IRISH

The question of Home Rule had been causing enormous problems before the war, including the Curragh incident outside Dublin where in March 1914 60 Cavalry officers threatened to resign rather than be employed to coerce Ulster into accepting Home Rule. In Ulster it led to the creation of the Ulster Volunteer force under Edward Carson and in the south to that of the Irish National Volunteers, both arming. It also led to the resignation of the Secretary of State for War, Sir Jack Seely, and the Chief of Imperial General Staff, Sir John French.

When the House of Commons passed the Home Rule Bill in September 1914, suspended to the War's End, Ireland supported our War effort and 3 Irish divisions were formed; the 10th and 16th from the South, and the 36th from Ulster, semi-trained by the UVF (Ulster Volunteer Force) which performed so magnificently on the first day of the Somme. (Scottish Divisions were the 9th, 15th and 51st).

Ireland was excluded from Conscription, although Westminster unsuccessfully tried to introduce it in 1918. Having produced the largest percentage of volunteers in Britain, Belfast had no need of it! The Easter Rising in 1916 in Dublin seems to have had very little adverse effect on the Irish War Effort.

THE DEVELOPMENT OF THE BEF'S ARMS, SERVICES AND HEADQUARTERS

Cavalry

The one Cavalry Division deployed in August 1914 had increased to five by 1916, and was reduced to three in early 1918 when the two Indian ones were sent to Palestine. The British cavalry was better than the German: it had Boer War experience; it was trained to fight dismounted as infantry as well as mounted; it carried the infantry rifle rather than the shorter-range carbine; and it wore khaki uniforms instead of colourful ones and it did not wear funny hats.

However, trenches negated its previous primary roles, reconnaissance and the charge. However, the Cavalry were kept on the Western Front in large numbers due to Haig's fixation on creating a breakthrough for them to exploit, but this never occurred.

However, there were times when they played a vital role:

On at least two in extremis occasions the Cavalry held the line dismounted; one was in October 1914 during 1st Ypres when the Household Cavalry held parts of Messines Ridge and lost heavily, decimating England's aristocracy. And another was in early 1918 during the massive German Offensives when the Cavalry was vital in plugging the gaps in our lines.

In 1918 Brigadier General Jack Seely, a larger than life character, who had been a Member of Parliament and Secretary of State for War until he lost his job as a result of the support he gave the Curragh 'Mutineers', and who had been appointed Commander of the Canadian Cavalry Brigade, was called upon to delay the enemy's advance which was on the point of getting too near to our vital railway centre at Amiens.

Seely had to attack German infantry in Moreuil Wood. He sent some of his force into the wood, mounted for speed, who then fought dismounted. One Squadron was sent around the wood to cut off the Germans. There they rode down the 200 enemy troops they found in the open. This cavalry action may have saved Amiens but the cost was about 50% casualties.

A book was written about Seely's horse, Warrior, how he and Seely went to France in August 1914, survived four years of bombs and bullets, and returned after the war to the area around Mottistone in the south west part of Isle of Wight, where they rode on together until they had a combined age of 100. And interestingly, the MP for Isle of Wight is currently, June 2018, still a Seely.

ROYAL ENGINEERS

In 1914 the Army had 24,000, by 1918 the BEF had 350,000.

Amongst the Royal Engineers many tasks, besides building and demolishing things:

- They would assist the Infantry to consolidate newly won positions.
- They ran the railroads and the inland waterways.
- They supplied the water at the Somme for 300,000 men and 40,000 horses.
- They were responsible for meteorology, surveying and mapping. Their mapping Departments grew from precisely 4 persons to over 4,000.
- They provided all communications above Battalion level.
- They delivered gas by cylinders and projectors.
- Later they did camouflage and searchlights. They could act as Infantry, and they tunnelled.

TUNNELLING

In 1914 we had no capability but by 1917 there were 33 Tunnelling Companies.

Their creation can be credited to a civilian, 'Empire Jack' Sir John Norton-Griffiths, a larger than life entrepreneur, Member of Parliament, Territorial Force Officer, and millionaire businessman. He wrote to the War Office proposing the formation of special Companies of what he called 'Moles'. This was agreed within days and in February 1915 'Clay Kickers' from his company digging sewers under Manchester were enlisted and tunnelling. They hardly had uniforms, couldn't drill, were issued rifles which remained a mystery to them and certainly were not given ammunition. Our miners got the upper hand, being allowed to concentrate on tunnelling and to stay in one area.

Around Ypres the strata was clay and sand with trapped water, on the Somme it was chalk, so different techniques were required. At the Somme each bit had to be gently and quietly eased out. At Ypres mining was quicker but had to be waterproofed.

THE DIFFERENT TYPES OF MINE
Defensive
A lateral gallery with listening posts would be dug just in front of our Front. If enemy mining was detected, a subsurface charge would be blown.

Offensive
Two types, the first to destroy whatever lay above it. The second, a Fougasse, to create a high crater rim to prevent or provide observation.

The tunnellers could also blow covered approaches across no man's land for the Infantry, and dig Russian Saps, i.e. shallow tunnels to forward tunnels for short range weapons. Initially mining was directed at inflicting casualties but later to support our assaults. For example: the Lochnagar Mine was one of 17 blown on the first day of the Somme. In June 1917 at Messines 19 mines were blown.

On the first day of the Somme, a covered approach across no man's land to the right of La Boiselle allowed the small lodgement we had gained, to be maintained, because it could be supplied and strengthened. Otherwise this would be impossible as artillery and machine gun fire was sweeping no man's land.

Six Russian saps were used by the 30th Division on this day on the right of our assault front where we had the most success. In these Stokes mortars added to the bombardment just before Z hour. **Note: Stokes Mortar,** *a smooth-bore muzzle loading weapon for high angles of firing that could fire up to 25 bombs in one minute to a range of 800 yards.*

The scale of the mining was astonishing; in June 1916 when mining was at its height, the Germans on our Front blew 126 and we blew 101. During the Advance in the last hundred days, tunnellers were tasked with checking for mines, delayed action devices and booby traps in dugouts. Tunnels were seldom more than 100 feet down. In clay, they might be driven in 30 feet a day, in chalk 3 feet. They were seldom longer than 1,000 yards.

ARTILLERY

Artillery was the main killer not machine guns. True, that the latter was the main killer during our attacks, but the Artillery killed all the time. Our Artillery massively increased: its manpower from 20,000 to 550,000; its field guns, those that supported the Infantry and Cavalry, rose from 500 to over 5,000; its 'Heavies', that is guns, but mainly howitzers, with calibres from 6" to 15", increased from 24 to over 1,200; and Trench Mortars, well we had none to start with but by the end we had hundreds of light 3", the 6" Newton and the 9.45" Flying Pig.

Types Of Shell
At the start we had shrapnel and high explosive.

Later - Gas
This was first used at 2nd Ypres by the Germans in April 1915. We first deployed it at Loos in September that year where it was discharged through 5,000 awkward heavy cylinders, and later by Livens Projectors, basically a huge and simple mortar, usually dug in dozens as a time. During the Somme, gas would start to be delivered by shell.

On April 22, 1915, German forces shook Allied soldiers along the western front by firing more than 150 tons of lethal chlorine gas against two French colonial divisions at Ypres, Belgium.
This was the first major gas attack by the Germans, and it devastated the Allied line.
Vancouver Corner was the site of the first German gas attack of the war. The gas came rolling across the landscape, first engulfing Algerian troops who, being superstitious and uneducated, believed this was magic. They ran in mass panic, a not unnatural circumstance, but in trying to run away they kept pace with the gas cloud.
The gas being used was chlorine, which has a greenish tinge so was recognisable to those with a degree of knowledge of chemistry or science. The Canadians were witnessing the effect of the gas on the Algerians, being better disciplined and educated, the troops realised that urine has a filtering effect on chlorine (which is why it is used in swimming pools) so they urinated on their handkerchiefs and held them over their noses and mouths thus negating to a degree the gas effects.
At the monument, a very tall column topped with a soldier's head, bowed in prayer and hands resting on the butt of his rifle in the manner used by soldiers at the burial of their comrades.
Around there are bushes especially chosen because they have a shape like a shell burst.

Smoke Shells
Previously delivered by cylinders or projectiles, smoke could also be dispersed, albeit in smaller quantities, by shell which arrived during the Somme. In 1918 Incendiary shells were added to the pick and mix.

Early Problems
First, the Field Artillery was not yet wholly convinced that guns should be hidden, with their fire controlled by forward observers. At Le Cateau in August 1914 this led to some 18 pounder batteries being positioned in view of the enemy. The result was that they were slaughtered and 38 guns lost. Secondly, the 13 and 18 pounders initially had only shrapnel and no high explosive (HE), but this was soon addressed. Finally, there was the Shell Shortage. Charles Repington, the Times Correspondent, reported its adverse effect at the Battle of Aubers Ridge in May 1915, and this contributed to the fall of the Asquith Government.

The Artillery did learn to position their pieces well back and hidden, and this they normally did. However later in the War, mortars and a few field guns might go forward with the Infantry to take on strong points or machine guns with direct fire. This was prevalent during the big advances of the last 100 days.

At the start of our assault our Artillery would be overwhelming, but as the Infantry advanced further this effectiveness deteriorated. This was due to the difficulty of getting the guns forward and to lack of information - where had our Infantry got to and where was their opposition? (Effective Ranges: 18 pounders, 6,500 yards; 4.5" howitzers, 7,000; heavier howitzers, 5,000-15,000).

The Artillery On The Somme
The preparatory 7-day bombardment fired 1.5 million shells, insufficient to deal with the enormous number of targets, often strongly constructed in the chalk. More Heavies had arrived. However, the rush to produce them led to defects: for instance, the 2 x 9.2" Howitzers intended to pummel Thiepval were put out of action by a premature, and the battlefield was littered with duds.

On the Somme our Artillery was becoming overpowering and causing very heavy casualties. John Masefield wrote home 'In an area 13 X 9 miles no single tree was left'. (This is from Warminster to Wilton and from the Nadder north to Shrewton.) The effects of this were, first that the Germans had to send reinforcements from Verdun to the Somme and secondly, they had to give up trench lines because we would destroy them and instead turned to a defence in depth with many lines. These were not lines of trenches. Each 'line' consisted of an outpost zone, a main battle zone and behind that a zone for counter attack forces. Each zone would be 2 to 3,000 yards in depth, with a similar distance between them, and containing strong points, often concreted, much wire, some trenches and individual firing points, often in shell holes.

Creeping Barrage
The Somme also saw the introduction of the Creeping Barrage. This meant our Infantry could win 'the vital race to the parapet,' that is between Germans emerging from their dugouts when our bombardment ceased and setting up their weapons, and our Infantry arriving there. Therefore, - the Infantry would advance just behind the Creeping Barrage, sometimes within 40 yards, as it closed up to and reached the German lines. Beyond it our Artillery would be engaging many areas with a delightful mix of high explosive and shrapnel souped up with a bit of gas.

Prior to the introduction of the Creeping Barrage the main theory of the assault had been 'towards the close of bombardment, shortly before Zero hour, the Artillery would put down an intense barrage on the enemy front trenches. At Z hour, when the Infantry advanced, this barrage would be lifted and dropped on the next trench'.

The delay in introducing the Creeping Barrage was because it was considered too difficult, but the ever-increasing sophistication of our gunnery meant it could now be handled. The creeping barrage could consist of up to seven lines of exploding shells; the nearest lines fired by 18 pounders or 4.5" howitzers and the deeper lines by heavier artillery. The speed of its advance - between 2 and 8 minutes for 100 yards, depending on circumstances and mud in particular.

Deception
Was often used. The 'Chinese Assault' would be where our bombardment would cease, and the Germans, expecting an assault, would man their parapets only to be caught by a renewed barrage.

Counter Battery Fire
Is the enormously important neutralisation of the enemy's artillery, but locating their positions could be difficult. It could be achieved by artillery forward observation officers, a very dangerous job. The final instruction from one battery commander

was; 'and remember, boy, your main job today is to stay alive'.

They might be located by aircraft or by flash spotting, but this became more difficult after the Germans introduced a flash-less propellant and began putting out dummy flashes.

By Sound Ranging

We have L/Cpl Bragg and Cpl Tucker, both eminent physicists to thank for this.

Bragg developed a system with microphones set up in a line over two miles. Eventually 40 lines could be established. By 1917 the system had been perfected, it could filter out unwanted sounds, and locate enemy guns within 50 yards.

Final success in sound Ranging was achieved by Cpl Tucker. He realized that the gun-wave (inaudible to humans) had to be recorded, as opposed to the gun-noise. This was detected by a fine platinum wire with an electrical current flowing through it. A breeze (gun-wave) cooled the wire, decreasing its electrical resistance, thus giving a faint electrical signal. Sound ranging was hopeless during major British Artillery barrages, but ideal at Cambrai when our guns had been silent before the attack. The team would meet every two months when they presented technical papers, posed for photographs and concluded with a binge of heroic magnitude. Sound Ranging had a theoretical maximum effective range of 9,000 yards. Nevertheless, at Vimy Ridge in April 1917 it located a heavy howitzer 11 miles behind the front, at 3rd Ypres it found 190 guns in the first three weeks of the battle and at Cambrai they located all major pieces of German artillery. But it did not work when the wind was blowing towards the German lines.

Also, it could discover the calibre and muzzle velocity of the gun, to indicate when it fired and where its shells fell, to indicate the fall of shot of our shells in relation to the enemy battery, and to calibrate our own field guns.

Other Advances In Gunnery

The instantaneous 106 fuse, introduced in 1916, cut wire more effectively, because its blast went horizontally, whereas the blast of its predecessor, the 101 fuse, had gone more vertically after it had dug itself slightly into the ground.

1917 saw the introduction of **Predicted Fire.** That is take the bearing and distance from the map, feed in other calculations and fire knowing you would hit the target. These other calculations included: frequent 'met' reports with the conditions at various altitudes, how worn the barrel was, and how hot, the characteristics of each batch of shells, and the calibration of each gun. Before that, guns usually had to be pre-registered on their target, which forfeited surprise. Now, with our short duration predicted barrage, the Germans would no longer have sufficient warning of our attack to position their reserves. Now they had to be strong everywhere, and this their manpower situation prevented.

But not until 1917 would Haig have enough artillery to launch one major offensive after another.

The growing power of our artillery is illustrated by a German letter from Messines in June 1917 'All night we lie ready for action with our gas masks on. The wounded and gas cases are carried off in batches. There are many killed by gas. We are quite powerless against the English', and that was before our 19 huge mines had been blown.

Gas

The Germans first used gas in April 1915 and ourselves that September. We first used Chlorine gas, then mixed it with Phosgene, which made it spread better. These only affected the face, i.e. eyes, nose, mouth and lungs. They were rarely fatal and could take 48 hours to take effect. Then in 1917 the Germans introduced Mustard gas, to which we responded in the following year. This caused blisters on skin, not only on the face, eyes, throat or lungs, but also elsewhere like legs. It was therefore the most effective of all gases. Gas was rarely a killer, but it had a huge psychological and nuisance effect. About 5% of our gas casualties were fatal or permanently invalided.

Respirators or masks steadily became more effective although the very notion of trying to fit masks to terrified horses in a muddy wagon line at two o'clock in the morning beggar's belief.

Machine Gun Corps

Despite the Battalion's two machine guns being increased to four in 1915 their advocates argued that they needed centralised control and deployment. This they got when the Machine Gun Corps was formed in October 1915.

During 1916 the Battalion's Vickers were replaced by the Lewis gun and the Machine Gun Corps appeared as Companies, with 16 Vickers, attached to each Brigade. In 1917 it appeared as Battalions, with 64 guns, for each Division. Examples of their deployment: a machine gun company at High Wood on the

Somme gave a sustained barrage for 12 hours onto an area 2000 yards away to prevent counter attacks. At Vimy Ridge in April 1917 the Canadian Corps' attack, on a 4-mile front, had 150 Vickers, grouped in 8-gun Batteries, firing to create a bullet-swept zone 400 yards ahead of the creeping barrage. (Alan Brooke, our CIGS in WW2, was on the staff of their Corps Artillery).

Later there were also a few Motorised Machine Gun Brigades, beefed up with medium mortars, infantry and sometimes armoured cars.

THE INFANTRY
Early in the war it comprised 54% of the BEF, by its end 36%. This reduction was due to the development of other techniques. The manpower shortage in the winter of 1917-18 led to the number of Battalions in a Brigade being reduced from 4 to 3, except in Empire Divisions and the Guards.

DEVELOPMENT OF THE FIREPOWER OF THE BATTALION
In 1914, it only had its rifles plus 2 machine guns, which were increased to 4 in 1915. Hand grenades: In 1914 we started with dangerous home-made devices. But in 1915 the satisfactory Mills bomb appeared. By the end, hand grenades/bombs could be incendiary, smoke or tear gas besides high explosive. Bombs were often used for bombing up trenches, 'throwing bombs over a traverse and then following up with the bayonet or entrenching tool'. They were also used for throwing down dugouts. One often reads of attacks stalling or defence failing because they had run out of bombs.

In 1916 came the rifle grenade, fired from the rifle – range: 60-200 yards. It could be either a Mills bomb or a smaller grenade, and high explosive or phosphorous. It could also be an excellent coloured grenade for indicating the Infantry's position. That same year the Lewis machine gun, light and portable at 28 lbs! came into use. Eventually Battalions had 36, including 2 per platoon.

And Battalions would often have the light 3" Stokes mortar, attached from Brigade.

Development of the light mortar
Two inventors, both called Stokes, one successful.

2" Stokes 'Toffee Apple', divisional medium trench mortar, 60 lbs bomb, 500 yards.

3" Stokes, brigade light trench mortar, initially 400 yards, HE, smoke, incendiary.

4" Stokes, for the Royal Engineer's Special Brigade, gas, HE, smoke or incendiary, range: initially up to 500 yards, later 1,500.

By the war's end, the Battalion could generate a blizzard of fire.

INFANTRY TACTICS

In 1914: short rushes supported by its own rifle fire and machine guns and Artillery, then a charge.

By 1916: The Infantry's primary assault formation was a series of successive linear waves, covered by Artillery. The following year, due to the new German defensive layout in depth, the platoon might advance in a diamond formation, or a line of skirmishers with worms behind. If the Battalion advanced in waves, these might have different roles: the first could consist of fighting platoons, the second of mopping up platoons, followed by support ones and finally by carrying ones. Or, another tactic or formation for the platoon: Manoeuvre and Assault teams:

SCOUTS	+	+	+	+
ASSAULT TEAM	RIFLEMEN		BOMBERS	
FIRE TEAM	RIFLE BOMBERS		LEWIS GUN	
MOPPERS UP		+ + + + + +		

Also, in 1917 at Divisional level, Bite and Hold attacks were perfected. These were attacks with much more limited objectives, therefore, within range of our artillery. The Germans had no answer to them. Their drawback was that whilst they enabled us to break in, the time they took to mount meant we did not have time to break out.

Then in 1918 came the All Arms Attack: with the infantry, artillery, mortars, tanks, machine guns and aircraft all working together. Also, in 1918, the platoon was usually split into two half platoons of 15-20 men each. Each half platoon consisting of a section of Lewis gunners and a mixed section of riflemen and rifle-bombers. The bombing (hand grenade) section having disappeared since almost all persons now carried bombs.

The most successful pre-dawn attack by 4 Divisions at the Somme on the 14 July should be mentioned. This was a novelty and a risky one. Haig doubted it could be done, especially by inexperienced troops, and had to be persuaded. It involved a night approach of over 1,000 yards by 22,000 men of the six assaulting Brigades, in order to form up within 500 yards of the German lines. There, staff officers and markers from Battalions laid out tapes for the troops to form up on. This was screened by Lewis gun detachments 200 or 300 yards further forward occupying shell holes made for the purpose by 6" howitzers. The assault was preceded by only a 5-minute intense bombardment to ensure surprise.

TRENCHES

Initially, on the Aisne in September 1914, we had only short sections of disconnected trench, by that Christmas, a continuous line, then later a maze. By 1918 we were copying the German's defence in depth.

Out on the Aisne there was no barbed wire so we nicked it from farmers' fields. Sandbags, timber, and trench periscopes were unavailable, and picks and shovels were worth their weight in gold.

When trench warfare started there was such an insatiable demand for trench stores that inventors, some eccentric or mad, rushed to meet it, often with downright dangerous devices, and so did London stores. The Army and Navy Stores had a Weapons Department which supplied Siegfried Sassoon with a pistol and wire cutters, and Gamages advertised their patent trench catapult.

The standard routine was 4 days in the Front Line. Then 4 in the Support Trenches, followed by 4 in Reserve Trenches. But when under extreme pressure, weeks would be spent in the line.

ROYAL FLYING CORPS

The Royal Flying Corps (RFC) was established in 1912. In 1914 the Royal Naval Air Service separated. In 1918 both were incorporated into the Royal Air Force under Major General Trenchard. The RFC went to war with 63 aircraft. By the end it had 1,700. They also operated Observation or Kite Balloons. At up to 4,000 feet these were located about three miles behind the front. They communicated by telephone cable. Their two-man crew had parachutes, whereas the aircraft crews did not; parachutes were too bulky and might encourage them to abandon their machines too early.

Its Roles

Reconnaissance was possibly the RFC's primary role. It was aircraft that spotted the German Schlieffen Plan advance on Mons and later the gaps between their armies approaching the Marne that persuaded Joffre, the French commander, to cease retreating and take the offensive.

They also spotted for the artillery, but how to get sightings to the ground?

At first, a note would be dropped, or they could report by morse with a lamp. In 1915 a wireless was installed, but it was only Morse and one way, air to ground. Not until late 1917 were planes equipped with two-way voice radio.

Aerial Photography

Was another role. At first the observer leant over the side to take his picture. Later a mounted camera was installed. By mid-1915 photographic plates, filmed at 16,000' would cover some 2 to 3 miles in sharp detail and take 18 successive photos, on which most operational planning would be based. By the war's end there were 5,000 photographic interpreters.

Eventually aircraft supported infantry attacks by machine gunning and bombing, dropping smoke bombs and resupplies, and by reporting their progress. Initially the aircraft were unarmed unless the crew took up a rifle or pistol. This gave way to machine guns firing through the propeller. In 1917 bombing of rear areas became common. The RFC usually had air superiority except during major German efforts and when they introduced new aircraft.

TANKS

Tanks were the long-sought answer to the dreadful trinity of wire, trench and machine gun. This wire could consist of three belts each over 30 yards thick. Tanks were armed with a mixture of 6 pounder guns and machine guns. Their maximum speed over perfect ground was 4 mph, their radius of action 12 miles, they bogged down very easily and were mechanically unreliable. Their 9-man crew suffered from heat and fumes and wore masks as protection from the metal splinters blown off the interior by rifle or machine gun fire.

Our tanks first saw action during the Somme, 49 were deployed, of which only 36 even made it to the start line, 14 later ditched or broke down, but the remainder caused panic and helped the infantry enormously.

In 1917 at 3rd Ypres, Passchendaele, the ground was usually too soft for them but on one occasion 9 tanks advanced up a single road and overcame the garrisons of 5 huge blockhouses. At Cambrai in late 1917 470 tanks were deployed, some being supply tanks carrying resupplies, infantry, mortars, and wirelesses to keep higher command informed.

The Whippet, a lighter, faster, at 8 mph, tank appeared in 1917. We produced 2,600 tanks. The Germans produced 100 A7Vs, all except 20 being used as supply vehicles. We placed too much emphasis on firing the 6 pounders while on the move. Ultimately the tank of 1916-18 was considerably less potent in practice than its propagandists would like us to believe. In 1918 there were 16 battalions, each with 36 tanks, of fighting tanks, 1 of armoured cars, 2 of gun-carrying tanks, and 5 of supply tanks.

Tank Tactics
They would assemble behind our lines and be guided forward at night at the last minute with their noise being drowned by artillery or aircraft. Tanks would usually proceed the infantry, they worked in sections of three or four. One tactic was, having mashed any wire, they would swing parallel to the trench and shoot it up before continuing.

Defence Against The Tank
Mainly the field gun, but also rifles and machine guns with armour piercing rounds, or bundles of grenades, and occasionally mines. At Cambrai, the Germans rushed up lorry borne ack ack guns and the tanks suffered appalling casualties.

HEADQUARTERS AND GENERALS
Brigade and Divisional HQs expanded enormously during the war. Anthony Eden in 1918 at the age of 21 was the youngest Brigade Major in the BEF.

Next up was Corps HQ. This level of command was new to the BEF. To start with the BEF had 2 Corps and 19 by the end, each usually containing 2 to 4 Divisions.

The main thing about Army HQs was that they grew to structures with powerful assets, particularly artillery, which they could shift about to support the main effort, some artillery having been withdrawn from Divisions.

Finally, the BEF's General HQ, (GHQ). This did not exist before the war except on exercises. In the scorching heat of August 1914, the Chief of its General

Staff, General Murray, was discovered worried, not by the situation displayed by the enormous maps spread out on the floor of his hotel room, but by the fact that chambermaids kept coming into the room and he only had his pants on. But GHQ grew like Topsy, to 3,000 by the end.

Its main Chief of Staff, Kiggell, was too loyal to stand up to Haig, and was replaced after 3rd Ypres by Lawrence, an ex-Boer war major, who had left the Army and made a fortune in business, to which he could return and therefore had more freedom to question Haig's judgements. He was a 'dug out' and one of the successful minority. He had been a Brigade and then a Divisional commander in Gallipoli and with the BEF.

But in the British Army only Regulars commanded Divisions or higher, unlike the Australians or Canadians, who of course only had very few Regulars in peacetime. Monash, who had been a civilian engineer and part-time soldier, rose to command the Australian Corps, and the huge profane Currie, who had had questionable business practices as a civilian when in the Militia, came to command the Canadian Corps.

BACKGROUND TO ARMY COMMANDERS
Rawlinson, Plumer: **Infantry**
Horne: **Gunner**
Gough, Allenby, Byng, Birdwood, (Haig): **Cavalry**

CASUALTIES AMONGST GENERALS AND STAFF OFFICERS

Sometimes headquarters were in chateaus, but sometimes in a cold damp dugout or damaged barns. Of the about 1,200 generals who served in the BEF, more than 200 were wounded and no less than 58 killed. Many were 'degummed' or stellenbosched, i.e. dismissed, sent home. By the end of 1914, Division and Brigade staff officers were instructed not to go forward, as 36% of them had already become casualties, and their experience was just too valuable to lose.

The expression 'Lions led by Donkeys' deserves some explanation. The enormous expansion of the BEF led to it becoming a massive deskilled organisation, that is until the Somme, which lasted four months, where there was much brutal on the job learning.

For instance, at Loos, in September 1915, in the two New Army Divisions that attacked disastrously on the 2nd day, only 1 of the 2 Division Commanders was a Regular, similarly only 2 of the 6 Brigade Commanders, and only 1 of the 26

Battalion Commanders. The rest were 'dug outs', dug out of retirement, who should instead have been sitting comfortably at home, and only 30 of all the 26 Battalions' officers were Regulars, the rest being wartime volunteers. The same would have applied to the Divisional and Brigade staffs.

However, a few dug outs were excellent. Besides Lawrence, another was Sir Bryan Mahon, a retired cavalry general, who was chosen to command the 10th Irish Division, who had a number of mild eccentricities which won him the affection of his troops, who smoked incessantly, spoke to almost everyone he met and who sat his horse like a subaltern.

TALES ABOUT GENERALS

Allenby, Commander of the 3rd Army, a cavalryman with a foul temper, when he left his HQ the staff would send out a warning message: BBL – bloody bull loose.

Birdwood, another British Cavalry General, who commanded the ANZACs in Gallipoli, and the Australian Corps in France, endeared himself to his troops by his very relaxed sense of dress. One day he was walking amongst them and was not recognised by an Aussi, who was hauled over the coals for not saluting his General Birdwood. His reply was something like 'Sorry, I didn't recognise him. Why doesn't he have feathers sticking out of his tail like any decent bird would'.

Then there was a Corps Commander's attempt to be well known within his command. Hunter-Weston, known as Hunter-Bunter, decided to wish troops departing on a leave train a Merry Christmas. An aide would open the carriage door and the general would intone "I am Lieutenant General Sir Aylmer Hunter-Weston, Member of Parliament, your Corps Commander and I wish you a Merry Christmas". From the smoky fug of the interior came the reply "and I am the Prince of Wales and I wish you'd shut the bloody door".

General Shute was the unpopular commander of the 63rd (Royal Naval) Division. He was a stickler for convention and had difficulty with Naval traditions and appears to have had an obsession regarding latrines. His critical inspections of the trenches were very badly received within the division. A.P Herbert who was then a Sub-Lieutenant in Shute's Division, and later a novelist and Member of Parliament, wrote the following poem.

The General inspecting the trenches
Exclaimed with a horrified shout,

'I refuse to command a Division
Which leaves its excreta about.'

But nobody took any notice,
No one was prepared to refute,
That the presence of shit was congenial
Compared to the presence of Shute.

And certain responsible critics
Made haste to apply to his words,
Observing that his staff advisors
Consisted entirely of turds.

For shit may be shot at odd corners
And paper supplied there to suit,
But shit would be shot without mourners
If somebody shot that shit Shute.

INTELLIGENCE

GHQ had six Intelligence staff officers in 1914. In 1918 it had 23. Charteris was its head from January 1916 to January 1918 and is generally considered to have been too optimistic, then Lawrence briefly, Cox, Butler and Clive. Dedicated **Intelligence Corps** staff were added, slowly and unevenly, from 1915 onwards, and downwards through Army and Corps HQs and then Divisions and Brigades, and even to some Battalions.

The Intelligence Corps was formed in 1914, before the war. These personnel would often work in tandem with dedicated Intelligence staff officers. The Corps was augmented by civilian assistants: military experience optional, drawn from all walks of civilian life, German/French essential, brains too. They were mainly interested in the size, location, intentions, morale and doctrine of German Army opposing BEF.

SOURCES

Frontline – observation.
Prisoner/deserter interrogation - the most productive. A deserter in Holland

provided the holy grail of the German Field Post Office Directory for which he was paid £100.

Debris: letters, pay books, papers. Dedicated 'searchers', established in 1916, would examine corpses, captured HQs and communication sites.

RFC spotting.

RFC aerial photographs.

Flash Spotting and Sound Ranging.

Signals intelligence from telephones and wireless, including the breaking of codes.

Spies

In 1909 the Secret Service Bureau was formed. It mainly worked in Belgium. After the German Invasion of Belgium, it usually reported via Holland and England. In October 1914 GHQ also became involved in running espionage systems in Belgium. As native locals near the frontline could not be bribed, Belgian refugees in England were employed to start with. Other methods tried included the insertion, by aircraft or parachute, of agents with pigeons, but this was rare and problematic.

Intelligence from Holland or Belgium took time to reach GHQ. Intelligence provided by agents on troop train movement and German rest areas in the rear were very important in enabling GHQ to build up a very accurate German Order of Battle.

COMMUNICATIONS

This was the responsibility of the Royal Engineers Signal Service, that is from Battalion upwards. Our ability, or more often inability to communicate, seriously affected operations.

In 1914: A Battalion's signallers were equipped with differently coloured flags, heliographs, and signalling lamps and telescopes. These were soon left by the wayside during the Retreat from Mons. At the higher level the BEF was going to rely on land-line telegraph, which during the rapid Retreat from Mons was impractical. Instead they had to rely on the French telephone network, despatch riders, requisitioned vehicles and the horse.

In 1915 with trench warfare, military land line telephones took over. Although the supply vastly increased it could never keep up with demand, and so kleptomania became a confirmed habit and Willie Bragg's specialised lines to his microphones were frequently pillaged.

In 1916 a standardised grid layout of lines was adopted, whereby each Division would have a centralised cable running from front to rear with side branches at the level of batteries, Brigades, other Divisions and Heavy Artillery HQs. If the front line advanced, new side branches could be added.

Problems With This System
It did pin down HQs. Cables strung up on poles or fixed to the sides of trenches were too vulnerable. Therefore, they had to be buried, manually, not less than 6' to protect them from artillery fire. 13,000 miles of it was used for the battle of Cambrai alone.

It was vulnerable to phone-tapping. The answer to which was, besides voice security, to double-check the insulation of cables against earthing and not to use this system within a mile of German trenches. Therefore, one of the alternative systems, the Fuller Phone, which transmitted its signals through the earth and which was more secure, was used forward of Brigade.

During our attacks it was vital to know to where the infantry had got. Imagine the difficulties: obscuring smoke and dust and sometimes a featureless waste of a landscape. Signal cables laid forward were usually cut by shellfire or our movements. Runners took time and often did not get through and as precautions against being hit, had coloured braid on both arms for identification and always carried the message in the top left pocket to aid retrieval. Waving flags was a bit dodgy. Also used were lamps, flares, coloured rockets and shiny disks on the backs of the infantrymen, and last but certainly not least, pigeons. Our emphasis on their use can be judged by the fact that during our retreat in March 1918 40 pigeon lofts were captured. There was one unfortunate brigadier who was desperately anxious to know how his battalions' attack were faring and was waiting tensely for a news-bearing pigeon. Eventually one arrived and the message was hurriedly taken from its leg and rushed to the waiting Brigadier, who read 'I am fed up with carrying this bloody bird around France'.

There was therefore usually a delay in the reporting of accurate information to the higher commands from the advancing infantry, from which all belligerents suffered, which meant that opportunities arising from fleeting opportunities could not be taken, and many disasters could not be prevented.

Wirelesses
In 1915 heavy, cumbersome and unreliable wireless sets were confined to linking GHQ with Corps. By 1917 wirelesses were appearing, but they were very bulky, weighed 100 lbs and were short ranged, 7,000 yards. They were sometimes placed in Signals Tanks to report back on the Infantry's progress.

ROYAL ARMY MEDICAL CORPS
Only three people have won the VC twice. The first was a Captain Upham of the New Zealand Infantry who won his in WW2 in Crete and at Alamein.

The other two were WW1 RAMC officers:

The better known of these is Noel Chavasse, the medical officer of the Liverpool Scottish, who won his first on the Somme and his second, posthumously, at the 3rd Ypres, besides an MC in 1915. The other was Arthur Martin-Leake with his first VC earned in the Boer War.

Captain Noel Godfrey Chavasse 1884-1917 was a doctor with the RAMC. He was awarded the Military Cross for gallantry June 1915 Hooge Belgium and the Victoria Cross for tending and rescuing men under heavy fire while wounded with shell splinters in August 1916. He was responsible for saving the lives of twenty wounded men. His second Victoria Cross was awarded posthumously when, despite being seriously wounded, he refused to leave his post, remaining on the battlefield for two days in September 1917. He died of his wounds and is buried in Brandhoek New Commonwealth War Grave Cemetery in Vlamertinge.

The most decorated other rank in the BEF was L/Cpl Bill Coltman, a nonconformist stretcher bearer in a North Staffordshire Battalion. He was awarded a VC, two Distinguish Conduct Medals, the next best thing, and two Military Medals. Somehow, he survived and returned to gardening, which he probably found rather quiet.

The Royal Army Medical Corps expanded from 20,000 to 144,000. Its organisation worked on the principle of going forward to collect the wounded. At the first stage was the Regimental Aid Post (RAP) with Battalions. Its stretcher bearers would collect the wounded and the Regimental Medical Officer and his 1 or 2 RAMC assistants would do their best for them.

Next, the Brigade's Field Ambulance provided three Dressing Stations, some within a couple of miles of the Front. Their stretcher bearers would go forward to collect the wounded from the RAP and prepare them for their removal to the Casualty Clearing Station, the CCS. Normally there would be one of these per Division, but this would be much increased before major offensives, like at 3rd Ypres where the additional ones were given names such as Bandaghem, Mendighem and Dozinghem.

The CCS would collect the wounded via tramways, light railways, horse or later motor ambulances. It was soon realised that surgical intervention should be available as soon as possible, in particular for wound excision to control Tetanus and Gas Gangrene. So, this was brought forward to the CCS from the Base Hospitals.

Some CCS specialised in head or chest cases, the abdomen, or fractured thighs, or gas. A CCS could handle 1,000 wounded at a time and were often grouped together and seldom less than 7 miles from the Front, usually situated near railway sidings or roads, in tents or buildings.

From the CCS wounded would go by train or barge to the Base Hospitals. During the Somme an average of 240 ambulance trains a week ran, each taking about 350 casualties. By then these were specialised trains, of which the BEF had about 40 by 1918. Barges were used when jolting had to be avoided and time was not of the essence.

Base hospitals were often near the coast. From them certain cases would be evacuated to England, to Blighty, a Hindustani word for home, on special hospital ships. It is interesting to note that the ship taking King George to England after he had had a bad fall, was mined on her next voyage.

In 1917 there were 300,000 hospital beds in Britain. One of the medical advances was the use of X rays which went further forward as the war progressed.

Casualties
An analysis of causes of wounds for one day during the 3rd Ypres shows 36% high explosive, 27% bullet, 20% shrapnel, 14% uncertain, 1.94% gas, 0.7% grenade and 0.16% bayonet.

Some 12% of the British Army's ordinary soldiers were killed during the War, compared with 17% of its officers. Eton alone lost more than 1,000 former pupils - 20% of those who served. UK wartime Prime Minister Herbert Asquith lost a son, while future Prime Minister Andrew Bonar Law lost two. Anthony Eden lost two brothers, another brother of his was terribly wounded, and an uncle was captured.

Venereal Disease: 400,000 cases were treated during WW1. VD was regarded as a misdemeanour as it was a preventable disease. Treatment took a month or more. Initially men had been repatriated to England for treatment but as the scale of the casualties rose, orders were given that all cases were to be treated in France until the soldiers were fit to return to their units.

Women
To finish this medical section without mentioning women would be utterly wrong. Many thousands served in France with Queen Alexandra's Imperial Military Nursing Service, or with other organisations such as the Red Cross, besides the many who assisted in Voluntary Aid Detachments (VAD), usually as care assistants, or in Motor Ambulance Convoys as drivers. In 1917 the Women's Army Auxiliary Corps was formed and 9,000 served in France engaged in clerical, mechanical, or cookery work.

CHAPLAINS
63 Chaplains went with the BEF in August 1914. By the end about 1,700 had served, of whom 176 were killed. Two won the VC with the BEF, the most famous, possibly, being the Revd Hardy, Church of England. Being over 50 and in poor health he had to pester the Authorities to accept him. Initially employed in the base areas, he managed in December 1916 to get himself appointed chaplain to a Lincolnshire Battalion. There is a poignant photograph of him receiving the VC from the King in France, to add to his DSO and MC, all earned within 11 months, and watched by his daughter in the VAD. He was killed soon after.

ARMY VETERINARY CORPS (ROYAL ON 27.11.18)
Animals: horses, mules, canaries, mice, pigeons and dogs. Canaries and mice helped the tunnellers by detecting if poisonous fumes were present underground. Pigeons carried messages, and dogs too occasionally, although the BEF used them less than the Germans.

Mules were more resistant to conditions and required less fodder than horses. The average wastage of horses and mules was 2% per week.

Mobile Veterinary Sections were with each Cavalry Brigade and Infantry Division.

There were also Veterinary Evacuation Stations. By 1918 there were 25 Veterinary hospitals each capable of looking after 2,000 horses or mules; all helped by the RSPCA. At the end of the War most horses were sold to local dealers, only a few lucky ones were brought home. In Palestine the Australian Light Horse, when they were told their horses would not be going home with them, decided to have a monumental last day of races and then shot them all.

LOGISTICS
The Army's pre-war logistics relied on the well proven but ad hoc system based on pragmatic staff officers providing a system suited to wherever they might find themselves. This made sense considering the wide range of places to which they might be deployed. But it certainly did not prepare the Army for a war of this scale, intensity and duration.

Two things did not help in August 1914: first, the Army's logistics organisation existed on paper only until mobilisation. Secondly, the Retreat from Mons was not down its line of communications which ran south west to Le Havre, instead it was south. Imagine being in charge of taking supplies to the retreating BEF; it was a new job, your team is new as well, you don't know where the BEF is because of poor communications, you don't speak French and their maps leave much to the imagination.

In 1914 and 1915 everything was in short supply and hugely increased orders had been placed with factories. New ones were being constructed, and those abroad were being given whopping orders, but they all took time to deliver.

The Ministry of Munitions, under Lloyd George, created in the spring of 1915, soon included Trench Warfare and Munitions Invention Departments, and just pre-war there had been tentative steps towards state-sponsored laboratories. Sir John

French set up the GHQ Invention Committee in early 1915.

The pre-war annual production of boots was 250,000, By December 1914 an order was placed for 7.8 million.

Come the Somme in 1916 and this ad hoc system was collapsing. It just could not cope with the enormous amount of material now being sent to the much-increased BEF.

Civilian expertise was the answer. Sir Eric Geddes, who had been the general manager of the North Eastern Railways and who had advised the War Office pre-war, was appointed Director-General of Transportation for the BEF. He appointed civilian experts to run the docks, railways, inland waterways, light railways and roads:

Docks

The supply problem was now in France, not in the factories. So much stuff was arriving on ships that it could not be handled. So, Geddes arranged with the French for more dock space to be under our control and for cargoes to be loaded in England in such a way that they could be unloaded straight on to trains, rather than via warehouses.

Railways

Two problems were solved. First, control of the railways in our sector was acquired from the French, and secondly, more railways, engines and rolling stock were obtained. It had been estimated early in 1917 that to maintain simultaneous attacks by three armies, whilst merely holding the rest of the front, 200 trains per day to all railheads would be required, but the number achieved never exceeded 160. By the War's end 4,500 miles of track would be laid, and the BEF would have 1,500 engines and 54,000 wagons.

Inland Waterways

Further use was made of them. By the end of 1916 564 vessels, all operated by the Royal Engineers, were in use.

Light Railways

These ran forward from the main railheads. Better and more extensive use began to be made of them. Often, they would run directly to heavy artillery positions to simplify ammunition supply. These, Decauville, light railways should not be confused with tramways, which ran even further forward, and on which ran small 'carts,' usually pulled by men or horses.

Roads

The French rural roads were not built to take heavy army traffic and collapsed. Under Geddes' influence more and stronger roads were laid. This was just as well as on the Somme Front, one of our two armies there, the 4th, on a front of less than 10 miles, had nearly 5,000 lorries, which together with enemy shelling and the moving forward of our heavy artillery had been making an awful mess of them.

With Logistics - No Labour, No Battle

Early on, lack of unskilled labour in the rear areas caused great difficulties. Local personnel were unavailable, having been conscripted. The organisation of labour was fragmented and rather inefficient until the BEF formed a Directorate of Labour in December 1916, which during 1917 was expanded.

Besides British labour and POWs, 145,000 foreign labourers were employed, of whom the Chinese Labour Corps is possibly the best known and of whom the BEF eventually employed 95,000 and the French 40,000.

There was a very wide variety of jobs for the labour, working in French quarries for example. There were salvage companies and tank track repair depots. They worked on the roads and railways and in the docks, and 20,000 Canadian lumbermen were employed in French and British forests by 1918. The BEF's labour corps had about 400,000 in 1918.

It may be said that Geddes' reforms and the proper organisation of labour staved off a potential collapse of the logistics and developed a system that would enable Haig to plan and operate without fear of supply restrictions for the rest of the War.

THE THREE MAJOR EVENTS AFFECTING THE BEF IN 1918

1ST THE MASSIVE GERMAN ATTACKS:
This was their last chance to force the Allies to the peace table by defeating the English, before the Americans arrived in strength. It was possible because the Russian Revolution of 1917 meant Germany could send massive reinforcements to the

Western Front from the east, where roughly one third of their army had been usually deployed.

The Main Attacks
21 MARCH Against the BEF's right wing, mainly the 5th Army, but also the 3rd, next to it, on a 50-mile Front.
9 APRIL In FLANDERS, against us.
MAY-JULY Three or so major attacks against the French sector to the south east of the BEF.

In APRIL 5 of our Divisions had been sent to 'quiet' parts of the French sector to recover and to relieve French Divisions so they could be put into reserve. In fact, they took the full force of the German assault on Chemin des Dames on 27 May.

Because of its gallant stand in the Bois des Buttes the 2nd Battalion, Devonshire's was awarded the Croix de Guerre. All of these attacks – to cause the Allies to use up or mis-deploy their reserves - were in preparation for the killer blow which was, again, to be in Flanders against us. This was where we had little ground to yield before all our base establishments would be within range of the German artillery. Unfortunately for the Germans their preparatory attacks and the French counter attacks in July meant they had insufficient divisions left to mount it.

A Brief Explanation
The causes of the BEF having such a bad time in the German attack of 21 March, which continued for about 2 weeks, were:

German Advantages
- Great superiority, 44 Divisions to 11, a very violent and excellent bombardment.
- Plenty of time over the winter for training and preparation.
- Fog hid their attack.

English Disadvantages
- Morale at its lowest and tired. The onset of disillusionment and weariness.
- Reorganisation of Infantry Brigades: The War Office named 141 Battalions which were to be scrapped or merged, and these were spread unevenly between our Brigades. This caused immense re-organisational and morale difficulties.

Haig was forced to take over more of the line from the French.
- The Allies were forced to support Italy after Caporetto, where Rommel made his name. Russia, Italy and France had cracked in 1917. But on the other hand, Austria-Hungary had put out peace feelers.
- There was insufficient time and manpower to improve unprepared French positions, and little time for training in the new defence system; we were now copying the German Defence in Depth. In fact, the BEF was inexperienced in defence, having been on the attack for most of the war.
- General Gough's 5th Army, on our right flank, was the most thinly held, because it was the least important part of the BEF's Front, being furthest from the Channel Ports, and this army bore the brunt of the German assault.
- Finally, there was the manpower shortage. This was mainly due to the opinion and policies of Lloyd George, the Prime Minister. (He had tried in February 1917 to place Haig and the BEF under French control, because he thought they were militarily more professional.)

This manpower shortage and the dire situation resulting from the German attack on 21 March forced the War Cabinet, within days, to decide what reinforcements could and should be sent to the BEF. The result was an immediate and steady increase that led, by the end of August, to over a half a million increase in the BEF'S strength.

Various sources: those under 19 but over 18 and a half could now be sent to the BEF; the upper age limit for Conscription was raised from 41 to 50 for 'light jobs', and to 55 for some special cases, i.e. doctors; the number of exemptions granted from Conscription was reduced; the number of battle-ready troops in England and those who had been sent to work in factories and mines were also culled; all men under 25 in the Civil Service were conscripted; and some troops were sent to the BEF from Salonika, Italy and Palestine.

THE 2ND MAJOR EVENT WAS THAT FOCH, THE FRENCH COMMANDER-IN-CHIEF, WAS MADE SUPREME ALLIED COMMANDER, THE DECIDING AUTHORITY ON ALLIED POLICY

On 26 March Foch was given authority to co-ordinate British and French forces. On 3 April he was given strengthened powers - the strategic direction of military operations (of British, French and US forces, of Italian Forces on 2 May, and later of the Belgians). We were happy with this, because the situation was so serious. The main result was a much more flexible use of reserves: French reserves sent to support us and vice versa.

THE 3RD AND LAST MAJOR EVENT OF 1918 - THE PURSUIT OF THE LAST 100 DAYS:
Towards the end of July Foch firmed up plans for the Allies to take the offensive since they now had the initiative and the moral and numerical superiority, the Germans having shot their bolt. Thus, the 8 August became one of the decisive days of the war, with the BEF's All Arms Offensive, with a French Army under our 4th Army's command, driving the enemy clear of Amiens. It was the start of the last 100 days pursuit of the Germans.

German defence during this pursuit was usually conducted by scattered machine guns and individual field guns (which got our tanks); their Infantry by now being fairly unreliable. The Germans also fortified villages and farms. The BEF's pursuit was usually conducted by divisional advance guards supported by artillery, machine guns, cavalry, armoured cars and if weather permitted, aircraft.

Bad and demolished roads, booby traps, delayed action explosive devices, and the difficulty in bringing forward railways, slowed the advance.

TO CONCLUDE
By 1918 the BEF was incomparably more skilled and technological than in 1914. Its casualties, though horrendous, were matched by those of the other belligerents. Nevertheless, the BEF stuck to its guns through thick and thin, and never gave up or mutinied, unlike some of the other armies. Its performance is worthy of our immense admiration.

In Flanders fields the poppies blow
Between the crosses, row on row,
That mark our place; and in the sky
The larks, still bravely singing, fly
Scarce heard amid the guns below.

We are the dead. Short days ago
We lived, felt dawn, saw sunset glow,
Loved and were loved, and now we lie

In Flanders fields.

Take up our quarrel with the foe:
To you from failing hands we throw
The torch; be yours to hold it high.
If ye break faith with us who die
We shall not sleep, though poppies grow
In Flanders fields.

John McCrae, May 1915
Canadian surgeon with the BEF who died of pneumonia 1918

VARIOUS NOTES AND OPINIONS

EASTERN FRONT
Treaty of Brest-Litovsk (between Germany and the Bolsheviks in March 1918: was draconian, 25% of Russian territory, 45% of its population, and 75% coal and iron acquired by Germany.

The difference between the Western and Eastern Fronts: the relationship between mass, firepower and space.

All men over 35 left in the east by Germany, those in the west transferred to the east, in preparation for their big efforts in the spring of 1918.

German success in Russia, Serbia and Rumania led to some increase in demands on her military in 1918.

Romania joined Allies in the summer of 1916 and was quickly defeated.

THE DEATH PENALTY
346 were shot by the British Army including 37 for murder and 25 Canadians (Aussies no death penalty, unless for desertion and if the Governor General approved) out of 3,080 who were given the death penalty. 4 types of court martial: regimental, district, general or field general, and only the last was used on active service and only it could impose the death penalty which had to be ratified by the C-in-C, Haig, who would confirm or commute to a prison sentence. Offences for death sentence: desertion, cowardice, sleeping at post, striking a superior officer.......

PAY 1914:	PRIVATE	1 SHILLING PER DAY
	Sergeant	2s 4d
	Lieutenant	6s.
1917:	Private	1s 3d per day

There were Trade and Proficiency payments and an 'Overseas' allowance (1d) as well as supplements for families. Pensions: total disability £1, 13s per week, smaller percentages for lesser disability.

LEAVE

Initially for one week every 15 months, with extra days for those going further. Certainly, senior officers got home more frequently than privates. At some time, this was raised to 10 days. From 1.11.17 raised to 14 days. July 1917 50,000 were on leave any one time. January 1918 this was 80,000.

OFFICER TRAINING

Many New Army officers were granted commissions without any officer training, especially if they had been to a public school. They had to learn on the job. Early on, if they had been in an Officer Training Unit (OTU), either at university, Inns of Court, or a public or grammar school, this would get them a temporary commission.

In 1915 Young Officer Companies were established, and in 1916 Officer Cadet Battalions were formed, where the potential officer would spend 4 months. Sandhurst and Woolwich were expanded, probably for those who had opted for a Regular Commission. The Staff College also, in the early days, trained new officers, as well as staff officers.

MISCELLANEOUS

Special Reserve: 6 months in barracks, 7 years on the Reserve with one month's camp per year.

The Germans were on the defensive for most of the War except for 4 major exceptions - August 1914, April 1915 (2nd Ypres), Verdun February – November 1916 and the Offensives of 1918.

Artillery formation: 'widely extended lines of sections in files'.

'A massively expanded army, particularly one that had been improvised as rapidly and chaotically as the BEF, surely needed guidance, and it got it, if only too much, varied and sometimes contradictorily.'

The best book on the BEF? Tommy *by the late Richard Holmes who latterly lived in Kilmington.*

GERMANS OR BRITS - WHO HAD THE BETTER EQUIPMENT OR METHODS?

It often varied during the war.

Infantry - They were probably usually better trained, until 1917 – 1918.

Machine guns - They had an early lead, having started with dedicated companies and battalions. Unsure about later.

Artillery - They had a preponderance to start with. Our gunners probably later became the more skilled and certainly the more numerous.

Engineers - Certainly with tunnelling ours were better.

Generals and staff - After ours had learnt the art of World War, ours were probably as good as, if not better than theirs.

Communications - Unknown. Germans used wirelesses more than us, possibly because they were short of copper, because of the Blockade of Germany, for telephone/telegraph lines.

Aircraft - We usually had control of the skies.

Tanks - We had superiority. The Germans, usually being on the defensive, possibly thought they had less need for them.

Medical - Don't know, but they were sometimes short of medical supplies because of the blockade.

Logistics - Our logistical support was probably better, if only because we could get labour and supplies from the rest of the world and they could not.

Alex Saunt
Was commissioned into the Somerset Light Infantry and later served in various Light Infantry battalions, in 22 SAS for one tour, where he says he was about Number 8 in their batting order, and on the staff, in appointments mainly in the SAS/Special Forces' sphere. He was awarded the MBE for Gallantry after a tour as a company commander in the Ardoyne in Belfast in 1972 where he says that his main claim to fame was that of the five killed and 20 seriously wounded suffered by his battalion, his company suffered only one seriously wounded. He retired after 35 years' service and having qualified as an Associate of the Chartered Institute of Secretaries, and then spent 21 years in the Care Home business with his wife, a Registered Nurse and Health Visitor. They have now lived in Corton, near Warminster, for 21 years, their two daughters having flown the nest long ago.

CHAPTER 2

The Australian Invasion
Salisbury Plain WW 1   1916

Australia became an independent country in 1901 having been settled by Britain in the late 18th Century. At the outbreak of World War 1 it was just one of the countries of the British Empire and its former colonies to begin preparations to send troops into battle. For young men around the world this war began as a great adventure, it was expected to be over quickly and there was an enthusiasm to get into the fray before it was all over. Australia raised a force in September 1914 to seize German territory in the Pacific while at the same time raising the First Australian Imperial Force (AIF) to be sent into conflict overseas. Young men came forward in great numbers, 20,000 men volunteered to fight. In Australia only sons were not allowed to join up unless both mother and father signed letters of consent, so adventurous young men sometimes enlisted under assumed names.

In November 1914 the AIF sailed to Egypt to protect the Suez Canal. The planned amphibious landings in Gallipoli to secure the Dardanelles saw the New Zealand forces uniting with the Australian into the Australian and New Zealand Army Corps (ANZAC) to join the British and their allies against the Turks. The expedition of unbloodied troops, five infantry and one light division from Australia and one infantry division from New Zealand went ashore in longboats at 0400 hours on 25th April 1915. The planned dawn landing at Suvla Bay was unsuccessful as the strong tide and currents took the troops to steep cliffs and well defended Turkish positions. The Anzacs fought bravely for nine months until December when they were evacuated and returned to Egypt. Of the original force landed 66% were killed or wounded. The decision was made early in 1916 that the infantry divisions would be sent to France while most of the light horse continued fighting against the Turks in Egypt and Palestine.

In Australia various training camps were established in each of the Australian states, Broadmeadows in Victoria, Kensington in New South Wales, Pontville in Tasmania, Greenmount in Western Australia and Enoggera in Queensland. Once in the training camps the men were told to choose their mates, they would train and fight together. Training complete the men would embark on the ships for England, a voyage that took approximately five weeks. A typical journey from Melbourne was to ports in South Africa (Durban & Cape Town) Cabo Verde (St Vincent) after this the ships were in a submarine zone, the troops were not allowed to show any lights, portholes were shut at night, the watertight doors were kept closed, there were daily boat drills and the men had to wear life belts day and night. The lack of ventilation in crowded troop carriers was a serious health hazard in the event of sickness, disease spread rapidly through the ship with disastrous consequences. The early twentieth century plagues, virulent strains of influenza, bronchitis, meningitis and measles were pandemic. In addition, the simultaneous presence of septic pneumonia, catarrhal infections, acute tonsillitis, cerebro- spinal fever and Rubella (German measles) were all aggravated by the conditions.

On arriving in England and taking the train to the training camps, the men had 48 hours before being added to the strength, which meant they were not fed so had to bring all their food for two days with them from Australia- so tinned meat and biscuits.

Their accommodation, certainly on Salisbury Plain, was comfortable and spacious. The huts housed thirty soldiers, they had seating and four tables for the men to eat on. Food appears to have been plentiful. In the morning they were allowed half a small loaf each man with a quarter tin of jam and half a pound of margarine for eight men, meant to be for the evening meal but inevitably gone by midday. Breakfast was cold ham and hot tomatoes, sometimes tinned pork, or bacon and fried tomatoes with bread, margarine and toast.

For dinner roast or boiled meat, sometimes beef, sometimes mutton; another time baked in a meat pie, one for each hut on a big dish, or, a meat pudding beautifully cooked; about once a week stew. Two sorts of vegetable, potatoes and haricot beans, cabbage, green peas, onions or turnips. Sometimes rice custard and bread, margarine, treacle and hot tea with milk and sugar at every meal.

The huts were large and warm, each one had heater and plenty of coal so the men could make toast on it and it could be kept burning all night. Each hut had electricity and gas with mantles. Every soldier had four big blankets and a waterproof sheet. In the depth of winter it was not unusual for two men to share a bed for warmth.

A week before leaving Australian each soldier was provided with leather accoutrements costing two pounds ten shillings. A week after arriving in Britain this was taken away and thrown in a huge pile to rot. The men were then provided with webbing which was more suited to the conditions to be found on the Western Front. In 1914 20,000 men had been raised for service overseas, £42,000 to provide accoutrements that would prove to be deficient, yet in 1916 with two- years' experience of trench warfare in France and Belgium, money was still being wasted. Before embarking each Australian soldier had been issued two pairs of stout tan boots, confiscated on arrival to be replaced with one pair of English black boots. In the British Expeditionary Force only officers wore tan boots - thousands more pounds wasted due to lack of communication.

The period of training before going on active service was supposed to be fourteen weeks but by autumn 1916 given the casualty figures across the Channel it was more likely eight to ten weeks.

In camp the day began at 6am, a run out for roll call; at 6.10am fall in again; 7.45 with full pack go on a route march for about eight miles; get back at 10am; go to drill grounds on top of a steep high hill, have to crawl it is so steep, full pack and rifle all the time. Get to the top and fall on the ground and lay there until they got their breath; then drill until 12.30, an hour at each thing; with a smoke for ten minutes every hour. The same thing in the afternoon without the march, fall in at 1.45pm until 5pm.

Later as training intensified the men would go on twenty- mile marches through the English countryside led by the regimental band. Villagers would come out to watch the phalanx of men pass by, the women would curtsey and sometimes offer cups of milk. For the soldiers who were born on the far side of the world, the small villages with quaint names, thatched cottages, ancient inns, manor houses, grey stone churches, rustic bridges, narrow twisting lanes and green countryside appeared fairy tale landscapes peopled with Dickensian characters.

In Australia the men had access to modern weapons, in Britain the rifles were outdated, of the type used in the Boer War and bayonets were in short supply. As sentries were required to patrol with fixed bayonets this caused difficulties as often there were no replacements.

In a letter from England dated 10th November 1916 Lance Corporal Henry (Harry) John Hatherley

46th Battalion Australian Imperial Force writes:

"Just a few lines on the Australian rag time Army. The nearer you get to the front the worse it gets, and by what I can see of the English Army it is no better. The first thing we had to do when we got here was to tie our puttees at the top instead of at the bottom. For a week we were taught nothing but saluting and had lectures on it, who to salute and not to salute. Although only a few weeks off the trenches we spend hours learning how to present arms and over two hours every day loading and unloading with no cartridges, old rifles made before the South African War, over eighteen years old and entirely different in every way to the ones we will use at the front, got no others.

In our camp of two thousand men we have exactly sixteen bayonets and as there are exactly sixteen of a guard on our Camp who must have a bayonet, when one is sometimes missing the whole camp is turned upside down looking for it. At the guardroom is the klink, where as a rule there are sixty men in it. They have a good time in there smoking and playing cards but get no pay while they are in there. The guard have to watch them and if they want to buy anything or have a shower the guard have to go with them with fixed bayonets, wait until they are finished and bring them back again.

The other night two prisoners wanted to buy something at the canteen so two of the guards with fixed bayonets took them down. After a couple of hours had gone and no sign of either guards or prisoners, an Officer went and had a look for them. He found the four of them dead drunk in the canteen. He tried to get them to come away but it ended in one of the biggest riots you ever saw; beer bottles, glasses and everything flying in all directions. All the guard had to be called to bring the four back."

On 12th April 1917 Warrant Officer Robin Selby of the Taranaki, Company, 3rd Wellington Battalion, 4th Brigade New Zealand Forces wrote:

"Am still in Blighty as you can see by the address – the date of leaving for France had not yet been fixed. I am now in a new Brigade which has been formed and we are delayed by having to wait for its completion. We are only half strength and today were issued with rifles- the first time I have handled one for just six months, so feel a trifle awkward. This forms New Zealand's fourth 4th Brigade of Infantry – while we have a Mounted Brigade in Egypt – or should I say Palestine- and of course we have our own Artillery in France-Field Guns and Howitzers- so are a very complete little army in a way. To date New Zealand has sent out just on 80,000 men out of a population of just over 1,000,000."

Harry Hatherley candidly describes his impressions of the different nationalities, speaking the same language but having almost nothing in common.

"Talk about a rag tag Army, it gets worse, I have not done any drill for twelve days, sit in the hut making toast, sometimes go to the village for a walk and have afternoon tea there. Have not had a rifle in my hand for three weeks and expect to go to France any time now.

Another draft of men from our Company were picked out yesterday to go to France next week and they are teaching them to present arms and to salute and to do right and left turn by numbers. This is a fact; I have not seen the rifle we use at the front since I left Australia; the ones we use here were made over twenty years ago, altogether different to what we will use at the front; got no others!

Of a morning when the bugle sounds to get up, nobody thinks of getting out of bed, not until the 'cook house' sounds an hour later does anyone start to get up, and they would not get up then only someone has to get the breakfast or go without.

The nearer we get to war the less sincere it seems to get, nobody troubles about it. In this big Camp here are English, New Zealanders and Australians and of a night they are all mixed up together, but they don't have anything to do with one another. You never see an Australian or a New Zealander speaking with an English soldier. We would not be more distant from one another if we could not speak their language. I have not had a conversation with one yet, why I don't know. If you were to ask all the other Australian fellows they could not tell you why, in fact I don't suppose they have noticed it. We mix more with the New Zealanders.

You hear a lot about the discipline of the English Army and that you can't drive it into an Australian. I have seen both sides of it here and I say that it is impossible to drive discipline into an Australian; if they drilled them for the next twenty years they would be the same, they are different altogether to the Englishmen. He will do whatever he is told to do the moment he comes into camp and everything he does, he does in the correct way.

Walking through the Camps here you will see a Tommie on sentry, he will turn in the correct way, march up and down, hold his rifle correctly, never smile or talk to anyone. Walk a bit further on and you will see an Australian on sentry, he will be sitting on his rifle or leaning on it, perhaps talking to someone or yelling out to everyone who passes. They are everlastingly putting them in the klink for it but it makes no difference! If you came along at night he would most likely be asleep. All they say is "it's a lot of damn rot this guard work here, they won't catch us sleeping when we get across the other side"- meaning France.

A Tommie has his hair cut very short, buttons polish up a treat and not a thing out of place on his dress, but our fellows dress does not trouble them. If it came to a fight between the two I know which side I would get on, our fellows would eat them!

The English soldier is very clean about his dress and general appearance, always carries a little cane, but our fellows never trouble about dress. Their boots are never clean, tunic on any way and if a button falls off it stays off. Some have caps on, others hat's on, put on any way, no badges on some and all badges on the other. Hats hit up the side on one and the next down all round. All the Tommie's hair is cut very short, ours is never cut unless you go to a barber and pay for it and you can guess a lot don't worry about it.

The Tommie is very quiet and you never hear him swear, but the Australian is awful. The Tommie's get one and fourpence per day and they know how to live on it. They will go into a shop and ask the price of this and that and finish up getting a quarter of a pound of something, seldom spend more than two pence at a time and easily makes his pay last the week. We get paid two pound at a time and it lasts the majority of three or four days. He will go into a shop, buy the best of everything and spend less than a bobs worth.

A Commissioned Officer in the English Army before the war broke out got four shillings a day, now they get ten shillings. A Staff Sergeant Major gets three shillings and sixpence and a Private one and fourpence. Now you understand why we are called the six bob a day tourist."

With training complete there was no prolonged preparation to go to France. Orders to leave the next day with one change of underclothing, one towel, the boots on their feet, shaving kit and a waterproof sheet were not unusual. Hasty letters home asking for tinned food, pineapple or fruit and something that could be heated up on a fire, (rabbit, sausages, sardines) Havelock tobacco, soap, socks, handkerchiefs, gloves and balaclavas. Watches were often sent home and requests for cash to be sent in the post rather than money orders.

Now the waiting was over, the battlefield beckoned and ready or not the soldiers were heading into the unknown.

EXTRACT FROM THE ANZAC REQUIEM
This day above all others we recall those who served in war and did not return to receive the grateful thanks of the nation. We remember those who still remain where they were left; amid the scrub in the valleys and the ridges of Gallipoli; on the rocky and terraced hills of Palestine and in the cemeteries of France.

We remember those who lie buried amid loving friends in Great Britain and in unknown resting places in almost every land and those gallant men whose grave is the unending sea.

We remember those who died as prisoners of war, remote from their homeland.

We recall too, the staunch friends who fought beside us on the first ANZAC Day and ever since, men of New Zealand – who helped create the name ANZAC.

May they rest in the knowledge of their achievement and may we- and our successor in that heritage- prove worthy of their sacrifice.

NOTES
Both Harry Hatherley and Robin Selby fought on the Somme and survived the war. Harry was a tailor living in Hawthorn, a suburb of Melbourne. He arrived in England in September 1916 and left for France and the Somme on 2nd December. He took part in the charge of the Hindenberg Line and fought at Messines, Bapaume and Bullecourt before being wounded at Passchendaele on 19th October 1917. Harry spent fifteen months in hospital, first in France then England and finally in Australia. He sailed for home on 4th April 1918. A permanent legacy of his wound was a stiff and shortened left leg. He died aged seventy-four of a heart attack 17th December 1962.

Harry Hatherley

Robin Selby

Robin was an accountant, before he enlisted on 18th October 1915. He was in Egypt during 1916, leaving for the Western Front in April that year. He was twice wounded in action, in 1916 and 1917, on both occasions hospitalised in England. He returned to the trenches for the second time 28th January 1918. Robin sailed home to New Zealand on 3rd November 1919 taking up land in the bush in sheep and cattle country. He died of throat cancer 3rd September 1969 aged seventy- eight.

Harry's story is told in my book 'Swords and Ploughshares- Codford During the 20th Century.' published Gemini 2007.

Robin's story is told in my book 'Warriors for the Working Day – Codford During Two World Wars' published by Hobnob Press 2002.

Australian 14th Battalion Band Codford, Salisbury Plain 1917

CHAPTER 3

The Long Road Home
Mesopotamia 1918-1919   Douglas Belchamber

EXCERPTS FROM THE WAR DIARY OF LT. COL. D. F BELCHAMBER MBE

MESOPOTAMIA
August 29th 1918
I am just now convalescent from an attack of fever. It was a pretty rotten time I had in Baghdad. Trying to get any work done there is pretty hopeless. Bridges are closed for long periods on the off chance of Major Generals passing through, and officers can never be found in their offices. For two solid days I barged about Baghdad trying to get things done, but all I got was an attack of fever. I rushed off back here (Hiilah) on Thursday afternoon and felt very rotten. Friday I tried to start work, but had to go to bed. I felt worse on Saturday and got the doctor - temperature 104 nearly. Since then I have been getting on but am still weak. I feel very bored with this country and News from France continues good. We seem to be going back over the old Somme Battlefields of 1916-17 and with two more months to go this year we may hope to put an almost unbearable strain on the Germans.

THROUGH FIRE, SHOT AND SHELL

August 31st 1918
The last day in August. Last evening, I started jotting down my recollections of the War and it was an interesting though melancholy business summing up the memories of four years ago. I have not seen Reuters today but am told it is very good and that the French papers state that the present actions in France are only diversions and that the main push is still to come. I suppose they are holding the main American Armies as reserves in which case we may see some startling developments this year.

The Colonel has gone to Baghdad again today. I don't think I have ever tried to describe the Colonel. He is a very tall, big man, with twinkling eyes and crisp black hair tinged somewhat heavily with grey. Col. James L O'Connor is a character in this country. He has a great belief in mileage as an index to work and will whiz about in his car from place to place with the utmost faith that this is doing a big job of work. He has a big voice and delights in reading the Riot Act as he calls it or going off the deep end as we call it. He is full of yarns in which he is the central figure. He has – verba eius (*'in his own words'*) - been a full general in the Venezuelan Army, and it is great to hear him talk. A specimen might be - Lord Somebody or General X or some big sort would look at him and say "JAMES I don't know how you do it but you are a wonderful man". He has a vivid imagination and it is difficult to pick out grains of wheat from the chaff. In reporting prospects of the harvest he doubles or trebles figures glibly and talks in thousands where hundreds are applicable. I am afraid but little credence attaches to O'Connorisms but he is a good-hearted man and is certainly no fool.

SEPTEMBER 1918
Sept 1st
Today is the last of my enforced holiday and tomorrow sees me back in harness again. The immediate problems which confront me are those of getting grain cleaned sufficiently quickly, storage and cover for the winter and the problem of bhoosa collection and baling. (*Bhoosa - the broken straw and husks from the threshing floor used as fodder. Stalk or stem of a certain species of grain especially wheat, rye, oats or barley. Urdu word for Bran.*)

A new officer turned up today so that we are now pretty fully staffed.

I have spent today pretty quietly doing a good deal of writing. I am busily engaged in getting down my recollections and though I am afraid they will not be of any general interest they provide me with some interest.

The news from France is still excellent and the papers forecast still greater happenings to come. Dreams of possible peace and homecoming tantalise my waking and sleeping vision and I build castle after insubstantial castle in the air.

Sept 2nd
The Doctor came to see me last night and gave me strict orders that I was not to go to the office today although I feel quite fit. I therefore had some papers sent in from the office this morning and just ran through them. I wrote up some more of my Recollections of the war and then finished reading Wildfell Hall (*'The Tenant of Wildfell Hall', the second and final novel by Anne Brontë, published in 1848 under the pseudonym of Acton Bell*). The Bronte writing is quite good and interesting and I read their books with interest, but the style of conversation is or seems to me to be so artificial and unnatural.

The news is again good. Bailleul and Peronne both seem to be in our hands and we seem to be attacking in one place after the other. One almost dares to hope that the Hun is at a loss what to do, and that the Americans of whom nothing is being heard just now, may be held back to throw in for a big push, e.g. at Verdun.

Sept 3rd
My first day back in harness. Not so busy as it might have been but that is due a great deal to the fact that I haven't been there to stir things up. I am a little worried about the wharf but I am trying to arrange a 24-hour day there and I want to get a hustle on. I think we can manage it but it will require a great deal of careful organisation. I went over to the wharf tonight and settled up a few points. The mail which we thought was lost has after all turned up and is due in Baghdad tomorrow or the next day. We also expect the next one about 4 days later so the next week should be a rich one.

The news is good again and tonight a special wire came in saying the German retirement in the Lys Salient continues and fires are observed in Armentieres and East of Lens. Every step forward now seems like a day nearer home. I wonder if the Germans will break this year. The other day there was a lot in the paper about a rebellion in Austria and today it was reported that two German regiments refused to go to the Western front from Russia. Our communiqués have so often been misleading that one has almost ceased to dare to believe all the good news one hears, and yet I cannot help cherishing the secret hope that the breakup of Germany is at hand. I believe now that quite soon we shall hear of the push of the American Army.

Undoubtedly since my attack of fever the work has fallen off tremendously and I have had a soft day's work today. At the same time I am not quite satisfied with matters because I feel that a lot of things which ought to have been pushed recently have been allowed to slide and I have not the energy at present to try to pick up all the threads.

Last night I dined with the Colonel and Col Snepp, Howell, Col Priestley and others were there. The conversation was absolutely filthy and I felt quite disgusted. Most of those present appeared not to have an atom of decency left. One man was detailing his experiences on leave and complacently observed that his month or so had cost him 6,000 Rupees (£400). He also narrated cold bloodedly how he had haggled the terms with prostitutes the conditions being stipulated on each side. It is really hard to say that we as a nation are any better than the Hun whom we accuse of so many gross immoralities, when one sees and hears about half a dozen so called gentlemen go on in this way. At a time like this when every feeling of patriotism should induce every man to use economy and invest in War Loan an officer, with a safe and cushy job, has the effrontery to boast of the squandering of £400 in a month on dissipation and debauchery.

The news from France continues good. A War Office Wire just in says that the British in the Somme Area took 3,000 to 4,000 prisoners in one day and that here the German losses have been proved to be unusually heavy. Bailleul is ours, Kemmel is ours and Peronne is ours and now it remains to be seen whether we can sweep through the Hindenburg Line. Apparently since 15th July we have taken over 130,000 prisoners.

Sept 5th

This morning I had to spend a great deal of time in investigating another charge against that wretched interpreter NAGIB SAAD, and tomorrow I have to go to Jerboiyah to take a summary of evidence in a second charge against him. He has really wasted a tremendous lot of valuable time lately and I have strong hopes that the Court Martial will this time give him a term of imprisonment which may act as a warning to other Egyptian interpreters who are giving trouble.

(An entry to the diary dated August 16th reads "I spent all day until half past two acting as prosecutor in the case of an Egyptian Interpreter. These wretched men are an awful nuisance and I did grudge the waste of time.")

Last night there was a lot of rifle shooting in Hillah. I have not found out what it was about but I should think 30 or 40 shots were fired. Shooting has occurred at various other times and one night the supply dump near our wharf saw quite a small battle between the guard and armed Arab raiders.

The news from France is even better than before. We are reported to have smashed the Drocourt Quéant line and taken Quéant (*Quéant had been stormed and captured by the Canadians on 2 September*). If so we have pierced the Hindenberg line at one point at least. 10,000 prisoners on Monday were taken and the latest communiqué claims big losses by the Germans. There has also been a move at Salonica and in Siberia, and America has recognised the Czecho-Slovaks. I cannot help thinking that we are really entering on the last phase. Oh how I long for peace and home.

Sept 6th
Went to Jerboiyah early this morning with Nagib Saad, escort and typist and took the Summary of evidence in his case. I found things going on fairly satisfactorily. On the way back I called in at Debla and fixed up to send cars there to carry the grain. I see that we have now collected almost 30,000 tons altogether of Grain and Bhoosa. The Mill on the wharf is disappointing.

Sept 7th
A rather busy day. I saw a local sheikh in the morning and fixed up to rope in camels and hire them quite shortly in this district. I hope to get 1,000 or more. Baghdad has just informed me that they will probably have to withdraw all Govt. Camels but hope to return them in 2 months' time. I suppose these are wanted for the Persian L of C (*Lines of Communication*) which seems to swallow up all our transport. This withdrawal must seriously affect our work but I don't agree with the Colonel when he wanted to wire that the Collection of the Harvest will cease entirely.

Various reports lead me to suppose that we shall get very little purchase grain now but I am going to try to get Political to put on the screw and enforce the terms of the proclamation. There are obvious signs of a slackening in the bringing in of grain everywhere.

The news from France is still good. Apparently Lens is ours and we seem to be recapturing a good portion of the ground lost south of Ypres. The Hun is retiring, prisoners and guns mounting up and the French papers commence to talk of the last lap.

Sept 9th
I mainly fixed up various points about Bhoosa collection today. I don't know quite how this is going to pan out as Political Officers care very little about anything except keeping their Arabs in good temper and most of them will not show the necessary firmness to make them bring stuff in. They would like us to pay exorbitant prices and bribe the Arab instead of paying a fair price and telling him to bring it in. However we must hope for the best and I hope we may yet manage to get 10 - 20,000 tons of Bhoosa.

Sept 10th
Most of this morning was occupied in trying Nagib Saad the Interpreter. He was evidently found guilty though I don't know what the punishment will be. The ordinary little worries of life kept me busy for the remainder of my office day.

The news continues good from France, but I hear that the Hun in now standing and his Artillery fire has increased. I wonder if this means the end of our push this year and winter quarters, or whether Foch will find a way of launching the Americans at an unsuspected place. I presume the Hun will not be able to counter though one never knows.

Sept 11th
Kifl grain petered out today and as the winnowers for the wharf have not arrived I have had to cancel the Grain trains for to-morrow and Friday. It is most annoying as the wretched Arabs have a holiday from Monday to Thursday next on which we shall get no work done at all. I have just practically fixed up the Bhoosa transport business to Baghdad and if only we get shaleefs (*sacks made out of sheets*) in plenty we ought to be able to rail quite a quantity of Bhoosa to Baghdad.

Rather curious today! The sky was quite overcast with clouds this afternoon. If that means early rain it will rather upset some of our calculations I reckon. I see that the Germans have turned and are standing in France so that either we shall see a tremendous battle develop or possibly they will settle down in their positions for the winter. It is just possible I suppose that Foch might push in his Americans somewhere unexpectedly.

Sept 12th
There is a fair amount of Cholera about just now and I went this morning and had my

first dose of inoculation. The event of the day was the Promulgation of Sentence on Nagib Saad who gets 2 years I.H.L. (*Imprisonment with Hard Labour*). It is a stiff sentence and might have been saved if only previous Courts Martial had given him a moderately heavy sentence. As it is for similar offences he has been repeatedly fined - which he doesn't mind - until he felt that he could be insolent to officers with impunity.

The rice harvest in the Sharmich is reckoned at 9,000 tons - 3,000 available for us. I am afraid these figures will disappoint Baghdad and the Colonel talks glibly about 200,000 tons.

Our advance in France has slowed down but to be able to anticipate more accurately what is going to happen one must wait a few days.

Sept 13th
Grain is now coming in much more slowly and Revenue payments are all but complete. We shall probably have a good deal of difficulty in getting in purchased grain. We are trying today to commence a 24 hour shift at the Mill but with the shortage of Engineers and British personnel it is rather difficult.

Both yesterday and today have been overcast and for the first time for many months the sun has been clouded over at times during the day. I suppose it is the first signs of approaching winter.

Apparently we are - only temporarily I hope - held up in France more or less. If only we broke through now what an effect it would have. The weather however seems to have turned wet in France so I presume our operations will be hindered somewhat.

Sept 14th
There are all sorts of rumours that we have evacuated Baku and that Dunster force has had a rough handling and been withdrawn. I don't know what truth there is in it. I have had a bad time on the telephone tonight. The exchange is beastly poor and nobody I wanted was on at the other end. Townsend has just come in and says that Reuters has it that the Americans have attacked at St. Michel and advanced 5 miles. I have been prophesying a big push by them in this district. I haven't seen the Reuters myself but if Townsend's report is true it looks as if it may come off.

Sept 15th
General Stuart Wortley and Slater came down from Baghdad today and spent the morning looking round the wharf with the Colonel. I was in the office during

that time but just as I was going into lunch the Colonel sent for me and I was introduced to the D.Q.M.G. Macpherson was there and a lively conference ensued on the best means to take to wring the grain out of cultivators, etc. Macpherson and the Colonel wished for another proclamation to be issued prohibiting the sale of grain in Nyif, Kirfa, Kesbala and Baghdad at prices higher than 160 or 170 Rupees. Below that limit sales were to be free but if grain ran short we were to ration. The objections I could see were that the terms of the proclamation might be evaded and that we should not know to what extent our stocks would have to be maintained for rationing purposes. In the upshot the D.Q.M.G. decided to have a conference with the Civil Commissioner, the F.R.O. (*Field Requisitioning Officer*) and Slater and settle a policy. Rice prospects also were discussed but we got very little forrader with that.

I lunched with the Col and his guests who also included General Tidewell (G.O.C. Area). Both Generals were quite pleasant and I enjoyed the meal. The DQMG said he didn't see how wewere to support our advanced forces in Persia and that he quite expected a lot of them to migrate unwillingly to Constantinople. He also talked of the prospect of obtaining one ship from the Home Government entirely for carrying leave men and officers and of an increase in leave accordingly. The Colonel stated on the authority of a Harvest officer who got it from some Arabs that Lions existed at Ghuismas (below Umm-al-Barrur) but the Company was incredulous.

Sept 16th

The news is good again. The St. Michel salient is wiped out with nearly 10,000 prisoners and apparently rail communication is open to us between Verdun and Toul. Germany begins to sing lower in her Peace terms but she is not yet on her knees. There seem to be curious hints of an effort to approach us on the part of the Turks and possibly the Austrians. Russian news is impossible to make out. Apparently from the latest Bolshevism is tottering to its fall. If only the Russian front could be formed again then the end would be soon.

Sept 17th

No work is being done today anywhere on account of the Mohammedan holiday. I am not sorry as I feel quite seedy. The holiday started yesterday and ends on Thursday.

We have had to hop it from Baku (*the capital of Azerbaijani on the Capsian Sea*).

Savage says that it was the 39th Brigade in Baku and that they got it in the neck. As to that we don't know yet but it is official that we have come back.

Sept 18th
The work has slacked off a great deal and of course things are specially slow during the Arab holiday. All the 5th and 6th Corps camels have been withdrawn today for Persia and I must say I am sorry because they were doing good work with very little trouble.

A case of cholera (a British rank) has occurred in the poultry farm. Our new establishment has been approved and I suppose as soon as the General returns from Persia there will be a bevy of new DD's (*Deputy Directors*), AD's (*Assistant Directors*) and DAD's (*Deputy Assistant Directors*).

There seems to be a fairly decent push now in Salonika and various minor shows in France. I hope the St Michel blow will develop as that seems to threaten Germany rather intimately. I see from yesterday's communiqué the Hun offers Belgium complete economic and military independence if she will remain neutral for the rest of the war. It looks as though she is preparing to get out.

Sept 20th
The baling press has commenced work in the wharf. We are converting one winnower to be run by power and if it is a success we shall replace all the power machines by converted hand machines and scrap the former. We must now commence to think seriously about next year's harvest. I have a good many ideas and I propose to get together a conference of Harvest Officers and settle a definite plan of campaign in the near future.

Today is the anniversary of the big show in France last year. How clearly I can remember that awful day with its agony of suspense waiting for news from the Company and when none came that rotten night in ruined and bombarded Dickebusch. I did not then have any great hopes of getting out of France and yet it was only 8 days later that we were ordered out here. Instead of feeling unfeignedly thankful, I am now only filled with an intense longing to get home. I believe it must have been about now that 2 years ago Will, Harry and I were at home together for the last time.

Sept 21st
The Colonel has gone to Baghdad. He means to collar the General directly he returned from Persia and to be on the spot when all the promotions are made. A new and increased allotment of home leave has come out which gives me a faint hope that next year I might manage it, if the war still persists. I have asked the Colonel to see that my name is included in the list of applicants.

This evening I have been round the wharf again. It is very interesting and I watched the new Bhoosa baling machine at work. The converted hand winnower is nearly ready and should be working tomorrow. The change which has taken place since July is nothing short of marvellous.

The news is good again tonight. Various counter attacks have been smashed and advances made and prisoners taken in France. A German led force has been heavily defeated in North Russia and the Salonika communiqué speaks of the pursuit of a routed and broken enemy. I think that the long delayed mail ought to be here today week.

Sept 22nd Sunday
Just now we are full of excitement over English leave. Quite a lot of officers and men have been ordered to go off immediately to catch the boat leaving on the 30th and I suppose more will be sent for the boat on the 16th October. If the increased allotment holds I am in hopes that I may come in for it next summer. The very thought of it makes me tingle with excitement. The recent communiqués are very hopeful. In Salonika they talk about the pursuit of a beaten enemy with thousands of prisoners and guns captured. In Palestine we have evidently made a big advance capturing Nazareth with 8,000 prisoners, 100 guns and 4 aeroplanes. It looks as if our operations in Baku were intended to draw off Turkish divisions and so give Allenby a chance which he had taken. In Russia we appear to have won a battle in the North and it talks about the re-establishment of a Russian Front on the Don. Altogether things seem to be straightening out and I should imagine the Hun is commencing to get the wind up. I suppose there is still time for a big show in the West this year and as 300,000 and more Americans arrived in France in August and presumably as many will arrive this month I should think we shall have the men to do it. Altogether one feels that it is now permissible to hope as it has not hitherto been possible.

Sept 24th (sic = 23rd)
I drew out a kind of agenda for a conference of all harvest officers to discuss next year's programme this morning. I reckon myself that we can practically organise a real business proposition and make many economies in labour and material. If we get going in good time we ought to be able very successfully to run a big show next year.

In the afternoon there were the Shebana sports but I did not go as I had to get my second dose of cholera inoculation. While I was at the Fort I looked at the latest communiqués. According to them Allenby's show in Palestine looks like being the knock out for the Turk. We apparently broke right through and Aleppo seems to be now well within our range. We have already taken 25,000 prisoners, 260 guns and all their transport and their Army has practically ceased to exist. The Serbians, too, have pushed on well ahead in Salonika. Altogether it is very hopeful.

I am rather worried at the approach of the wet weather. On the wharf, at Dighara and Afej we have thousands of tons of grain and bhoosa which are lying there unprotected from the wet and the weather begins to look decidedly unsettled. We shall probably get over it somehow but it is a big problem. This last Arab feast seems to have been a kind of Entente. The G.O.C. entertained a lot of Sheikhs in Baghdad and we seem to have lent cars to all and sundry to take them about.

Sept 24th
This morning it is quite cool and the air feels damp. The sky is quite overcast with heaveish clouds. We started new office hours today, 7.30 - 12 am and 2-4 or until work finishes. I was most delightfully interrupted in my afternoon's work by the unexpected arrival of the Mail up to 17.7.18. I gave myself up to the enjoyment of it. (The general tone at home had not yet become optimistic but I expect that the next letters will reflect the better news.

Sept 25th
There was a nasty accident at the wharf tonight as an Arab had both legs cut off by the train. I felt awfully sorry for the poor devil.

Sept 26th
The sky looked very threatening this morning and it has been quite cool today. However 650 Tarpaulins have arrived so that I hope we shall be able to protect the corn in the event of rain. The Bhoosa baling press works satisfactorily but slowly. We

estimate that given some bonus or piece work system it should be possible to turn out a bale from each side in 2 minutes or about 600 a day.

Sept 27th
We have had a lot of difficulties with clearing grain this week, what with stoppages of the Engine, inoculations of the Labour corps etc. and I have just had to wire cancelling the train for tomorrow.

It is extraordinary how one may dream dreams and see visions. Last night I was just sitting in the mess listening to the others talking and joking when Martin put on a very inspiring march on the Gramophone. It was a fine record with a full brass band and as I listened I seemed to see vast columns of Khaki clad soldiers in time. As far as the eye could follow these columns came marching on up the hill but when they crossed the ridge they vanished into darkness which swallowed them up. I felt very sad about it all as it seemed like a vision of the myriad of our young manhood pressing into the war and being swallowed up.

Sept 28th
In the evening the 'Magics' from Baghdad gave a most enjoyable concert. As we came away a heavy thunderstorm was making itself heard at a short distance and a few drops of rain fell which quite put the wind up me when I thought of the thousands of tons of unprotected grain we have lying about. However no real quantity of rain came down and we are respited for a bit.

Tonight's communiqué contains intimation of a double offensive in France, one South of Arras apparently aimed at Cambrai and the other on a 40 mile front NW of Verdun. The latter has progressed 7 miles and 5000 prisoners are already taken. It looks as if we are trying the pincers dodge and threatening to cut the Hun's communications. Apparently the Serbs are giving the Bulgars a lot to think about and the British have crossed the border. Brilip, Ishtip and Veles have fallen and Uskut is the next objective.

Sept 29th (Sunday)
I have told Johnson to get on with the job of sheeting the stacks with Tarpaulin and am also putting up a request for priority to erect some shelter on the wharf.

OCTOBER 1918

Oct 1st

The anniversary of our entraining at Ghyvelde for Mespot. I have had an awfully busy but worrying day. I seem to be nothing but a strafer (*harsh task master*) today. I have written an ultimatum about labour saying that unless my demands are complied with I cannot be responsible for the handling and safety of grain. As a matter of fact we have been complaining for months and have been put off with promises that the situation would improve. Jobs of comparative non urgent nature have been put off until they are now of the first necessity. Labours fault has been that when we have tried to enlist extra help from Baghdad they have checkmated us by saying that they would be able to do everything with local labour, and it has always been next week or next month the situation would improve.

The Railways too are impossible. I prepare a careful programme each Thursday for the following week and wire it to Baghdad. It is almost never adhered to unless by chance it is some item I have subsequently cancelled by wire. Trucks are placed where there is no grain and where I have no labour on that day, and where I have arranged grain and labour there are no trucks. I am writing a sarcastic letter but I don't know whether it is any use.

However I took just a minute or two to finish off my letter. While so engaged the most exciting communiqué of the war came in. Unconditional surrender of Bulgaria, Messines and Wytochute Ridge captured. Cambrai suburbs entered, Zeebrugge heavily bombarded, Germans in a scare getting out of Rumania and Germany with the wind well up. I thought the turn of the tide had arrived when Italy repulsed the Austrians and it is getting now to full flood in our favour. The whole Belgian coast should go soon and I believe the Germans will be back across the Rhine this year yet. Oh how once more Peace and Home loom within measurable distance. Unconditional surrender of Bulgaria. All our enemies must surrender on the same "no terms".

Oct 2nd

We have had a very heavy gale of wind this evening with thunder and some rain and I got the wind up absolutely about the unprotected grain on the wharf. I wonder whether tonight's communiqué will be as good as last nights. I hardly think so myself as it is not possible to maintain such a pace but in these days, one never knows.

Oct 4th

News has come through that Turkey has asked for an armistice and it is expected that Bulgaria's surrender will be copied. I believe St. Quentin has fallen, Lille is outflanked and it appears to me that any day may now bring news of the capture of the Belgian coast and the fall of Lille, Cambrai and St. Quentin. I shouldn't be surprised if Austria soon follows Bulgaria's excellent example and perhaps even yet the war may end this year.

I don't think I mentioned that the other day the Grand Duke Dimitri (*he was to be executed in January 1919 by a firing squad, because he was a relative of tsar Nicholas ll during the Russian Revolution*) was dining with the General and we had to send up a Turkey for the food. The dinner was a great success. The menus were all hand drawn by Sgt Marshall and the pipe band of the Deolis turned up. After the dinner we had several solo turns with pipers marching round the table and then they finished up by the whole band with the drums and fife and their lamb marching round the table. Speeches were made by all; the best being the General's.

I stole off at 11.30 but did not get to sleep till nearly 1.0'c.

Oct 5th

I got up at 4.30 and had rather a lot of trouble waking up my drivers and the Colonel's cook and others. However I got off soon after 6.0'c and arrived in Baghdad at 10.0'c just in time to get over the bridge. I find that things were apparently seething in Baghdad. Without actually asking for direct information I saw enough to convince me that the General, the Colonel and others are playing a low game. Apparently when the Colonel said that my name had actually been sent in for a D.A.D. he was deliberately lying. I don't think he even attends very vigorously to anybody's interests but No1's and his policy of waiting on the doorstep (his own expression) in Baghdad until the General came back from Persia seems for the time being to have borne fruit for him. I am afraid our own Department like most others out here is rotten to the core.

Oct 6th

After spending the morning reading in the club I strolled back to the office and found a rather interesting document. It was the Demobilisation Regulations and as I read them through I almost seemed to be living in those wonderful days when we shall be quit of the Army for good. The news is still good and it seems as if the

Belgian coast will soon go. I don't think Turkey is quite yet outed though I suppose that may come at any moment.

Oct 7th
I left Baghdad this morning and arrived in Hillah about 1 o'clock. Tonight's Reuter is full of Prince Max of Baden's speech (*German prince and politician, heir to the Grand Duchy of Baden. Appointed Chancellor of Germany in October 1918 to negotiate an armistice with the Allies*). It is a great climb down and talks of restitution, rehabilitation and even indemnity for Belgium. A note has been despatched to President Wilson and apparently Austria sent one some days ago. I should not be at all surprised if, after all, peace should dawn this year and peace with victory.

Oct 9th
The Communiqué gave the terms of the German Peace note in which they agree to the fourteen points of President Wilson. Apparently they have lost about one quarter of their total of guns on the Western front and are again retiring. They ask for an immediate armistice. King Ferdinand (*Born in Vienna, he became Tsar of Bulgaria until the Allies destroyed the Bulgarian army in Greece, whereupon he abdicated in favour of his eldest son, Boris*) has abdicated and Boris reigns in his stead.

We have had all trains stopped for the next week which looks like urgent troop movements. Rather a worrying day again today.

Oct 10th
I see by tonight's Reuter that President Wilson has asked several questions before replying to the German note. In the meantime heavy attacks continue in France, the Bulgarians keep on surrendering as per agreement and the Montenegrans are reported to have risen against Austria. Beirut has been taken. I fancy out here we are going to nab Mosul and I shouldn't be surprised to hear any day that Allenby has got to Aleppo. I fancy Peace before Christmas is now quite a practical proposition.

Oct 11th
Tonight's news gives welcome intelligence of a victory in France. Apparently we have broken the front between Cambrai and St Quentin. This may have big results. 10,000 prisoners and nearly 200 guns in one day. Cambrai is ours. In Serbia we are pursuing the Austro Germans. In Syria we have occupied Beirut. In this country

troop movements continue and we shall probably hear news of another show quite soon.

Oct 12th

The last week has seen a great step towards peace I think because the Germans are squealing or appear to be. Last night's communiqué showed us as having taken Le Cateau and by the Baghdad Times it looks as if the line ran through Douai.

Oct 15th

The Maharram (*the first month of the Islamic calendar*) is now on and the Arabs have great processions each evening. They march in column of sections each headed by a man or boy carrying a pole on which is a cross piece with several braziers flaming away. One of these was as wide as the street. At the head of the procession was a party of semi-nude men who kept in a hollow square and moved forward facing inwards, performing a kind of slow dance and flogging their bare backs with chains. A kind of standard bearer follows them and then come the sections chanting alternately some refrain and the next replying.

I see we have taken Laon and La Fere and Douai and the Serbians are in Nish. I wonder what is happening up on the Flanders front as we haven't heard much from there.

Oct 16th

Today I have managed to finish off my proposals for next year's harvest with the exception of one or two points which Outlaw can supply. The chief other events in the office were that I wrote a rather rude letter at the Director of Labour through the Director of Local Resources. I read my essay to the Colonel before lunch and he fell asleep and as I noticed this I stopped in the middle of a sentence and sighed. This woke him up when thinking I had finished he said, 'That's very good indeed'.

The Reuter is again good. Wilson has practically told Germany that he will have no truck with the Hohenzollens (*the German monarchy since the 11th century*) and that outrage by sea and land must cease before we will talk. A new attack has started in Flanders and Rouless has fallen. Apparently Lille is in an awkward position and also Ostend. The Serbians continue in Bulgaria but Palestine and this place are quiet. We must shortly hear from both. Turkey has sent a peace note to America.

Oct 17th

This is the last day of the Maharram. For over a week we have had thousands of Arabs in torchlight processions as described on Oct 15th but today they paraded all the morning until one o'clock p.m. when the festival ended. Thousands of Arabs bare to the waist paraded the streets in platoons of single line each platoon having a kind of platoon commander in front. At the head of the procession was a primitive band consisting of a foghorn, cymbals and drum.

Hundreds of urchins with palm branches marched in front. Then followed some banners and emblems and then the platoons. As they marched in slow time alternate platoons chanted some dirge in true Gregorian style and the other platoons answered them. The platoon commanders exhorted their followers to more strenuous efforts the chief of which was the beating of bare breasts with the hand. I didn't see the more remarkable manifestations but I am told that bands of fanatics were parading covered with blood flowing from wounds inflicted by chains with which they scourged themselves and swords with which they cut themselves about.

I should imagine Mosul is to be taken shortly as the G.O.C. in C told the Colonel that he hoped the Turks would not give in at least for another 10 days. The communiqué today gives further progress in Flanders where Menin and Nervicq have been occupied and the outskirts of Thousont entered. Durrazzo is ours and the Serbians have occupied the heights north of Nish.

Oct 18th

Tonight's Reuter refers to sensational rumours of Germany's capitulation but denies them. The Colonel says there is a later one stating that we have occupied Lille and Ostend and have outflanked Bruges. The end of the war appears to me to be sensibly approaching.

Oct 19th

I see by tonight's Reuter that Ostend, Zeebrugge, Lille, Douai are ours and that Bruges is practically ours. New attacks also are being made. It looks as if the Hun is making up his mind to fight to the last but if we can only bring him to some disaster during his retreat we may make it impossible for him to put up a show.

Oct 21st

I see Austria has agreed that they have lost the war. Apparently we are pushing the

Hun back through Belgium though he is still resisting strongly. Denmark apparently is beginning to think of Schleswig Holstein.

Oct 22nd
Last night's communiqué did not contain very much news except that we now hold the whole of the Flanders coast and are halfway between Bruges and Ghent. Wilson has practically told Austria that what was good enough in January last is not good enough now. Tonight's communiqué does not contain much news; it rather hints that Germany's reply may be rather harder than her previous notes.

Oct 23rd
I went to Khawas this morning. The road (sic) was awful but the place itself is quite pretty. Grain has practically ceased coming in and I think quite shortly we shall withdraw the men. I went to Tiery before coming back to Hillah. The present bhoosa Khan is rather dangerous I think from the point of view that the bhoosa might catch fire and I wish it has been stuck outside of the town altogether. There was an accident at the Mill today which might have been nasty. In attempting to start up the Rice hullers the belt got caught and tore up the standards for the shafting bending the latter badly. The one rice huller was torn from its pedestal. The whole mill had to stop for about half an hour and the crushers are out of action for some days. It is a pity as I wanted to get on with the Rice. I have guaranteed Baghdad 600 tons before the end of December. It has been a rather worrying day. The Colonel wired down that Barley was going up to Baghdad very dirty and I am sending Johnson up tomorrow to Baghdad to look into it.

I see Germany's reply which is vague as usual appears to have roused the suspicions and wrath of the whole press which accuse Germany of merely marking time. Meantime we are nearly at Toumari and I see the French are at the Danube.

Oct 26th
Four years ago today we embarked for France. Last night after I got to bed (on the roof) it came on to rain and I had to come down hurridly (*sic*). There was quite a smart shower about 8 o'clock this morning. I am feeling uncommon homesick again tonight. One gets so impatient for the end of the war that when the communiqué does not contain great and startling victories one is quite disappointed.

There is a distant storm going on now and I can see the lightning though the thunder is not audible. It is quite oppressive in spite of a breeze.

Oct 27th Sunday
One of our Arab boys was discovered trying to sell a stolen lamp in the bazaar and I had to interrupt my letter to investigate this. Some evidence alleged that footprints were observed near the place from which the lamp and other articles were taken and these had been preserved by boxes placed on them. I felt like Sherlock Holmes as I had them measured but they turned out to be larger than the boy's.

Aleppo has been captured and we are nearing Mosul.

Oct 31st
It appears that we have collared practically all the Turks between here and Mosul. Apparently we are harrying the Austrians in Italy and I should fancy their unconditional surrender is pretty near. I should imagine Germany is much the same and I see Balfour, Lloyd George and others are in Paris apparently to discuss the terms of an Armistice. Altogether I am beginning to be full of hopes of an early home-coming. How I long for it!

I wonder whether we shall get any profit out of this place after the war. My idea is that they should stimulate production and take over a fixed proportion of the crops as we have done this year at a fixed price. It should be exported to England and taken over by Government and put on the market at the guaranteed rates. If export is controlled from this country the people here won't suffer and if the exchequer pockets the profits in England that should help to pay some of the costs of this campaign and of the development. The English consumer will in the long run pay but as if guaranteed prices are adhered to, he would have to pay in any case, he will benefit indirectly by the subvention to the exchequer.

NOVEMBER 1918
Nov 1st
A short wire has just come in to the effect that an Armistice has been signed with Turkey. This opens up various possibilities. It might even mean that a number of us should get back pretty soon. A holiday for tomorrow and Monday is proclaimed in orders to celebrate the defeat of Turkey. The Austrians are getting it badly in the neck I see and are entirely withdrawing from Serbia and apparently from Italy. The Kaiser (*Wilhelm ll, the last German Emperor and a grandson of Queen Victoria. He abdicated*

on 9 November 1918 and fled to exile in the Netherlands, living until 1941) has said that if it seems the best course for his country he will abdicate. I really believe peace will come before Christmas.

Nov 2nd
In orders it is stated that today and Monday are holidays to celebrate the defeat of Turkey. This doesn't make much difference to us because we have to carry on just the same. Reuters tonight seems to show that Austria is on her last legs and apparently she managed to get plenipotentiaries over the line on the evening of the 30th so quite possibly by now she has caved in

Nov 4th
Definite news of Austria's surrender has now come through and the armistice takes effect from 3 o'c today. At last Germany stands alone faced with the impossible task of trying to make reparation for its outrages against the whole of an incensed world.

This afternoon I attended a reception of notables by the G.O.C. (*General Costello*) to celebrate Turkey's defeat. All the chief people of Hillah and district assembled and supporting the General were officers from every corps and detachment. A guard of Shibornas gave the general the Salute. After a speech from the chief priest of Hillah in which he extolled the British and which finished with the wish to long life to the King, his Army and the Political Officer, the General make a speech. He referred to Bulgaria's collapse and Turkey's surrender and then read out General Marshall's speech delivered two days ago in Baghdad. In this reference was made to General Maude's promise to do all he could to alleviate the necessary restrictions of a military administration. General Maude did not live to redeem his promise but now almost on the anniversary of his lamented death the war being ended so far as this country was concerned it was possible to put into effect some immediate measures as a part redemption. These included the release of war prisoners not of Turkish nationality now in India, the removal of restrictions on trade and the movement of individuals; the resumption of burials at Najaf and Karbala subject to certain hygienic restrictions, the release of certain civil prisoners, and certain gratuities to civil employees. General Costello ended by announcing the surrender of Austria.

Peace must be at hand and that means home. That is the one surmounting thought in mine, and I do not doubt, many other minds tonight.

Nov 5th

There is a rumour today that when the Armistice was granted to Austria, Germany was offered it, if she accepted within 48 hours. If not she was not to have another offer at all. Apparently the Emperor Karl is about to abdicate or has already done so (*Charles l of Austria, the last ruler of the Austro-Hungarian Empire. Technically, he did not abdicate but rather 'renounced participation in state affairs' on 11 November 1918*). If the rumour was true and Germany does accept it we ought to hear tomorrow or the next day and then I suppose the weary world will once more be at peace. It seems like divine impudence for the Huns to make their proposals for no more aerial bombing behind the lines. They seem to forget Paris and London and countless other places. The hospitals etc. Ah well! it is another day nearer home.

Nov 6th

The chief event today was a visit I had to pay to Khawas with Dacres and Cosby to investigate an affray. The tale was as follows: The IWT Sergt lives with two sappers and our men at Khawas. On Tuesday evening he sent a Nokada and two Khalassies (*or Sepoys – Indian soldiers in the service of Britain*) into Hillah for rations. On the way they came across some Arab villagers who took them for thieves and set upon them. Apparently their clothes were torn and they were beaten. The Headman then appears to have had compunction and released them and took them to his own house. The Nokada however escaped and ran back to the Armbur and fell down exhausted outside. Being found by another of his Khalassies the latter ran into the Armbur and informed the Sgt. He sallied forth with four BORs, about a dozen Khalassies and carrying four lamps. They saw the lights in the village which however were doused at their approach and when they got near fire was opened on them. The party opened out and lay down and two shots were fired one of which killed an Arab. Then the Headman sallied forth with hands up and the two Khalassies were brought out. The Headman was tied up and taken back to the Armbur and kept for the night. I suppose the Sergeant is at fault in having taken any part in the inter Arab scuffle.

Nov 8th

There is a strong rumour though that Germany has agreed to our Armistice terms. I should have thought in that case we should have heard of it. If it is true it is the day which for more than four years has been the heaven of our hopes.

Nov 9th

I see that they have more or less driven Prince Rupprecht's 71 divisions into a corner and quite likely the armistice has been signed (*Prince Rupprecht of Bavaria had been given command of the German Sixth Army*). Delegates from Germany are with Foch and quite likely the armistice has been signed (*Marshall Ferdinand Foch was by now Supreme Commander of the Allied Armies and it was he who accepted the German request for an armistice on 11th November*). The German navy has mutinied and there are serious disturbances in Hamburg and other places.

Nov 11th

A series of tremendous storms burst over the whole country last night and this morning the whole place was flooded. I was sleeping on the verandah and for hours I watched it lightning from every corner of the heavens at once, whilst the thunder continued as a constant rumble and not as distant claps. The Kifl line is closed till further orders and the roads are impossible.

At the present moment we are all expecting the news of the German acceptance of the peace terms. The latest Reuters shows that they are in a hopeless plight and have practically no alternative. The hour for accepting the Armistice expired at 11 o'clock today, i.e. 2.0 o'clock our time and we are expecting the news through every minute. If it has been signed then the people at home know by now and England will be in a blaze of victorious happiness. Bavaria apparently has declared herself independent of the rest of Germany.

Nov 12th

The news we were so eagerly expecting is through. The Hun signed the Armistice at 5 a.m. yesterday and hostilities ceased at 11 a.m. and so after 4 years and 3 months this cruel war is over. I expect there were tremendous scenes in London yesterday. I do hope the authorities at home have got the situation in hand and clear plans for settling down. It will be interesting to hear the terms of the Armistice which are, I expect, pretty drastic. I wonder what will happen to us out here.

Nov 13th

G.H.Q. last night ordered a display of fireworks so Hillah rejoiced in flare lights, star lights, parachute lights and all sorts of military devices and quite a brilliant show was made. Today and the two following days are holidays.

Lloyd George has announced the chief of the Armistice terms including complete evacuation of all territories occupied also all Rhine bank to depth of 30 Kms on right bank, surrender of 3000 guns, 30000 machine guns etc, handing over of fleet etc, occupation of forts in Baltic.

Nov 14th
I see that all officers and men with experience in Army Pay work are to go to India to clear up soldiers' accounts. That is a definite move towards demobilisation. I see that the Huns are squealing about the terms of the Armistice and asking for relaxation but I hope it will not be granted. It says that scenes of the wildest enthusiasm prevailed in England when the news of the Armistice was received but at the front it was accepted with a quiet thankfulness. That is what one would expect. I wish news would come of a mail from England or better still that I should be recalled.

Nov 29th
We have started by cancelling wood contracts which is a step towards demobilisation as wood will be sent as ballast in transports from India.

Nov 30th
Four years ago today I arrived at St Omer from Bailleul to help form the French Machine Gun School.

DECEMBER 1918
Dec 16th
Men over 41 and promoted men and demobilisers are to go off as quick as possible.

Dec 22nd
Each day comes fresh signs of demobilisation. Today two more people, one an officer and the other a man were sent for. It becomes rather difficult to adjust the depleted staff to the work. The General has given the staff half a dozen turkeys and some whisky and beer and the office will be closed.

JANUARY 1919
January 1st
A new year, and may I soon be home. It is just a year since I started this diary and I

have just jotted down the one or two things which have struck me each day.

Jan 3rd
I managed to finish reading through the proceeding of the Court of Enquiry into Expenditure. Apparently Persia was stirring and the Democratic party didn't want us. Further north the Bolsheviks did not want us and what with inexperienced and inadequate staff, political reasons for bribing tribesmen and parties, the employment of rogues, and enemy action we seem to have wasted some money up there. The case is full of references to food shortages for troops and populations, contracts were iniquitous and seldom carried out, money was scarce and only to be exchanged at a loss.

FEBRUARY 1919
Feb 2nd, Sunday
In the evening the General, Ladd and myself with 6 of the office staff started off for Hillah. We had dinner at the officers' hospital with Harding and then motored to Baghdad Wick. We had a special sleeping carriage and travelled very comfortably to Hillah arriving about 6 o'c in the morning. I had brekker and shaved and then joined a party for Babylon (*Akkadian city-state founded in 1867 BC, whose few remains are to be seen in Al-Hillah about 55m south of Baghdad*).

We were very lucky today in getting Capt Hall (a professor) to take us round. Townsend lent me a roll of films so I hope I shall have some photos of Babylon. We first visited the German's quarters which are just as they left it. There was a calendar with the date 24 March 1917 the day they left. It is a tear off calendar. Their rooms contained their books and private effects (many photographic appliances) and a number of very tall collars, cuffs and dicky shirt fronts. There were also a number of bones, skulls and bits of pottery and other curios. In the courtyard was a heap of rounded stones, the ammunition of catapults probably employed in Alexander's time (*Alexander the Great died in Babylon in 323 BC at the age of only 32*). The stroll round the ruins was very interesting. This time I saw the remains of the old stone bridges across the Waters of Babylon and the site of the authentic tower of Babel (*the site of the Biblical Tower of Babel is not certain but archeologists discovered what appears to be the foundations of a tower in Babylon*). Ishtar's Gate of course I saw again and the covered way and also the temples of Marduk and another (*Ishtar's Gate was the eighth gate to the inner city of Babylon built in about 575 BC on the orders of King Nebuchadnezzar and Marduk was the sun god of Babylon whose temple was built at about the same time. It was a ziggurat estimated to have been about 91 metres high*).

It was topping weather and I thoroughly enjoyed the day. The General came up by car but I came on the train and got back at about 8 o'c tired but having had a most enjoyable day. The country looks very green and fresh.

The Dragon representing Marduk the chief God of Babylon on the Ishtar Gate.

Feb 12th
Apparently the General has put in an application to be allowed to proceed to England with all his notes, memoranda, etc, and take an officer and two clerks with him and a sort of mission from Mespot. I hope it may come off and that I may be the lucky officer chosen to go with him.

Feb 14th
Hart has adopted a system of marking for Officers to determine their priority in going home, e.g. each year's service counts 4 marks, so many for each year of age, so many for being maimed, etc. etc. I think I might get home fairly early on it. I have

got to be inoculated against plague tomorrow which is rather a bore.

Feb 15th
Slater and I were inoculated this morning and my arm is quite painful.

Feb 16th
I stayed in bed all the morning, not so much because I felt seedy, but being Sunday and feeling lazy I used the inoculation as an excuse and just stayed.

Feb 17th
We are gradually getting plans out for the transfer of the Dept and I think I shall be kept on for a month or two more. I am simply getting most frightfully impatient now. I hear that the Railway has broken down between Kut and Hainaidi.

Feb 25th
A red letter day. My order for demobilisation has come through and I am to go home as a demobiliser. I hope this means I have a good job awaiting me. Slater wants me to wait till the middle of March so I have wired the Base for permission to do so. I must cable home tomorrow. I hope to start on the 16th March. I am getting so excited that I can hardly bear the few remaining weeks in patience. Beside this I have received two letters from home but compared with the order to go home even the Mail for once takes second place.

Feb 26th
I am still pretty full of my shortly arriving demob day, though I find plenty to do to keep my mind off it. The General is going off about the same time as I am so I have fixed up with him that I should travel down on the S32 which will be quite jolly and comfortable. I wrote to Doris (*his wife*) in the morning to break the news and managed to conceal it for two whole pages. I decided not to cable as it takes at least 10 days to get through and I don't much see the object as there will be a 2 month's wait after the cable whereas by announcing it by letter I may hope to follow up the news myself quite quickly.

Feb 27th
I am trying to arrange for the release of as many people as I can before I go and have

written to all and sundry for various particulars.

Feb 28th
The last day of the month and the last of this Department's existence. It has been exactly 2 years and 1 month in existence and I have been with it for exactly half of that time to a day. I have been feeling rather seedy this morning.

MARCH 1919
March 1st
Today the Department comes under new control. G.H.Q. signalised this event by removing our telephone again, but they will have to put it back again as before. Some soldier administrators (sic) are curiously inept. Another mail should be due in Basra today. I am very keen to know all news from home now I am so near to starting. I have just been running over my accounts as far as I can in order to size up the possibilities for when I get back. I do hope the fact of my being a demobiliser means that I have been given a decent job.

March 10th
The Baghdad week starts today. Early this morning officers of the Department commenced to roll up from all corners of the earth for the General's dinner. The office has been cleared out and is being transformed into a dining hall.

March 16th
Final day today. I spent all the morning packing and gave instructions to Cameron to see them on board this afternoon.

March 17th
Red letter day. We are off and my thoughts have already done the few thousand miles home. We had a busy time getting the things aboard and saying good bye, but eventually started off just after 10 o'c. We are most comfortable. I have a cosy little cabin and there is a decent bath room. The General, S.M. Pankhurst, Cameron (my batman), Cpl Hodgson (the General's) Cullen, Wilson and Sanderson (of the footer team) are all the passengers and so we have plenty of room. The boat is ugly looking but very comfortable and has belonged to the Department as an inspection ship for some time. A little while ago we passed the Diala (*River*) and we are now well in

view of Ctesiphon (*one of the great cities of ancient Mesopotamia. In the 6th century, Ctesiphon was reputed to be the largest city in the world*). I forgot to mention yesterday that I have got a British Empire decoration, I don't know whether MBE or OBE.

March 18th
Last night we got a little below Zeur before anchoring. We had a beautiful days run and everything is as comfortable as possible. The night was a rough one with wind and rain but I slept well. I had a very curious dream. It appeared as if Doris and I were not married and that something I had done had upset her very much so that she broke off the engagement. I can remember how I argued and entreated and persuaded but she would not relent. It was a frightfully vivid dream and I was very distressed. However, at its worst and just as I had given up hope I woke up and was greatly relieved to discover it was only a dream.

The General (*presumably General Dickson*) is apparently booked to return in November. He is going to England now for about 5 months and then comes back here for the remainder of a year, receiving about £1,500 for it. Apparently he is to act as a sort of Secretary of Commerce. While at home he is going to publish his book on the work of the Department. We have just concocted letters and telegrams to the base trying to get all our men through with us to England. I can hardly realise that I am on my way really and truly.

I understand from the General that I have been recommended for the C.B.E. in the Peace Gazette.

March 19th
We arrived at Kut last night about 4.0 o'c and tied up for the night. All day long we travelled down the winding river. The country is perfectly flat and at one time looking through glasses there was not a single tree to break the monotony. It is all wonderfully green however as far as the eye can reach and quite different from[C] when I came up. At Kut last night Lt Col. Gordon Browne the commandant came aboard and stayed to dinner. We had a first class meal and got to bed early. We started off this morning at 5.0 o'c and by 8.30 had passed Sheikh Saad. We are now nearly at Aligargh and the Pushtikuh mountains are relieving the monotony on our left. The floods are out and apparently most of the country between the river and the mountains is flooded.

March 20th

We stayed for an hour yesterday at a spot on the river just short of Aligargh for minor repairs and I took a stroll on shore. The grass is about 18" long and the country is a mass of green. We caught a fish whilst there and the General and I have had fresh fish at every meal since. Later on we put in at a spot where there is alleged to be the remains of a very ancient brick bridge (Sassanian – *the last pre-Islamic Persian Empire 224 to 651 AD*)) but we could not discover the traces. For the night we put in at Kumert. The Sheikh, a fine old boy, came on board and made himself at home. He brought many eggs and fowls and in return bore off a photo of the General and a cigarette box of Najaf ware and much whisky. Conversation with Sheikh Nejuin was carried on by the General in English to his Indian servant, the latter passing it on in Hindustani to an Arab boy who then turned it into Arabic and vice versa. The Sheikh stayed some time and produced his portfolio with photographs. One of his chief treasures was a picture on silk of the King out of a packet of BDV cigarettes (*from late Victorian times in the UK and USA, cigarette manufacturers enclosed printed crests etc on satin in their packets, similar to cigarette cards. BDV were made by Godfrey Phillips Ltd*). This morning he sent about 2 gallons of milk aboard at sunrise and we were off soon after. We are now getting to Amara. Again the most striking feature is the marvellous greenness and freshness of everything.

March 21st

We arrived at Amara about Breakfast time and put in for the day. While the General went to see General Wanshope and Col. Gordon I went across to see Prior. We phoned up the Base where our letters had been received and they said they were making arrangements for the whole of our party to go on the EKMA. (S S Ekma, *a ship in the B.I. Line, built in 1911*) on the 25th.

Later on we met a man John just back from England and he said the Varsova was just about due at Basra and was going direct to Suez (*in fact the Varsova had been converted into an ambulance transport*). We asked Col. Bartholemew who was going off to Basra last night to see if he could fix that up for us. If this can be done it would save a lot of trouble and expense. I spent the afternoon in the Club reading and in the evening, we dined with Prior, Glenworth, Harfield, Hawkes, Aldridge and Morgan. Then on board about 10.30. This morning we got off about 6.0 o'c and I suppose we shall get to Kuma, the reported site of the Garden of Eden, sometime today (*Genesis located the Garden of Eden as being at the confluence of four rivers, one being the Euphrates*).

March 22nd

We did a rather slow passage yesterday. Before Kuma for many miles the river is very narrow and tortuous. Throughout its course the Tigris winds about in a most amazing way but just before Kuma it describes its champion loop, at one point the river describes a circle about a mile in diameter and it comes to within 80 yards of itself again. The intervening ground is only marsh and it seems extraordinary that a swiftly flowing river does not just break through and flow straight on. I borrowed a few films yesterday and took one or two photos, one of Lyra's tomb. We had to tie up once or twice yesterday with boiler trouble and in the famous loop we and another boat played a regular game before we could get past. We tied up early last night some miles short of Kuma and the men caught us some fish for dinner. We were off very early this morning and passed Kuma soon after 5.0 o'c. At that point the Euphrates joins us and now we are on the broad Shatt al-Arab. I expect we shall get to Basra about 10.0 o'c.

March 23rd

Basra has developed enormously and must now I suppose take rank as one of the large ports of the world. From Gurrat Ali right down well below Ashar there are miles and miles of wharves, and the river is crowded with shipping of all sorts from the B.I. (*British India Steam Navigation*) boats to launches and mahelas. There are slipways and dockyards and ship building places. Basra now boasts a first class hotel and some miles of asphalted road.

Yesterday morning we went up to 3rd Echelon and got the whole party booked on the Aronda which sails on the 26th (*S S Aronda was built in Glasgow and launched in 1912. It was torpedoed but sank in shallow waters; the mail it was carrying was rescued and sent on, and the ship was repaired and put back into service. Mahatma Gandhi later travelled in it*). We then lunched with Col James at the DDS&T's office. In the afternoon I did some shopping and had a refreshing hair cut and shampoo. In the evening we dine with Col Bartholomew: Ashton was there and also Graham Brooks who has not yet gone and the base contingent of officers. We are still staying on board the S32. This morning we have been in to see accommodation to verify our ship. If I can get away I am going to accompany Fitzgerald on a fishing expedition. There was a whole school of funny little fish all round the boat this morning. About a foot or 8 inches long they had a sharp projection in front about 2 inches long. The EKMA came in this morning.

March 24th
I went out with Fitzgerald and another officer fishing. We drove to Gurrat Ali across the railway pontoon bridge and settled on the piece of land between the Tigris and the lower arm of the Euphrates. It was very beautiful there and I found a shady spot where the luncheon basket was unpacked and I settled down for a lazy day. I had picked up my mail on the way out. The letters from home are rather pessimistic in tone. The pater seems now to regret having given up the business. Doris and the mater are anxious about Christine (his *sister*) and of course the labour disputes overshadow everything. Ah well, we must hope for the best. Doris is leaving the office and I think very rightly intends to study housekeeping till I come home.

Boyce, the other man with us, caught two salmon (10 and 12 lbs) and we returned after tea having had a topping time. I dined with Fitzgerald at the hotel - a really first class show. It is fine to see the European ladies arriving in the country now. Today we fixed up some minor matters and hear that we are to embark on the 26th.

March 25th
I finished up yesterday by dining with Fitzgerald and Bartholomew at the Hotel. We have had a fairly uneventful day today. The old S32 was towed out in midstream this morning to a position nearer the dockyard. We went ashore and I got some English money and ascertained that we definitely embark tomorrow. Tonight Fitzgerald and Bartholomew dine with us on board

March 26th
Today is the great day. In the morning the General and I went ashore to fix up the last few details such as readdressing letters, etc and sending wires to India to help us forward from Bombay. We had a motor-bellum alongside at 11 o'c to take all our kit up to the Aronda with the men. An early lunch at 12 o'c and then off in our launches up the 6 miles to the wharf. We had very little trouble getting on board and she is a very nice boat. The General has a cabin quite close to mine and they are roomy and very comfortable. I share mine with Col Wellborn. We managed by an audacious piece of wrangling to get all the men into second class cabins so they are also very comfy.

This evening we went ashore and said goodbye again to Fitzgerald. His Depot is a wonderfully big place. Sir John Hewitt when he came to Baghdad told the General that when he saw Basrah it made him proud to be an Englishman. It is certainly a wonderful place now and the activity is amazing.

March 27th

We sailed at 9 this morning and passed the old S32 about 9.20. Hodgson and the General's Indian bearer were waving to us. We hear that the Aronda stays at Bombay for about 10 days and then goes home. I hope they will let us stay on board but I am afraid we shall be transhipped. The Shatt al-Arab is a pretty river the numerous creeks especially being delightfully green and rustic looking. Abadan which we passed this morning has grown enormously and is quite a vast place. Its numerous gasometers and chimneys stretching far back into the desert give the air of a big manufacturing town to the place. We crossed the bar about 5 o'c and are now making for Bushire (*on the Persian Gulf*). At last I feel that I am really on my way home.

March 28th

This morning found us anchored off Bushire. We were about 4 miles out as the water is very shallow. As we were to stay here till about 4 o'c p.m. it was arranged for several of us to go on shore. We started off about 10 o'c and proceeded by a devious channel. On the way we passed the solitary representative of the Persian navy, the gunboat 'Persepolis'. She looks quite trim and neat but I don't think she is much practical use. I understand that she only goes to sea once a year to take the Persian Governor at Bushire 'The Lion of the Sea' to Bombay and that she had just returned from this trip.

When we got on shore Grant Peterkin and I were thrown on our own resources as the remainder of the party, Generals Dickson and Brownlow, a Major Wellborn and three sisters were off in cars to the British Residency. We wandered through the bazaars and found the town consisted of filthy narrow winding streets between broken down houses. All articles in the bazaar were outrageously dear and for the most part were cheap English goods.

At 11.30 we had had enough but we had to kill time till 3 o'c. One pitiful sight we saw. A poor little girl was wandering through the bazaars crying her heart out. She had a tremendous open syphilitic sore on her ankle. No one paid the least attention to her and doubtless she will wander about neglected until she dies.

We found the naval officers offices and quarters and they very kindly took us in and gave us lunch. It appears that all drinking water for Bushire has to be brought by boat as the local supply is too brackish. We stopped here to deliver water. After lunch the Commander very kindly lent his car to take us to the Political Residency some miles away. The road was a very good metalled road (made, of course, and kept up by us) and the country was not half bad. The corn was very sparse and short and in many places showed signs of shrivelling up. For the first time for many months I was on a road which undulated slightly. The residency itself is a huge and well-built house with a large garden, but this latter in the absence for a week or so of the Resident and his wife is being neglected and looks parched and dried up. We got back to the ship soon after 4 and started up again about 5 o'c. We are now running down in sight of the Persian Mountains on our port.

March 29th
Today the great excitement was arranging a sweep on the days run. I took 5 tickets and drew two numbers. I sold one of these for 12 rupees so that I profit 7 chips.

March 30th
We ran through the entrance to the Gulf during the night and we are now heading across the Indian Ocean. The days run was 320 knots and I had a ticket 337 which was within one point of 2nd prize. We are running very slowly as we are not wanted in Bombay apparently before the 4th. I don't know whether I have mentioned it but we have a number of sisters on board. This afternoon I had tea with two of them in the Chief Engineer's cabin and spent the time before dinner chatting to one of them (the prettier of the two). Besides the sisters there is an abominable person on board called Mrs Norbury. She spends most of her time dressing (including painting) and the remainder smoking, drinking cocktails and discussing the possibilities of platonic friendship with the different officers on board. A very affected, worthless sort of creature.

APRIL 1919
April 2nd
We have just arrived at Bombay. It has been a very pleasant passage and the weather though overcast has given us a smooth passage. My table companions are quite pleasant and I spend a good deal of time chatting to the sisters. Two of them on board I have singled out as being the nicest and curiously enough both are in many ways very like Doris. This seems to me to show that my taste is unchanged and is quite a helpful sign. I have spent quite a lot of time with one of them Miss Rothery and find her quite a quiet natural type of girl, a very pleasant companion. I have just taken some photographs of the Matron, a Miss Leach and Miss Rothery and also of the Chief Engineer a very decent Boilerman. I don't know whether we shall go ashore today but I rather fancy we are likely to stay on board till the 4th.

[C] April 5th

On the 3rd all the Sisters had to go on shore whilst those five who were to go on the Port Lyttleton stayed on board till yesterday (*S S Port Lyttleton was requisitioned in 1916 as a troopship*). I went ashore with the sisters and we landed at about 12.30. I had asked Miss Walker, Miss Leach and Miss Rothery to lunch with me but in view of the late arrival had to leave them to sort things out and arranged to call back for them at 4 o'c for tea. I had lunch at the TAJ Hotel.

Bombay is a very fine city and the streets and building appear to be better laid out than in any city I have been in except Dresden. I felt very lonely at lunch and overhearing that it was good business to drive to the Malabar Hill I formed the bold resolution of calling early for the sisters with a taxi and taking them for a drive. I got there round about 2 o'c and was fortunate in finding Miss Rothery in the entrance hall which saved me from the shy business of asking a strange sister. The matron couldn't come but Miss Leach could so the three of us started out and had a ripping drive.

Malabar Hill a very pretty place and gives a good view of the city and harbour. We went on further and saw public gardens, the Race course, a snake charmer, the towers of silence where the Parsees expose their dead to the Vultures (*Parsi tradition is to place their dead-on towers to be eaten by birds of prey*), a Mohammaden temple built out on an island in the sea, the Maharrajah of Gwalior's palace, some wonderful houses and gardens. Altogether we had a ripping drive and it seemed all too soon when we got back to the boats at 3.35. We there picked up Miss Walker and went to the Taj and had a tremendous tea. General Brownlow joined us and we sat in the palm terrace listening to the band.

Later on we adjourned to the lounge overlooking the harbour and watched the élite of Bombay going to and fro. The Sydney and the New Zealand were in harbour and Jellicoe was dining ashore that evening (*HMAS Sydney, launched in 1912, was an Australian light cruiser, from which the first launch of an aircraft from an Australian warship was made in 1917. HMS New Zealand, launched in 1911, was a battlecruiser presented to Britain as a gift from New Zealand. It carried Admiral John Jellicoe on a world tour to review naval defences in the Dominions*). A curious spectacle was to see the number of expensive motor cars gliding about full of Parsees. It was all too soon when 7 o'c came and I had to take my companions back to the huts and I was quite sorry to have to say goodbye. All three were very charming and Miss Rothery so constantly reminded me of Doris that I sometimes felt that I must be falling in love with her.

Yesterday we came on board the Port Lyttleton. After the Aronda it is a most disastrous change. I am sharing a very small stuffy cabin with the General and a padre. I was feeling seedy when I came on board and I felt very unhappy at the change. During the night I got one of my old attacks of stomach trouble with violent pains and I was up most of the night. Amongst other things I was violently sick. However I feel much fitter this morning although I have judged it wiser not to eat any breakfast.

April 9th
We are now raising Socotra on the Port side (*a small archipelago of four islands in the Indian Ocean, about 150 miles east of the Horn of Africa*). Up to the present we have had a quiet and uneventful voyage. Weather conditions good, food excellent, officers' quarters cramped but it is a good ship for the men. I have been very seedy all the time but am feeling a bit better. We are playing quite a lot of chess on board but I am very out of practice.

April 11th
Nothing much to report. Passed Aden at 12 noon today. It is very hot and practically no breeze. Chess still occupies most of our time. Am feeling somewhat fitter. We expect to pass Perim at midnight (*a small volcanic island off the coast of Yemen*).

April 14th
Nothing much to report. We have had a fairly even run up to the present. On the 12th and 13th we passed the Twelve Apostles, little islands. This morning a good breeze sprang up ahead and now is blowing half a gale. The ship is pitching a bit but is marvellously steady as there is quite a sea running. We expect to get into Suez about Wednesday midnight.

April 16th
The breeze still holds. I felt a little squeamish on Monday night but survived alright. We have just passed a Japanese Torpedo boat destroyer escorting a submarine. They passed quite close to us. There is high land in view on the West and I fancy we are at the entrance of the Gulf of Suez - 5 p.m. We are now well in the gulf with the peninsula of Sinai on our starboard and Egypt to port. Should arrive at Suez by 8 tomorrow morning.

April 17th
Arrived at Suez at 8.30 this morning. During the day a crowd of other boats arrived a lot of them with troops on board. Three Jap TBDs (*Torpedo Boat Destroyers*) and 2 submarines came out of the canal this afternoon apparently on their way home. I believe two of them were the identical ones which convoyed the Menominee (HMS Menominee) when we came out. We started up again about 4.30 and now just after 5 have entered the canal. I wrote a short note last night to Doris which I hope to post tomorrow at Port Said.

April 19th
Arrived Port Said at breakfast time yesterday. Went ashore and looked in the shops. I nearly bought a tea service for Doris at £11 but the shopman would not accept a draft without reference to his boss who was at church and I had no money. I then lunched and got Fairfax to come back to the shop with me and he advised me that the price was excessive. As it appears that in all cases shop keepers out east have been rooking the British officer right and left, I decided not to get anything.

Arrived back on board at 3 o'c. Coaling going on. This owing to lack of labour did not finish till today at 4 o'c and we weighed anchor at 5.25. Several liners with Australians have passed through the other way. And there were lots of ships in harbour going our way and I hear we are going to Plymouth.

April 20th
Easter Sunday. I went to a Communion Service in the Captain's cabin. It was a nice little service taken by the Padre who shares our cabin. The Ormonde passed us this morning (*HMS Ormonde, a minesweeper, built in 1906*). The weather is delightful though cool and there is quite a heaving swell on. The boat is pitching a bit but I am beginning to get my sea legs and don't notice the motion.

April 22nd
Both yesterday and today the ship logged 260 miles at midday for the preceding 24 hours run. We are due to pass Malta tomorrow and Gibraltar on Sunday evening and should reach Plymouth on Thursday week the 1st May. There was a good deal of swell on yesterday and today the ship is quite lively. We had some heavy squalls of rain last night and today.

April 23rd
I felt a bit qualmy (*nauseous*) this morning when I got up and was a bit off my breakfast. There was a high wind and a cross sea running. However the feeling wore off and during the morning the sea and wind moderated and I felt better and did ample justice to lunch. We passed Malta before midday having logged 270 miles in the 24 hours and by 6 o'c we were in sight of Pantallera Island (*Pantelleria is an island in the Strait of Sicily*). At that point we shall have to turn slightly to the north to avoid a danger area round Cape Bon (*a peninsula in Tunisia*). The wind is dead ahead and is quite strong and the sea is coming up again. This time next week we shall be getting ready to land, I hope. Anniversary of Harry's (his *brother*) death. Requiescat in Pace.

April 24th
Last night we ran into a heavy wind and between 12 and 4 a.m. we only made 7½ knots an hour. The ship bucketed about quite a lot and I couldn't sleep between 1 and 4 o'c. However I managed to survive and felt quite fit this morning. The sea is still pretty high and the wind is strong. We lost a good deal of time giving Cape Bon a wide berth owing to a mine field suspected there. I see that in the log last night's weather is entered up as 'High N.W. sea and Fresh gale'.

April 25th
The wind has dropped and the sea is calm again. We did 228 miles to midday yesterday and 244 to midday today. Africa is on our left hand. I am afraid Plymouth will not be reached till next Friday.

April 27th
Fine but dull smooth sea and wind light dead astern. Logged 265 miles by midday. Should pass Gib before noon tomorrow. Got our first glimpse of Europe just before tea.

April 28th
Passed Gib at 11 o'c. Tried to take three photos but light is bad and doubt if they are much good. Can just see Africa through the haze but have a good view of Gib. A whale passed us spouting just before breakfast.

April 29th
We saw a lot more whales in the Straits. Yesterday morning we passed St Vincent and turned north. A fresh wind rose and presently increased to a moderate gate. We logged 251 miles up to midday. By this time there was a high sea running and I tried to take some photos of the spray over the bows. Our pace decreased considerably and by 8 this morning we had only logged 124 miles nearly 100 short of our average. Now, (11 o'c) it is clearing up both the wind and sea having fallen considerably.

April 30th
A fairly heavy wind and sea kept up throughout the night. Passed Finisterre about 6 this morning. I am afraid we shan't get to Plymouth till Friday afternoon. We only logged 156 miles to midday yesterday and have been doing barely 8 knots since. Now we are in the bay the sea and wind is less than it was off Portugal.

IN THE BEGINNING
Douglas Belchamber had served the first years of the war in the Machine Gun Corps. In his diary he describes how it came to be serving in Mesopotamia.

FEBRUARY 1918
Feb 1st
A fine day and for the most part uneventful. I had my abrasions dressed by the doctor this morning and the rest of the day passed in ordinary office routine. I had finished up and was sitting in the mess about 7.30 this evening when Maj Gretton called me and told me the General wanted to see me. When I reported the General said that he had seen Col. Dickson and the Director of Local Resources and found that the latter was wanting a lot of extra help. If I cared to take on a job like that, he would give me a letter of introduction and I could call to-morrow. Needless to say I jumped at the idea and went to bed dreaming of tremendous possibilities.

Feb 2nd
I feel somehow that today will prove to be the turning point of my life. Something tells me that my Regimental Soldiering days are over and that I may shortly enter a career whose course may shape my whole future life. I saw Col. Dickson today. He is a big powerful man who strikes one at once as being master of his job. He has a genial manner and he received me in a most kindly way. He is lodged magnificently

in Baghdad and once more I appreciated all the refinements of civilisation. Large and spacious rooms, beautifully furnished and carpeted with all the little knickknacks that minister to one's minor conveniences and love of ease. But what more than all else impressed me was the magnitude of the work in which he is engaged. It is nothing less than an attempt to roll back 2000 years of ruin and restore this country to its ancient prosperity. Irrigation, communications, cultivation and above all organisation are needed and Col. Dickson kindly told me that he would be glad of my help in these vast projects. To me the idea of being engaged again on solid constructive work, work of civilisation as contrasted with my efforts for three years needing to learn and teach how to destroy, this idea alone filled me with tremendous joy. I cannot help idealizing and looking ahead to the time when once more this wasted desert deserves its old name of the Garden of the World. From a point of view of ambition I might be gratified by the implied promises of advancement given to me, but in honest truth I would prefer to serve in this scheme as a subaltern, to helping in any destructive work as a general. I do not say that my vision has not sought in the future some fancy hopes for myself. I build my castles in the air and think of myself as doing great deeds and earning a name. Doris could come here and live with me. Meantime I must get the General's permission to go and make a formal application for a transfer.

Feb 14th
I was Orderly officer today and got up at about 6.15. It was a lovely morning and since I was up I did not regret the necessity which forced me to such early rising. Just before I was going on parade at 8.50 Gore came round and told me that my orders had come so that I should have to report to the Director of Local Resources at once. I promptly made arrangements for all my things to be packed up in the Cook's cart and started off at 11.30. It is rather interesting to note that the West Kent's are engaged today in raiding all the Arab Villages near the Camp on account of various thefts which have taken place lately.

As I was crossing the bridge into Baghdad a Bosche (*sic*) plane came over and our Sentries promptly started to waste shells at a great rate. As far as I could see no bombs were dropped.

We had rather an adventurous time getting here. The roads leading from the main street to the river front where my quarters are (*sic*) very narrow and the Cook's cart got hopelessly jammed in one place. We had come a long way down the lane and came to a place where an angle of wall jutted out and made it impossible for us to pass. We took a brick out of the wall but could still not get by. Finally we had to take the mule out and back the cart right back.

I have got very comfortable quarters here indeed. After a 40lb tent it seems strange to be in a room which must be about 20' x 15' x 15' high as far as I can judge. I have two electric bulbs in the room and a decent stove and Hodder has managed to find a table and rig up another one and also a chair. In fact I am in clover. I sat out in the verandah overlooking the river this afternoon and read Arabic (when I was not dozing). I expect to start work tomorrow and I feel quite ready for it.

Feb 15th
I have now done my first day in the office. I am fitted up very comfortably in an armchair with a roll top desk and it feels quite like old times again. I could not do very much today but I looked through a lot of papers and I saw enough to satisfy me that the work embraces a very large area and will be very interesting. All sorts of problems are linked, political and financial and commercial, agricultural, labour questions, questions of transport, machinery, communications etc. etc. and I can see that the whole undertaking is even more vast than I thought. I find that office hours are about 7.30 am to 7.30 pm so that it will be quite a long day.

Athariston was quite interesting as he described the country and he is just going off with the Hush-Hush Brigade probably beyond Kermanshah. He has invented and built a model of a wooden device for sifting grain which should be quite useful I should think. Hodder went into Hospital today and I am afraid I shall not get him back again, worse luck.

The Belchamber family December 1916
standing (L to R) Christine Sophie, Ernest Henry (Harry) Douglas Foster, Winifred Mary
sitting (L to R) Christina (mater), Sidney William, (Will), Sidney Charlie (pater)

DOUGLAS BELCHAMBER

Having just reached the age of 26 at the outbreak of WW1, my father, Douglas Foster Belchamber, like so many hundreds of thousands of other young men, lost some of the best years of his life in a bloody and brutal war. At least he emerged physically unscathed in 1919, though his younger brother Harry was killed in France in April 1917 and his other brother, Will, was seriously injured in the trenches in France by a grenade blast.

The three brothers had all enlisted shortly after the outbreak of war in 1914, my father as a private in the Artists Rifles, having held a Territorial Army commission since 1910. In October 1914, he was sent to St Omer in France and soon after was appointed a "temporary" Sergeant Instructor. As he noted four years later in his diary, he helped form the French Machine Gun School. After about a year, he returned to England and was attached to the Machine Gun Training Centre at Grantham, having been appointed to a commission ("on probation") in the Artists Rifles.

In 1917, he became an acting Captain and possibly Adjutant of the 238th Machine Gun Company. In July, the Company was sent out to Passchendaele, where he was second in command of the service company responsible for supplying the troops in the front line. His letters to my mother, Doris, make for very interesting reading for the few months that they were there, but in October the company was then sent out to Mesopotamia (modern Iraq) as part of the 54th Brigade, the 18th (Indian) Division.

In the middle of February, he was seconded to the Department of Local Resources (DLR), first in Baghdad and later in Hillah, to help with the logistics of feeding the military and the civilian population. During his time in Mespot (as it was familiarly called) he kept a diary, as so many people did. This was not intended for publication and was more a series of jottings. He made no attempt to correct, edit or improve the text, so, even for such a highly educated person, there are mistakes of punctuation, spelling and grammar that I have made no attempt to correct on his behalf.

The diary is of particular interest, as it operates on several levels. There is the day-by-day record of what his work entailed and his interaction with his colleagues and subordinates. Underlying this main thread is his concern for those at home and his bouts of homesickness: his partially blind father (or the Pater, as this classically educated scholar was wont to call him) trying to maintain the boiler and laundry machinery, which his parents operated as a business and his mother's (or the Mater's) courage and resolution in keeping the family afloat, despite all the trials and tribulations of the war. For her, especially, the loss of one son and the grievous wounding of another must have been hard to bear, while trying to run a business, as well as having a partially disabled husband to look after and two young daughters to bring up.

And then of course a major concern was for his wife, Doris, whom he had not seen since their wedding when he was home on leave in December 1916. Doris lived initially with her parents-in-law in Clapham and, as a labour of love, she transcribed all the letters that father wrote to her while he was serving in Flanders. This was very convenient, since her writing was very legible, which his was not, and it is her transcriptions that have survived.

Apart from his home concerns about food shortages and the air raids, his constant anxiety was about the way the war was going in France; even until quite late in 1918, the Germans (or 'the Boche' or 'the Hun') seemed to be holding their own and even gaining back ground that the Allies had won, which is why he found it difficult to understand why the Americans were so long in entering the fray.

Finally, we see the scholar. Father had received an excellent education at Battersea Grammar School but, as his parents could not afford to send him to university, he had already obtained an external BA from London University before the war and then passed out first in the testing Civil Service examination. In Mespot, he did not allow his mind to stagnate; he started to learn Hindi and Arabic and brushed up on his maths. Above all, he read voraciously and quickly. His taste was catholic to say the least: Dickens, Austen, the Brontes, Zola, Hugo, Sven Hedin, Borrow, various Lives and Biographies among others.

As a mathematician, it is hardly surprising to read that he was delighted to find some kindred spirits in the Mess to play Bridge with and he even recorded the details of the four hands of one especially memorable game.

Not the least interesting matter in the diary is the question of father's army rank; one is never quite certain what his substantive rank was at any given moment. Before enlisting, he had held a Territorial commission, which he resigned on enlistment. He rose from a Private in the Artists Rifles to a Lieutenant Colonel with an MBE but the passage from the one to the other was a bit of a roller coaster.

In December 1914 he was appointed a 'Temporary' Sergeant Instructor and in March 1916 he was appointed to a commission 'on probation' in the Artists Rifles and attached to the Machine Gun Training Centre in Grantham. In 1917 he became a 'temporary' Lieutenant, then an 'acting' Captain until February 1918, when in Mesopotamia he reverted to 'temporary' Lieutenant with the Department of Local Resources. In March, he again became a 'temporary' Captain and in May he was given the 'temporary' rank of Lieutenant Colonel. Having reached England at the beginning of May 1919 he relinquished his rank of Lieutenant Colonel and so presumably went back to where he started nearly five years earlier, a humble Private.

The one commissioned rank below Colonel that he hadn't held was Major but two years after the war he had the satisfaction of being granted the rank of Lieutenant Colonel.

Finally, as my father became a senior civil servant, it must have given him real satisfaction to read General Dickson's final report on him:

"Hard working and of exceptional administrative capability. His handling of the many problems connected with the Euphrates Development were most successful and of very great service to the Department."

Thanks

I am very grateful to Colonel Sir William Mahon LVO for translating some army acronyms my father used; to Anthony Richards from the Imperial War Museum for revealing the meaning of others, to Majid for telling me the meanings of a number of Indian and Arabic words and finally to Graham Sacker who very kindly researched father's service

David Belchamber – July 2018

NOTE

I am grateful to David Belchamber for permission to reproduce part of his father's Mesopotamian diary and to Helen Belchamber, not only for her painstaking work in transcribing the letters and diary but for but pointing me in the right direction to include Douglas Belchamber's reactions to the final weeks of the war. RW

CHAPTER 4

Mazra'a Internment Camp
Commandant's Office Diary   Palestine   1942
Michael Higgins

Sunday, 4th January 1942
The inmates of Camp 2 have sent a petition to the Chief Secretary and a telegram to the Spanish Consul protesting against the accommodation and the food. They have heard that there are a number of empty houses in Sarona[1] and they want to get them.

Monday, 5th January 1942
A very cold day. There is snow on Carmel. Visited all huts. The inmates are complaining of the cold. Afternoon cleared up and camps 1 - 2 - 3 - 5 were allowed out for football. Rations were fair.

Tuesday, 6th January 1942
The cold weather continues. A large number of Jewish visitors arrived in spite of the cold weather. Inspected meat ration. Cabbage three days in succession. Night inspection. All sentries alert and on their posts.

---

[1] Sarona - German colony north of Jaffa - internment camp during WWII

Wednesday, 7th January 1942

A very strong east wind blowing. It is very cold. Mr **Grant** (Officer *in charge of Acre*) visited camp and spoke to the supervisor of No 2 Camp. They have not yet decided whether they are going on hunger strike or not. Mr **James** visited camp with a Mr **Bryant** to inspect the accommodation of the internees. The wind died down during the night.

Thursday, 8th January 1942

Mr **Scott** visited camp and continued his inspection and interviews until 6.30 pm. He heard all the complaints. especially those from No 2 Camp.

Friday, 9th January 1942

Half gale blowing from east again. Tried **Jansan** and **Szerbensky** for missing *Tamam*[2] and sentenced them to 7- and 4-days S.C. (*solitary confinement*) Internee **Mastearz Jerzy** released for service with the Polish forces. Sea mine exploded at military camp at 11.45 hours. Military Intelligence Officer captain (Captain **Humphries**) visited camp at 3.30 pm. He spoke about the communists interned here. He also interrogated **Stavanowski**, leader of the Poles. Spoke to the canteen contractor about the price of Devon Beef Loaf which he is selling for 70 mils per tin. This is advertised in Spinneys for 50 mils per tin.

Saturday, 10th January 1942

Mild day. Phoned Mr **Scott** about the camp requirements which are as follows:

	Number required	Number received
Suits	191	100
Underwear	317	100
Shirts	244	-
Pairs of shoes	338	100
Towels	317	300
Pairs of socks	287	100

---

2   Tamam - Arab word meaning OK - refers to the roll-call of inmates

Mr **Scott** has arranged to send the following today
500 blankets
100 pairs of trousers
100 jackets
100 pairs of socks
100 vests
100 pants
300 towels

Tried **Ahmed Assad Shaheen** for creating a disturbance in his hut and sentenced him to 7 days S.C. 4 days B.W. (*bread and water*). Message to say that the Spanish consul is visiting the camp at 11 am tomorrow. Clothing arrived from clearance camp at 3 pm. I issued out the blankets and towels. Night inspection, all sentries alert.

Sunday, 11th January 1942
The Spanish Consul visited the camp at 11.30 am and remained here until 2.30 pm. He interviewed the Italians and Germans, and he went inside both camps. He saw **Billy** who made a complaint about his medical treatment. He hurt his leg last night. The M.O. examined him and ordered complete rest. He made an admission order on Sunday and promised to send the ambulance this morning.

Monday, 12th January 1942
Mr Grant arrived at the camp and visited No 1 and No 2 compound. He also charged B.C. (*British Constable*) **Edmondson** for Court of Discipline. The rations were good and there is a definite improvement. I only hope the contractor will keep it up. Day cold but pleasant. Billy who sprained his ankle on Saturday night has not yet been removed to hospital. The ambulance did not arrive. I have seen the baking done by the Arabs and I consider it 'not good'. Since **Dashan** left, there is no baker capable of doing the job. Accordingly I am ordering the contractor to bring bread with the rations.

Tuesday, 13th January 1942
Cold dry day. I managed to get **Billy** away to hospital in the prison van. One of the internees **Charles P Arboud** complained about his treatment while he was at the clearance camp hospital. He states that he remained there 8 days without treatment and nourishment.

General complaint from Camp 1 about the canteen. Devon Beef Loaf is not now available in the canteen. Since I pulled the contractor up about the price, he charged 70 mils per tin, while Spinneys is advertising it for 50 pence per tin. Out of the 22 items demanded he was able to supply only 10. Also oranges were scarce. Notice came through about **Gegg**'s transfer to Waldheim[3]. Rations good and they arrived early.

Wednesday, 14th January 1942
A dry cold day. The three Czechs left for the Advisory Committee at 10 am. Inspected rations which were good and arrived early. Inspected huts 3 & 5. Have not yet completed putting the blankets on the wall of the huts.

Thursday, 15th January 1942
Cold, dry day. **Edmondson** was tried by a Court of Discipline in Haifa. I went to Barclays Bank in Haifa and arranged the exchange of LP192 Egyptian pounds and returned at 2 pm. Gegg was transferred to the Waldheim colony. **Faoud Othman** was released and handed over to the Police at Acre. **Black** was admitted to Haifa hospital suffering from worms. Spoke to Mr **Scott** *(person in charge of prisons)* on the phone regarding the camp, clothing, etc. The three Czechs arrived back from the Advisory Committee at 5 pm. A tender load of wood arrived from Acre. Visited guard and sentries after midnight. All alert. Visibility fair, no moon.

Friday. 16th January 1942
East wind blew up about 9 am, which made things in the camp rather miserable. Rations came early and on the whole the quality was good. The vegetables were cauliflower and potatoes. Inspector **Strong** went to Acre for board on unserviceable kit. Cheese was not supplied today. The contractor wanted to supply figs in lieu. I have demanded that cheese be brought to the camp this afternoon. Gave B/I (*British Inspector*) **Scully** permission to go to Jerusalem to arrange family affairs. **Egged** together with **Salamie** were released this afternoon. Gale blowing throughout the night. Lights went out at 8.30 pm.

---

[3] Waldheim - German Colony in Galilea - internment camp during WWII

Saturday, 17th January 1942
Strong gale blowing today. A Russian priest with his choir arrived and said mass in the recreation room. Rations inspected. Generally good, but no cheese again today. **George Fokialis**, a Greek, was handed over today to 2nd Lieut. **Abadgoglou**, the Greek liaison officer. 3.30 met the hut leaders of No. 2 camp regarding a change in the [*1 word*] regarding baths. I warned **Richard Mayer**, the outgoing bath-man, about his conduct.

Monday 19th January 1942
A mild day. Orders were received that 28 of the Jewish convicted in the camp were to be released. They were transferred to C.P Acre at 11.15 am. This cuts down the number of convicted to 4 persons and I hope to receive others to replace them to carry out work in the camp. **Harry Farley** returned to the camp today and at 6 pm a release warrant was again sent from CID. I visited the British Police Mess in the evening. They are in a bad way for cooking utensils.

Tuesday, 20th January 1942
A wet day. Went to Acre to arrange to get some kit for the BP mess, Spoke to Mr **Grant** about the conditions there. Inspected the rations on my return. Meat for PBX was not good. No cheese was brought. The contractor did not bring any meat for No 1 and No 2 camps. The attorney General arrived at 3 p.m. and started his interviews. He left at about 4.45. Took a mess meeting at the British Police mess. All the grievances seem to be about the lack of supervision in the kitchen. The mess canteen came in for a lot of criticism. News from Tel Aviv that Mr **Schief** was killed in a bomb explosion. A considerable amount of rain fell during the night.

Wednesday, 21st January 1942
Cold and bright. The Attorney General visited the camp at 9.30 am and finished his visit at 1.30. The rations were not good today. The contractor did not bring the full quantity of cauliflower, so I had to order 88 kilos from Kaskai. I also had to order 12 kilos of cheese. The contractor phoned for Mr **Grant** to lodge a complaint. I went around the camp with Mr **Grant** re proposals for British quarters. The hut leader of No 1 hut of Camp 1 came and complained about a certain Italian who changed his place in the hut without permission. On investigation I find that the Italian was justified in moving his bed. Changed over Camp 5 to Camp 3. I also confiscated

9 primus stoves from Camp 5. Four people out to Advisory Committee. Three to hospital.

Thursday, 22nd January 1942
A cold wet day. The rations were a bit better today. The drains of No 1 & 4 Camps have not been functioning properly since Tuesday. I only managed to get the PWD (Public *Works Department*) to send out a man today, but nothing could be done about it and it is left over until tomorrow. Went to No. 1 camp to see what arrangements were made regarding No 1 hut. I took down a partition which was erected between an Italian and a Czech. 100 pairs of shoes received at the camp. Visited guards and sentries after midnight. All were alert and regular.

Friday, 23rd January 1942
A cold wet day. PWD came to repair the drains. Inspected No.1 Camp. Rations were good except for the fact that there was a little too much bone and skin, which I cut off and returned to the contractor.

Saturday, 24th January 1942
Mild day. Strong off duty. Rations were very bad. The doctor condemned 34½ kilos of meat. The contractor sent another consignment of meat which was just as bad. I had to order this through Kaskai. He was ordered to bring another today but he could not supply it. Rations did not come until 1230. Meat arrived from Kaskai and a bill submitted for LP 7.425. Sixty suits of clothes arrived from the Clearance Camp. 1, 2, 3 & 5 campos were out today on football.

Monday, 26th January 1942
Mild day. Inspected No.3 & 5 camps. No 3 camp was in a terrible mess. I took away some bed boards which had large nails stuck in them. I also took the trestles which were broken. No 2 camp did not put the rubbish outside the gate today. No 5 camp refused to carry out any task outside their camp. Rations were fairly satisfactory. I asked PWD to carry out some repairs to the bathroom door in No 1 camp without [*1 word*]. I also asked them to install the new boilers I had received but nothing doing. Telephone message from **Luskerm** to say that 10 persons are coming tomorrow. Night inspection before midnight. All sentries alert and regular.

Tuesday, 27th of January 1942
Strong east wind blowing this morning but by noon it cleared up and the day turned out fine. Saw the rations today; the meat was fair but the milk looked bad. I sent a sample of it to Acre for analysis. It was deficient of 2.1% fat - not fit for consumption, and there was a recommendation for prosecution. Mr **Grant** came over at noon and discussed various topics. He left at 2 pm. The Ration Contractor from Haifa came to speak about the rations but I knocked all the wind out of his sails when I showed him the doctor's report about the milk. Seven persons came in from Jerusalem at 5 pm - 5 Arabs, 1 Jew and 1 Pole.

Wednesday, 28th of January 1942
Mild day. Four persons - **Thomas Farris** and three others left for the Advisory Committee and one Italian left for Tantura to join his family. Dr **McQueen** arrived in camp and he had a look at the huts. He visited Camps 1, 2, 3 and the sick bay. Issued clothing to No 3 Camp. A bad wet night. I warned the sentries and guards to pay particular attention to No 2 hut, No 1 camp. I have information that **von Rottick** will make an attempt to get away.

Tuesday, 29th of January 1942
A very wet day. Seven Arab convicted arrived from Acre prison and started to work cleaning up the camp. Rations were fair and the contractor brought eggs for the first time since Mr **Scott's** last visit. 24 kilos of beef were returned to him. I insisted he noted that potatoes were insufficient for a period of 14 days.

Wednesday, 30th of January 1942
Cold dry day. Working on cleaning up the camp. Rations - mutton. potatoes and eggs. The mutton was good but was short by ten kilos. The contractor explained that he had arranged with 3 camp to give them something in lieu. **Jalton Jacobi**, **Albert Sengfield** have been instructed to CID Jaffa for a pass. Mr **Scott** visited the camp in the afternoon and inspected all camps and Baracandas. I complained about the rations but apparently the contractor got a complaint against me in first.

Sunday, 1st February 1942
Very mild day. General clean up in camp for DIG (*Deputy Inspector General*) visit. Mr **Grant** arrived and later Mr. **Ballantine** and Mr. **Sayer** came. He went to No 1 &

2 Camp. The leader of the German Barrack started his usual demands. He was pulled up for his insolent tone. DIG arrived at 1035 and 1140 he inspected the rations. They were good with the exception of a few kilos of bad meat which I returned. A general fight in No. 3 camp. I sent three persons to Acre Prison for solitary confinement. The ambulance arrived at 12 noon to take 2 persons to Athlit Hospital. Mr and Mrs **Grant** came to tea. Inspected camp after midnight. All sentries alert and regular. B. Sgt **Brosman** on night duty.

Monday 2nd February 1942
Cold dry day. **Oxley** on transfer to Clearance Camp. Inspected rations. Meat fair. I cut a lot of skin and bone off. Mutton was ordered but not supplied today. Inspected kitchen in Baracanda and sent for both supervisors. Czech officer called in the afternoon and paid out LP10 for the detainees. **Arbid**, an American, and **Alfanco** had a fight in No. 2 Camp about cookhouse supervision. I had both of them out. **Arbid** is suspicious that **Alfanco** is not doing his job as quartermaster properly and was doing a bit of spying.

Tuesday 3rd February 1942
Cold dry day. Inspected 1 and 2 Camps. Kitchen in No. 1 camp very bad. I have told the supervisor all about it. Inspected the A.R.P (*Air Raid Precaution*) shovels and scoops and found a number of them broken. **Pawel Waleski**, a Pole, was handed over to the Polish Recruiting Camp at Haifa, **Eugin Taenger** [*or Taenzer*] received from Refugee camp at Athlit.

Wednesday 4th February 1942
Inspector **Schwilly** for D.M.B. at Jerusalem. Electricity supply cut off from 8.30 am - 4 pm. Escorts left for Haifa Hospital and 8 Arabs left for the Advisory Committee, Jerusalem. Rations were fairly good today. Mr **Scott's** office phoned through to say that the contractor cannot supply mutton. A case of fighting in No. 2 Camp settled. **Mohd Shetat**, an Arab internee, was sending his boots home to his village today. He was one of the prisoners who was going barefooted around the camp until he got a new pair of shoes. Signed and affidavit that **Herbert Ollies** is an enemy subject and he is detained in this camp. Checked up on sentries at 10.30 pm. All alert. Water not turned off by Cpl of guard.

Thursday 5th February 1942
Dry cold day. Rations came early. I returned 10 kilos of meat which was bad. There is still a question of 63 tins of sardines which are outstanding since 20 -21.

Friday 6th February 1942
Went to Jerusalem and swore an affidavit before the Crown Counsel. Stayed with **Wiggie Bennet** and went and saw **Peter Gallagher**. Left camp at 7.30 am.

Saturday 7th of February 1942
In Jerusalem a big job to get a car to return. Went to Mr. **Millar** CID who arranged to send a detainee to the F.L.C. I arrived at the F.L.C. at 1.15 pm. Mr **Grant** was inspecting the camp, Checked up on accounts. **Jones** handing over to **Steward**. Got new fan belt for car. Returned at 2 pm.

Sunday 8th of February 1942
A splendid morning. Made a good clear out in B Camp Baracanda. Rations today were as follows:
    15 kilos of bad meat - returned
    26 tins of sardines and 399 eggs or a substitute outstanding for a long time.

Edmondson got 6 months imprisonment today. **Thomas Farris** is afraid he will die in this camp and wants to know what we are doing about it. Walked around the camp at midnight. All sentries alert.

Monday 9th February 1942
Cold bright day. Inspected the meat and it is as follows:
    Beef 13000 kgs
    Kosher 11.500 kgs
    bad and unfit for consumption. Inspected 1 and 2 barracks and the Baracanda. The Baracanda at "B" was not inspected by Sgt. **Black**. His excuse of no time cannot be accepted. **Turralion** is now supervisor of No. 1 camp, the previous supervisor got the sack because he struck one of the Italians.
    12.30 the contractor brought 11.500 kgs of kosher meat but Dr **Khairy** returned half of the meat again. 3 p.m. air raid alarm. Haifa A.A. guns went into action.

Tuesday 10th February 1942
Mr **Parkhouse** visited the camp and interviewed the following:
Dr Salliltis Markos
We discussed various problems. He left the camp at 10 am. The stores clerk from Acre Prison and I worked on stores until 1.30 pm. Insp. **Strong** inspected the meat today. I had a general complaint about the oil. **Herbert Ollies** left for Supreme Court Jerusalem. Tractor plough arrived from the stock farm and ploughed the area south of the camp, also a patch on the east side.

Wednesday 11th February 1942
Habeas Corpus case **Herbert Ollies**. Hearing in High Court today. The under mentioned left for the Advisory Committee:
  Walter Hedelma
  Rafiq Baki Hubkani
  Sherif Abdul Mabhani
  Khalil Shawkat Kisani
  Masrallah Odeh
  Javynis Navas Supreme Court.
Inspected the meat and found 6 kilos of the kosher meat was bad. The rations came early today. Acre Prison played 1st round of Dowbiggin[4] Cup and beat Haifa Rural 6 - 0. Warder Faiz Kassab of Central Prison died as a result of burns received when a primus stove exploded.

Visited the sentries at 9.30 pm. All alert and regular.

Thursday, 12th February 1942
Rations - 2 kilos of kosher meat returned to the contractor. Inspected all the camp today and was very dissatisfied with No. 3 Camp. I had all the hut leaders out and told them what I want for my inspection tomorrow. Took my car out to go to Acre and burst up my batteries at the new Rly crossing. Mr **Grant** spoke to me regarding certain information he had received about 4 & 6 huts, No. 4 Compound. I put on an extra British sentry inside the compound. Visited sentries at 10.30. All working well. No. 8 hut, 4 Compound were singing at 10.30 pm. I sent the Jewish Cpl to

---

[4] Dowbiggen Cup named after Sir Herbert Dowbiggin, Inspector General of Police in Ceylon - visited Palestine in May 1930 to carry out an efficiency review of the Palestine Police.

take the names of the detainees.

Friday 13th February 1942
Saw supervisor of No. 4 regarding the singing. He asked to see Mr. **Grant** regarding permission to sing in the camp after 10 pm.

Went to the bank at Haifa to check accounts and to get money from "Cooks" and from the port for internees. Returned back to camp at 2 pm. Mr **Grant** was on inspection and was very pleased with the camp. The rations were reported to be good. Six persons returned from Advisory Committee. Three British constables arrived from Athlit on temporary transfer and I made new dispositions around Camp 4.

Saturday 14th February 1942
Lovely sunny day. I inspected the meat ration which was very good today. Inspected camp and kitchens. Everything was in good order. Took on case of discipline against Altman for refusing to do duty on the morning of 8. 2. 42. Rations came today at 1 pm. Walked around the camp at 10 pm. Everything in order.

Sunday 15th February 1942
Day off. Heard of the fall of Singapore on the wireless. Took the children back to school and called at Bells in the afternoon. Checked up on sentries after midnight. All alert and regular.

Monday 16th February 1942
A bright sunny day. Several applications from British convicted for such things as tooth paste and other things and a request for swimming. Tried a Jewish internee from No. 2 camp for cursing the Cpl. during the morning roll call and sentenced him to 7 days S.C. in Acre, the rations were fair but there was some bread short.

Tuesday 17th February 1942
A mild day. Tried two Italians from Compound 1 but the corporal made a bit of a mess of the evidence, so I had to admonish one of them and sentenced the other to extra fatigue in his compound. Father **Eugene** called at the camp. He spoke to **Markis** and **Bodassian** and to Father **Lesain**. Rations were inspected by **Strong**.

THROUGH FIRE, SHOT AND SHELL

Wednesday 18th February 1942
Inspected rations which were good. In the afternoon I went to C.P. Acre to see Mr **Scott** regarding escapes. Inspected camp after midnight.

Thursday 19th February 1942
Got 12 recruits from Acre and fixed up the new disposition around the camp. Two petitions received from detainees and internees regarding rats and drainage. Found the contractor trying to do business with the Jews regarding the sale of tea. The Jews wanted sugar, cigarettes and tomatoes

Friday 20th February 1942
Cold wet day. Inspected rations and found everything in order. Issued out tooth paste and tooth brushes to 1 & 2 Camp. No 4 Camp demanded to be issued with them also, but I could not see my way to issue them.

Sunday 22nd of February 1942
A dull wet day. The transfer of the Jewish Sgt. was postponed until tomorrow. 11.30 am yellow light alert from Haifa. 11.40 all clear. Mr **Bird** arrived and stayed for lunch. Sgt **Hoskins** had my car out and had an accident with it. Walked around the camp and inspected all sentries.

Monday 23rd February 1942
Prison van left for Clearance Camp, Athlet with 4 internees and one detainee. No 3 Camp was not up to standard and I sentenced the following to seven days fatigue:
Mohd il Abid Shalat
Abdul Rahman Mohd Herabi
Ibrahim Awad Ali
Sgt **Skoflevitch** was transferred to Athlit Camp today and a Sergeant was transferred here. Tuesday

Tuesday 24th February 1942
Mr Grant arrived for inspection and inspected the whole of the camp with the exception of No 6 Compound. 1 and 4 Compounds were not good but the rest showed up well. Sgt. **Thomas** called, C.I.D. Jerusalem called and collected **Haim Marqvitch** who is wanted by Jerusalem Court. Visited sentries before midnight. All alert and regular.

Wednesday 25th February 1942

Went to Acre to meet Mr **Grant** but I missed him. Phoned him later at the Clearance Camp and arranged with him about the search which is to take place tomorrow. Wilhelma[5] phoned up to say that a captain representing the Red Cross was visiting me at 3.30 tomorrow.

Thursday 26th February 1942

7.15 am met **Bill** in camp and started a search in Camp 4. Among the articles seized were the following: 2 wire cutters, a number of files "6", hammers, chisels, hand saw, hacksaws, torch lights, pliers. a packet of letters prepared for transmission outside. Parts of a form which was cut up, bed trestles cut. At 2.15 Dr. ? of the International Red Cross called and interviewed the following leaders of the party in camp:

Leader of Germans
Leader of Anti-Nazis
Leader of Italians

He remained in the camp until 5.30 pm. He seemed pleased with everything he saw in the camp.

Friday 27th February 1942

Close, slightly dry. Inspector **Wade** came from Haifa regarding the letters which were found yesterday. Complete list of articles seized:

Knives, large pocket	5
Rasps various	9
Chisels	6
Hammers 2 lb	2
Wire cutters	3
..... large	1
Pan scrapers	1
.....	1
Small hammer	1
Saws various	8
Saw frame	8

---

[5] German Colony - internment camp in WWII

Torches, hand	3
4 pieces of	
Small wrench	1
..... hammer	1
Knives, French, large	1

Bundles of papers and letters sent to C.I.D. Haifa
5 Finns arrived in camp from Haifa
Visited sentries after midnight.

Saturday 28th February 1942
It was reported to me that B.I. **Strong** had an accident early in the morning whilst riding in the Acre. He was admitted to the Government Hospital suffering from a bad knee. Fourteen Jews from No 1 and No 2 wished to pray today. So I would not let them into No. 4, but I gave them a hut in No. 6. I received instructions from Mr **Parkhouse** to release **Ollies**. He was released at 3 pm. Went to Acre for pay and paid out in the afternoon. Saw the second round Dowbiggin Cup where Prison beat Acre Div 9 - 1.

Sunday 1st March 1942
A good day with east wind blowing. Insp. Hook came with my pay. W.O. **Zusis Patyckas** came to the camp to see Dr **Zakariah**. He had no pass. He had a small parcel with a pair of socks and a shirt.

Monday 2nd March 1942
Haim Masseyck for court in Haifa. A nasty east wind blowing. A large part of today's mail consisted of letters to the advisory committee in connection with the release of **Ollies** by the High Court. **Gallalie** to Athlit hospital. Greek intelligence officers visited the camp today and interrogated Jean. **Haim Masseyck** returned from Haifa Court. B.C. **Hutton** from Haifa to serve a term of imprisonment. The scroll, letters of Esther, arrived today and it was handed over to the Jewish supervisor this being the eve of Purim.

Scott was drunk in camp yesterday and **Williams** was absent from duty on the night of the 1st. Visited sentries before midnight. All alert and regular.

Tuesday 3rd March 1942
A bright sunny day. **Scott** came and weighed off two B. Cs, **Sacott** and ..... Three Arabs from Gaza were released and during the search I found a lot of my comp property going away to Gaza.

ADC called regarding the cart which is used here at the camp. It came here from Central Prison Acre. I will send it on.

Wednesday 4th March 1942
A dull cloudy day. Seven Arabs left for the Advisory Committee and on searching them I found seven letters (6 concealed in shoes and one in a pocket of the internees). A quarter of the meat was bad and it had to be returned to the contractor. The leader of the Germans complained that Hut 6 was displaying something in their hut which they objected to. I went in and found that there was a drawing of an aeroplane with Churchill, Stalin and Roosevelt. It was displayed near the door where it could be seen by all. I asked them to take it down and they did this.

20 kilos of meat sent by the contractors was again rejected as unfit. Went to Acre to collect family and met Mr **Grant**. A bit of trouble in No. 3 camp. **Selsby** left on transfer to clearance camp today. PWD came in to clear the drains in No. 2 compound.

Thursday 5th March 1942
A strong east wind blowing today. Investigated a case of swearing by a warder in No. 4 camp, but I could find no truth in the allegation. The drains of No. 3 camp are blocked up again. I sent for the PWD at 10.30. After inspecting the drains the workman withdrew; he could do nothing with them. I spoke to **Sheik Shakey** yesterday regarding his conduct in a put-up case against a warder. I tried two disciplinary cases. Walked around the camp after duty. **Brosman** on duty.

Friday 6th March 1942
Cold wet day. PWD sent their men to work on the drains in 'A' Camp. **Richard Chey** released for the Air Force today. The PWD took an aluminium cup out of the drains. This may have fallen in accidentally. I cannot see why anyone would want to block the drains.

Saturday 7th of March 1942
A mass was said in No. 1 camp for the **Duke of Aosta**, the Italian Commander in

Chief Abyssinia who died in Africa. Went to Haifa and conducted some business at Barclays Bank. I checked all the money in the safe and then exchanged some Syrian money for the internees. Called at the school and took the children home.

Sunday 8th March 1942
Had a day off. Went to mass with the children at the camp. This mass was in the form of a High Mass for the Duke. I understand some people in the camp are making propaganda on this point. I went to Haifa and saw Strong in hospital, He had his operation yesterday, and he is more cheerful today. Around the camp after midnight.

Monday 9th of March 1942
Good clear day. The drains in No2 Camp choked up. PWD was informed yesterday but nothing happened. The camp is absolutely flooded out. I phoned PWD again about the matter. They promised to send someone in one hour's time. At midday a party arrived to start clearing the drain. Dr **Bigger** arrived and remained in the camp for about half an hour. The PWD man left at 3 pm, he did not complete the job. I phoned **Newman** but without success. He said that the job would have to remain until tomorrow. A Pole, Captain **Cichocki** called and asked to see **Kasimowski**, a Polish internee. This captain said that he was wounded at Tobruk and he had just come from hospital and was soon returning to the Western Desert soon.

Tuesday 10th March 1942
PWD started early on the drains. 3 Czechoslovakians started a hunger strike in protest against their detention. Mr **McGillivary** the DDC arrived at 12 noon for his inspection. He had time only to see 'A' Camp. PWD finished at 4 pm, when all drains were reported clear. I visited sentries at 10.10 pm. Sgt **Hoskins** inside 'A' Camp inspecting doors and windows.

Wednesday 11th of March 1942
Seven persons left for Jerusalem for the Advisory Committee. Inspected No 1 and 2 compounds. No meat received from the contractor today. I will accept fish if it is possible to get it. Two internees left for X-Ray treatment in Haifa. **Hustler** was one of them. He is supposed to be planning an escape. I sent **Brosnan** in charge of the party.

Thursday 12th of March

Czech officers came to the camp today to carry on the interrogation of Captain **Zeckler**. Tried a number of disciplinary cases and sent one Arab 17 (1) C to solitary confinement for 8 days for trying to smuggle 6 letters out of the camp. He had the letters in his socks during Tamam today. No 4 Camp demonstrated against B. Sgt **Hoskins** because he locked them in for an extra 40 minutes in the morning. **Hoskins** should not have done this without my approval. I went to Acre to see the investigation officer about the case of wire cutting and the case of assault in the Arab camp. I visited the camp before midnight. All sentries alert and regular.

Friday 13th of March 1942

A doubtful day. I inspected the whole camp. Mr **Weingart** from the Swiss Consul General called regarding one of his people interned here. The Greek investigation officer is in the camp to interrogate Greek internees. Jean **Polypos,** a Greek internee, released for service with the Greek Army. Checked the guns and ammunition with Sgt **Black**. Sixteen Arabs out to the Advisory Committees.

Mr **Scott** came at 3 pm. He inspected the whole camp. Mr. **Grant** arrived at about 4 pm.

Saturday 14th March 1942

A bright sunny day. Two more Czechoslovakians are on hunger strike. This brings the number up to six. This afternoon a letter came to say that **Fillipovic, Miroslav** and **Joseph** (brothers) and **Novotny, Vladimir** were accepted into the Czech forces and they discontinued their hunger strike.

[C]Monday 16th of March 1942

I had a deputation out from the Anti-Nazis of No. 2 Camp. They want to be separated from the Nazis. A Polish priest came and said a mass for the Poles in No. 1 Camp. The Palestine Electric Company came to the camp and repaired the lights. I instructed the Acre Police to investigate a case of attempted sodomy in No. 3 Camp. Went to Acre in the afternoon and saw Mr **Grant** regarding changing over camps 1 and 2.

Studying new camp orders in relation to the previous orders.

I phoned for rations and ordered eggs. Contractor said he had meat in the fridge at camp.

Tuesday 17th of March 1942

Mr **Grant** to camp where we discussed the possibilities of Air Raid Precautions (ARP). We saw the various leaders of the camps regarding the transfer of the Nazis and Fascists into one camp. Lt. Col. **Yiavroumus** of the Greek Army called today to see the ex-Chief of the Greek Police and his deputy.

Panovic, a Yugoslav, made a bit of a nuisance of himself in Camp 2 today. I had him out and warned him regarding his conduct. Three Czechs on release to the forces today.

No eggs were received in rations today but the contractor brought the usual of eggs.

Wednesday 18th of March

Panovic was in camp 1 today. I had to send him to Acre. It appears to me that his mind is a bit unbalanced. Three Greeks and 4 Arabs left for the Advisory Committee in Jerusalem today.

The contractor only brought eggs for yesterday and promised a double issue of meat tomorrow. **Hamoude** phoned up and asked about the eggs received. Later the contractor bought a further 1000 eggs.

Thursday 19th of March 1942

I issued clothes to the undermentioned from No 3 Camp, but they refused to accept them because they did not receive underclothes:

Mahmood Naim
Ismail Abdulla Jabail
Mohd Maser Sharif
Mohd Jousuf il Jouan
Mohd Abid (M)issu

Greek Intelligence Officers visited the camp and interviewed **Constance**. Went to Acre and spoke with Mr **Grant**. It was decided to make No. 1 Camp 'Enemy Alien Camp' and all others to remain in No. 2 Camp. Rations were good today.

Friday 20th of March 1942

Mr Grant arrived in the morning and inspected 4, 5 and 6 Camps. He did not inspect 1 and 2 Camps owing to the change over. The change took place at 1.30 pm and about 45 persons changed over. With the exception of a mild protest from the Poles and Czechs and the dismissal of Dr **Galillea** from his post as Supervisor as he would not cooperate in the move, everything went according to schedule and the whole move was completed at 2.30 pm. No 1 Camp is Enemy Alien Camp, No 2 Camp is the Anti-Nazi and Anti-Fascist. Ex-BC **Kent** left today after serving 3 months.

The meat was very good today.

Saturday 21st of March 1942
An unsettled day. Seven Communists were released from the camp (3 Arabs and 4 Jews). I dealt with one Arab convicted prisoner who refused to carry out his task. No 1 and No 2 Camps having been duly separated, do not now want to play football or mix in any way. I think this will stop after a week.

Rations were good today.

A fight started in No 3 Compound and I have asked Acre Police to come to investigate it.

Monday 23rd of March 1942
A cold day. Rations were good. No. 2 Camp cannot do anything with the Bougal, they want vegetables or flour instead. Inspected the meat. It was good. Father **Eugene** (*Order of Franciscan Minors* - Roman Catholic Chaplain to the Force) called in the afternoon and saw Father **Lesain**. Two Jewish detainees were sent to Central Prison Acre and two Jewish Internees were released.

Tuesday 24th of March 1942
The weather improved and today was very pleasant. I was kept going all day with Jewish visits. I visited No. 3 Camp and supervised the cleaning out of the huts. Went to Acre and collected money from the bank and the sub-accountants. A Greek, Captain **Constance**, came to the camp to see **Pascano**. I visited the sentries after 10 pm. All alert. BC **Ayling, Bailess** and .... released this morning.

Wednesday 25th of March 1942
A strong East wind blowing up. Two Arabs for the Advisory Committee today, **Schwilly** is going to Jerusalem for his 2 days leave. Mr **Grant** started his investigation but he had to leave early. Went to Haifa in the afternoon for the semi-final of the Dowbiggen Cup and saw our team getting licked 4 - 1. The team put up a very poor show and showed no drive whatsoever. I called in to see **Tubby Glaysher** before we left for home.

Thursday 26th of March 1942

I tried **Singer** from No 4 Camp on a disciplinary charge and sentenced to 6 days solitary confinement. I tried four cases of discipline from the staff. Yugoslav officers came to see the Yugoslav internees. Merchant Navy Captain came to the camp to pay the Finnish seamen. **Balawski** to Haifa Hospital, Dr **Karl Grenseys** to the Ajanib Acre. He requested to be sent there as a protest against his removal from Camp 1 which he says is the best barracks. Mr **Pike** and his family called for tea. Visited the camp after midnight.

Friday 27th of March 1942
I phoned the Jewish Committee regarding special food for the Passover and the representative promised to call in on Monday at 9 am. Rations were good, but the contractor brought cheese instead of the eggs ordered. PWD came but did not do anything. They promised to come again on Monday. Went to Haifa in the afternoon to collect the children from school. I called at the hospital to see **Strong**. He is not very cheerful.

Saturday 28th March 1942
All available prisoners working on grass cutting. I am sending the two Jewish prisoners who refused to turn out to Acre to finish their time there. I inspected the rations. The meat was fair but I cut off 13 kilos of skin and returned this to the contractor.

Sunday 29th of March 1942
Moslem holiday - feast of the Prophet. Attended mass at No 1 compound with the children. Visited No. 3 Compound and saw the warder let out people from the compound to speak to and signal to persons who pulled up outside the camp. There are four doors broken in the latrine of No. 4 Camp. Visited camp after midnight. Nothing unusual to report. Phoned up Jerusalem about the affidavit regarding **Karl Scherer**, but the sergeant does not seem to know anything about it.

Monday 30th of March 1942
East wind blowing. Went to Acre Prison to see about some stores, but could not get anything. Later I went to the bank and collected the pay which I distributed in the afternoon.

Tuesday the 31st of March 1942
Met the Chief Rabbi who came to the camp to look into the Jewish kitchen and see the supervisor. He also went into the Synagogue. Today is Jewish detainees visiting day. Two cases of wine were brought into the camp but I refused to pass them on and had them returned. I inspected No. 3 Camp and was not pleased with the state of the bed boards. Inspector **Schwilly** on leave to Jerusalem. The old boiler man, a Czech left the camp on release and **Karal Schyer** left for Jerusalem to attend the High Court.

Wednesday 1st of April 1942
My 44th birthday.

Went to Haifa to get some money from the bank for Mr. **Trutairian** who is discharged tomorrow. Mr **Grant** came and inspected the camp. All Jews from 1 & 2 Camps transferred to Camp 4 for the night. I am taking special precautions for the security as the lights of the Huts will be left on until 12 o'clock midnight.

Sgt **Christie** of the Field Security Police called in to see me. All arrangements for the Jewish feast.

Thursday 2nd of April 1942
I visited sentries at 4 am. One was not alert on his duty. He was reprimanded. I had 3 B. Sgts conducting the Jewish visits. Many appeals were made to have visits outside with their families but I could not allow this. If I had given permission to one I would have had to give it to all.

Friday 3rd of April 1942
Good Friday. I attended mass at the camp church. Later **Panovic** struck an Italian and nearly caused a row in the camp I phoned Mr Grant and sent **Panovic** to Acre. I have now stopped all visits between No. 1 and No. 2 Camp.

Saturday 4th of April 1942
Easter Saturday, a dull day. Stores informed me that the shoes we were expecting would be sent on today, so I shall be able to issue them. I visited all the camps. Mr **Grant** visited the camp and discussed the Standing Orders and checked the Clothing Issue Book.

THROUGH FIRE, SHOT AND SHELL

Sunday 5th of April 1942
Easter Sunday. Various officers; Czechs, Yugoslavs and Poles called to see the various internees today. Early in the morning Italian prisoners left for Tantour to spend the day with their relatives. Germans also left for Sarona and Betlehem.

Monday 6th of April 1942
Easter Monday. A nice day. A Russian service was held in the camp while the R.C. padre celebrated an Arab mass for the benefit of number 3 Camp. Mr **Grant** called regarding some disciplinary cases. Got 500 tomato plants from the stock farm, and I had them planted. Six Arab internees came from Jerusalem today under heavy escort.

Tuesday 7th April 1942
A real summer's day. Visits to Jewish detainees started at 9 am. Went to Acre to see Mr **Grant** about the new arrivals today and to discuss the question of summer clothing for the internees. News of the release of **Jansen** and **Finar** (a Dane and a Finn) came through today, Haifa CID collected them at 4 pm. Telephone message via **James P.**

Wednesday 8th April 1942
(Swansea 1905) **James Phillips** left for Jerusalem today with the Advisory Committee party consisting of 4 Arabs and one from mixed Camp 'C'. Passports of 6 ex-British Police and of BC **White** sent to Jerusalem by the i/c of the Advisory Committee escort. Today is the last day of the Passover feast and a lot of visitors arrived by bus and car. Ex-BC **Clark** arrived to serve a 3-month sentence. 144 visitors came to the camp today.

Thursday 9th April 1942
Visited the Guards and Sentries at 4 am. All alert and regular. Visibility was good.
Three Greeks into camp today from Acre prison. Wireless message from Jerusalem to send BC White to HQ offices by 12 noon tomorrow. I tried a number of disciplinary cases and sentenced one Jew **Abraham Vilenchik** to 14 days solitary confinement for assault and abusing a prison officer and refusing to give his name. He admitted that he did not give his name to the warder. Eight ex-British Policemen were sent to the Central Prison Acre. They are going along to Jerusalem tomorrow and they will probably be repatriated to UK tomorrow. A Major Blackmoore called and asked to see Dr. **Cuamato**. The detainee **Abrahm Vilenchik** did not come out

of his compound today. I reported the matter to Mr Grant at 8 pm and he gave me instructions to have him out today.

Friday 10th April 1942
Abraham Vilanchik came out this morning and apologised for his conduct yesterday. PWD came to the camp to check up on requirements. Went to Acre to see Mr. **Grant** about various things. Spent the day issuing clothing to camp 3 & 4.

Issued razor blades to camps 2 & 4. Captain **Readman**, Army Intelligence Beirut, came to interview the two (**Fajies**). Went to Acre to collect the children from Grant's and returned to the camp at 7 pm.

Saturday 11th of April 1942
Practice ..... aircraft .... at Haifa today. Issued kit to No 3 Camp this morning. **Hamonds**, the Chief Clerk, called in at the camp this morning. Tamam in camp today 522. Telephone communications out of order today. Phoned Mr **Grant** for permission to leave camp tomorrow and proceed to Wilhelma.

Sunday 12th April 1942
Left at 8 am and went to Wilhelma with the family. We had a good trip and we returned at 6.30 pm. I called in on the Greys at Ramleh.

Monday 13th of April 1942
Nothing unusual to report. A dirty day with plenty of sand. Inspected all the camp. B.P Quarters not good. The Mess Caterer is not exercising supervision. He has sufficient staff who just need shaking up a bit.

Tuesday 14th April 1942
Bad khamseen wind blowing. Mr **Grant** made an inspection of the whole camp. In the afternoon I went to Haifa to take the children back to school. We all called in to see **Geordie Strong** at the hospital. Returned to camp 7 pm. A fight broke out in No 4 Camp; one person to hospital. Left for the High Court - a habeas corpus case.

Wednesday 15th April 1942
Eight persons left for the Advisory Committee in Jerusalem. **Jayousie** was tried by magistrate court, Acre for assault. PWD plumber did not come to camp today to

carry out the required work. I heard that Sgt **Brosman** was admitted to hospital Haifa today for an operation on his old corns on the soles of his foot. Got permission to wear drill on Friday.

Visited the camp during the night. Checked British Police blackout arrangements. Blackout arrangements in Compound 6 hut very bad.

Camp ready for inspection by Mr **Scott** who arrived at 10.30 am. He inspected all the camp and interviewed a number of individuals in the afternoon. He left the camp at 5 pm. The Solicitor General was at the camp and interviewed 6 persons.

Friday 17th of April 1942
Went into summer dress which is very comfortable for this weather. Went to Acre to see what I could collect from the stores. Apart from a drum of grey paint I was unlucky. Went around the camp it 10 pm. Sentries are all working well.

Saturday 18th of April 1942
Electricity was cut off early today. I also had some difficulty with water. The supply today is bad. Mr Scott honed from Jerusalem about some papers he left behind here on Thursday.

Sunday 19th of April 1942
I visited the sentries and guards at 5 am. I inspected rations and I returned a part of the meat consignment, which was nothing but skin and bones. **Adil Hajan** No. 250 Acre, **Kamal Mustafa Saleh** are suspended. Dr **Hankibil Mauries** should be watched. According to information received from Acre Police. The two first ones are carrying letters.

Monday 20th April 1942
Checked up on the canteen manager and found him selling at reduced prices, ie.

	Canteen	Marked
Potatoes	220	130
Oil	150	120
Eggs	12½	10
Onions	60	30
Baked Beans	100	60
Pilchards	150	9

He wanted to reduce his price as from tomorrow. He sold 2 tins of mixed fruit for 140 each and he told me the price was 120. Hitler's birthday today - nobody seemed to take much notice of it in the camp.

Tuesday the 21st of April 1942
Jewish visits to camp. A large working party out from all camps. Two detainees and 1 Italian internee to Haifa hospital. **Hoskins** took them. **Cosmato** still owes the sum of 200 mils to **G. Cocchlan**. He gave a cheque but it was turned down. Went to Acre to see Mr **Grant** about the canteen manager, Camps 1 & 2 played football but owing to the roughness of the play I had to stop the match.

Wednesday the 22nd April 1942
Mr **Parkhouse** arrived from Jerusalem to discuss various matters. Paraded all Palestinian personnel in the afternoon. The regular warders were not too bad but the TAC (T*emporary Arab Constable's*) were terrible. I visited the guard at 10 pm. One of the sentries was not alert.

Thursday 23rd April 1942
Billy left for Sarona until such time as he is cured. Got a message this morning. Checked up on No 3 Camp, they had been hanging blankets on the wire and on the corners of the huts. Saw four persons from No. 3 camp who were found in possession of money yesterday. I have ordered that the account be frozen until further notice. Mr **Scott** CID into camp with **Wilkinson**. They interrogated a number of Jewish detainees and took one away with them to Acre.

Friday 24th of April 1942
One Jewish detainee was taken to hospital at 4 am. He was seriously ill. **Kerstin**, a Pole, was released today after 18 months internment. Met ration contractor and discussed various problems regarding rations. Took orderly room. Two warders, one to forfeit 7 days pay and the other to pay a fine.

Saturday 25th of April 1942
Mr **Grant** visited the camp for inspection and was not very pleased with camp No 2. Discussed ARP (Air Raid Precaution) measures and arranged with Sgt **Wilson** to come to camp at 3.30 pm on Monday.

Monday 27th of April 1942
Mr **Richardson** came to see one of the internees. Had ARP instruction by the B/Sgt from Acre Police (**Wilson**). Eight men from each compound attended. Mr **Grant** came to the camp and discussed fire fighting and ARP. It was decided to put 15 fire buckets and 25 sand bags in each compound.

Tuesday the 28th of April 1942
Jews refused visits this morning owing to the restriction placed on visits generally. I sent for the supervisor but he refused to come. During the 15 minutes he remained there. In the afternoon the visits were taken by 25 persons and they came out for their rations. The Spanish Consul visited the camp. ASP **Kramer** interviewed the **Homsi** brothers and he stayed in the camp the whole day.

Wednesday the 29th of April 1942
Went to Haifa to transact business at the bank on behalf of the internees. Stayed in Haifa all day and returned to camp at 6.30 pm and found BI **Parker** waiting impatiently for my return. **Anton Retta**, an Italian internee attempted to commit suicide today by cutting his left wrist.

Thursday 30th of April 1942
Went to Acre to get the money for pay from the bank. I spent the day paying out and arranging ARP. A very strong khamseen blowing.

Friday the 1st of May 1942
Labour Day. No holiday in this country. A terrible day, the second of the khamseen. It was very bad about noon today. Mr Grant arranged for two instructors to come from Athlit to instruct on the digging of ARP shelters. Had to send a Pole to Acre. He was creating a fuss and struck a German over the head with a primus.

Saturday the 2nd of May 1942
The khamseen broke today. Started digging Air Raid shelters today. Mr **Grant** visited the camp and inspected 1 & 2 Camp and Baracanda B. Went to Haifa in the evening to attend the re-union dinner of the Gendarmerie and got home at 1.30 am. Met a lot of old faces. General **McNeil** presided and the IG (*Inspector General- the highest rank in the Palestine Police*) and **Spinney** were guests. News of **Parker's** promotion.

Sunday 3rd of May 1942
On duty. Nothing unusual happened throughout the day. In the afternoon two Greek officers, Capt **Skerduplus** and Lt. **Demaris**, arrived to see **(H)anavite**.

Monday the 4th of May 1942
Three Yugoslavs on hunger strike today as a protest against their detention. One is an ex-Sergeant Major, one is an ex-Captain of the Yugoslav Air Force. The third one is a civilian. Captain **Farrar** of the Allied Reception Camp called and I informed him of the visit of the two Greek officers who had called yesterday. Had a fire fighting display by the Acre Fire Brigade.

Tuesday 5th of May 1942
Visited the camp at 4.30 am. Guards and Sentries alert and regular. I had a look out for persons interfering with the fishing nets of No. 1 Camp. Jewish visits today. No extra staff and CID Haifa promised help. The promised help came at 1 pm, but nobody came. A terrible hot wind blowing this afternoon. PWD came and marked out the trenches in Baracanda 'B' and started a party digging.

Wednesday 6th of May 1942
The khamseen continues. Mr **Parkhouse** arrived from Jerusalem and interviewed **Lasan, Gallille, Rois** and **Segal** regarding a letter to the Chief Justice. PWD engaged in digging trenches. in Baracanda 'B'. Supervisor and three others transferred to Central Prison Acre today. Nine other Jews arrived from there.

Thursday 7th of May 1942
PWD working on trenches in Baracanda 'B'. No cooperation from the Jews or Arabs. No. 3 was in a filthy condition. I have ordered the removal of all primus stoves from there until such time as a better effort is made. Three ex-T.J.F.F (*Transjordan Frontier Force*) released today.
  Today's Tamam:
  Camp 1   123
       2   132
       3   112
       4   124
       5   1 attached to 3

         6   22 convicted
         Total   514

Went to sub-accountant to draw a cheque for £189 but he had no money. **Strong** came back from hospital in the afternoon with his leg in plaster. He is excused duty for seven days. Around the camp - guards and sentries alert and regular.

Friday 8th of May 1942
Inspected the camp. Camp No 4 was not up to the mark. Went to Acre to cash a cheque with the sub-accountant. Sixteen labourers are at work digging trenches. Mr **Scott** phoned and asked for a list of names of visitors to the Jewish detainees for the last four weeks. He also spoke about the provision of fire extinguishers. Went to Haifa in the afternoon and collected the children from school. Had a bad headache and went to bed early.

Saturday 9th of May 1942
A cool day. 27 PWD workers in camp started removing the fence and digging trenches at 'A' camp. Mr **Grant** arrived for inspection. He was not very pleased with No. 2 compound. The huts were pretty untidy.

Sunday 10th of May 1942
Usual routines in camp. Went to Haifa in the afternoon with the children and called in on the **Glayshers** for tea. I inspected the guard and found one of the sentries, **Hanna Nasrawie**, asleep. I took his Greener Gun away from him and handed it over to the Cpl i/c Guard.

Monday 11th of May 1942
PWD continuing digging trenches. Went to Acre to see Mr **Grant** regarding disciplinary matters.
Tamam in the camp today is as follows:
    Camp   1   123
            2   131
            3   120
            4   122
            5   -
            6   21

Tried a number of Arabs from No 3 Camp for not complying with orders, ie not handing over their primus stoves to the camp store. A deputation of 8 from camp 3 came to see me. I explained to them what I wanted and after a mild protest about sending four people for punishment to Acre, they left the office.

Tuesday 12th of May 1942
Jewish detainee visits today. CID Haifa arrived at 9.30 am. There were not many visits today - 25. The supervisor of No 3 Camp John **Marion** replaced by one of the **Faroukies**. Three people sent to Haifa for X-ray examination. **Balisky** from Malta No. 2 Camp sent to Acre Prison for 7 days. He would not do any work in the compound. PWD working on trench digging today. I spoke to **Hinman** about the fly netting for the BP Mess and mess room. Mr Grant authorised the removal of the rush matting from the windows.

Wednesday 13th of May 1942
Inspected the whole of the camp this morning and I supervised the removal of the rush matting from Camp 4. Two Czechs **Kovacovic** and **Maurice Hutman** were released to join the forces. There was a dispute in No. 2 Camp in which **Shane Goldstern** was implicated. Everything was settled and the hut leaders gave him a job of work to do.

Thursday 14th of May 1942
One internee to Haifa Hospital for X-Ray examination. Sgt **Downey** and family arrived for a visit. The release of **Akerman** was approved by the government. **Thomas Farris** was examined by a British eye specialist at Haifa Hospital this afternoon. Sgt **Brosman** was admitted to Haifa Hospital due to his foot complaint.

Friday 15th of May 1942
Akerman and **Tovan** left camp this morning on release. Haifa CID in to interrogate two of the Jewish detainees.

Tamam:

Camp		
	1	123
	2	131
	3	119
	4	124

```
         6              19
       Total           516
```
The cook-house of No 3 Camp was very untidy today. Mr **Scott** visited the camp in the afternoon and inspected the Air Raid Shelters, etc. He remained in camp until 6.10 pm. The party of Arabs which I had sent to Acre for punishment on 11.5.42 returned today.

Saturday the 16th of May 1942
Usual camp routine. Nothing unusual happened with the exception of a bit of a fight between **Rugun** and **Panovic** in Camp 2.

Sunday the 17th of May 1942
Went to church in the camp at 10 am. Afterwards inspected the rations which were good today. Swimming in the afternoon. Sgt **Bickley** came back from leave to take the place of **Brosman** who was admitted to hospital.

Monday 18th of May 1942
Inspector **Strong** resumed duty today. A fighter crashed in a field beside the camp. The pilot got away with it. Lieut. **Sullivan**- Army Intelligence - arrived to speak to **Misel**. Supervisor on request. Mr **Grant** phoned to say that all visits to '15B Emergency Regulation' persons were discontinued and that they would be allowed to write and receive one letter each two weeks. Visited the sentries around the camp during the night. All alert and regular.

Tuesday 19th of May 1942
I sent out Police to the crossroads to stop visitors from coming to the camp to visit persons detained under '15B Emergency Regulations'. Mr Grant arrived and inspected No. 4 Camp. He was not very pleased with it. The inmates of the camp were a bit upset about this news.

Wednesday 20th May 1942
I interviewed four people from Camp 2 today. Phoned up Acre concerning the supply of coal and wood. **Mohamed** promised that he would get some out today. I met the hut leaders of Camp 4 and spoke about the filthy condition of the huts, Mr **Parkhouse** arrived in the camp today to carry out interviews. I visited the camp

during the night. The road at the back of 'A' camp needs some attention now that the Air Raid Shelters and the fence is made up.

Thursday 21st May 1942
Dr **Turner** arrived from Jerusalem and saw a number of persons who were on the sick list for ear, throat and tooth trouble. A bottle of Arak was confiscated from the Greek Quartermaster of No. 2 Camp. It was bought in by the sub-contractor for rations. Eleven Romanians came into the camp last night at 8.30 pm. They were accommodated in the recreation room in Camp 1 for the night and they were well looked after.

Permission was given to No. 4 Camp to have the huts open until 10 pm and their lights on in their hut until 11 pm. Everything went off very well.

Friday 22nd of May 1942
Quite a number of visitors arrived for the Jewish detainees contrary to expectations. The eleven Romanians who arrived at the camp last night wish to go to No. 2 Camp this morning. They are mostly all Jews. I went to Haifa in the afternoon to collect the children from school. Inspector **Robinson** CID visited the camp to see **Wentland** and he stayed with him for about two hours.

Saturday 23rd of May 1942
Major **Matherson** from ME Head-Quarters came and interviewed the Romanians. He saw **Dragus** and finished up by seeing **Ruguna** in the hospital. **Ahmed Yanis** came to see me in the camp this afternoon. During the night 11 - 12 there was an Air Raid Alarm. I turned out all the staff and got them into positions around the camp. By midnight the all-clear sounded.

Sunday 24th of May 1942
Day off. I went to church in the camp and later I attended the opening of the new café in Camp 1.

Monday 25th of May 1942
Joseph Wentland, a Polish internee visited me this morning and spoke to me about Inspector **Robinson's** visit. He is going to write a letter to the DIG CID. Lieut. **Sullivan** - Army Intelligence - came and saw one of the Finns with a view to his release. One Italian and one Greek were brought into camp by a military escort.

THROUGH FIRE, SHOT AND SHELL

Tuesday 26th of May 1942
A warm day today. **Colin Wade** came from Haifa to see one of the Jewish detainees, but he was in Acre prison again. I have a general shortage of coal and wood. After a number of telephone calls I managed to get a few sacks of wood and coal from Acre.

Wednesday the 17th of May 1942
Went to the First Aid class and saw a number of persons passing their exams. I was very impressed by their progress after only eight lessons. I went to Acre and picked up the pay, and then paid out until 4 pm. Three Arabs from Gaza released today and two Jewish detainees came in from Jerusalem. The wood contractor sent some men to chop up the large pieces of wood in the camp but they could not do anything with it.
   I went around the camp and inspected all sentries - all alert and regular.

Thursday 28th of May 1942
Inspected the camp today. No 3 cook-house was not up to the mark. Dr **Hedelman**, the dentist arrived from Haifa. Not much news through from Lybia, where a big tank battle is going on. Mr **Grant** visited the camp and inspected the wire on the west side of the camp which is in no way complete. PWD sent one man to repairs windows. I phoned Jerusalem about **Hochstetten's** condition. He is now in his eighteenth day of hunger strike and his is in poor shape. He will not break his hunger strike unless he is visited by one of the Jugoslav mission.

Friday 29th of May 1942
The store-keeper came from Acre and checked through the stores prior to his handing over the stores. Information was received that a member of the Yugoslav mission is to visit **Hochstettem** today, but he failed to turn up. I walked around the camp. Guards and sentries alert and regular.

Saturday 30th of May 1942
A rather hot day. The Yugoslav mission visited **Hochstetten** at the sick bay and had him examined by a doctor. The mission also saw Capt. **Panovic**. **Hochstetten** did not stop his hunger strike and he is now in his 28th day without food.

Sunday 31st of May 1942
The Chief Rabbi visited the camp today and spoke to the Jewish members in No. 4 Camp. He also saw the Jews in Camp 2.

Monday 1st of June 1942
I went to Acre and checked up on my stores with **Mohd Effendi**. I collected the ration money for the BP. A Greek Captain from the British Intelligence Service came and interviewed **Pasconoff**. A Polish priest accompanied by a Polish officer called in here and paid £22 for the benefit of the Poles.

Tuesday 2nd of June 1942
Trouble in Camp 2 again about **Panovich**. I had to send him to Acre for 14 days s.c. I tried **Saroussi** for insulting the Cpl and I let him away with a caution. **Hochstetten** who has now been on hunger strike for 31 days is to be transferred to Acre Prison Hospital on the instructions of Mr **Scott**. B/Sgt **Brosman** was discharged from hospital today - on light duty. I put him in **Cowell's** job in the office.

Wednesday 3rd of June 1942
Mr **Grant** arrived for inspection and remained until 2 pm. There is a general shortage of wood in the camp. I took the afternoon parade. Visited sentries in camp before midnight. All alert and regular. The fruit which arrived today was bad and it was refused by 1 and 2 Camps.

Thursday 4th of June 1942
..... called in to see his fellow-countrymen in the camp. I took orderly room - 2 British and 2 Palestinians. Nothing appeared in today's papers concerning the fact that we are now under military control. The tomatoes which arrived were of poor quality and they were returned to the contractor. Inspector **Black** and his wife called in the evening.

Friday 5th of June 1942
A real khamssen wind blowing today. **Jonnie** at the High Court. **Marcel Covel** to Haifa for X-Ray treatment. **Schwilly** is part of the court. Went for a swim in the afternoon. Visited the camp at 2.30 am. All sentries and guards alert and regular. Sgt. **Hoskins** on duty.

Saturday 6th of June 1942
A very hot day. I settled a difference in No. 3 Camp between **Inja** and **Anton Azam**. PWD working on the wire at the west of compounds 1 & 2. They are also making gates and repairing windows.

Sunday 7th of June 1942
Went to Acre and checked through the lists of the Stern Gang members with Mr Grant.

Monday 8th of June 1942
Worked all day on the list of Jewish detainees and changed the non-Stern Gang group to camp 5. Capt **Lifoglou** called here and carried out his investigation of the Romanian affair. **Belaski** left for Athlit Camp today. No one in the camp was sorry for him.

Tuesday the 9th of June 1942
A khamseen wind blew up about 10 am and made the camp a bad place to live in. **Lifoglou** visited the camp again today to interrogate the Romanians. The Greek captain paid his last visit to the camp today and interrogated three of the Romanians.

Wednesday 10th of June 1942
The day was not bad in comparison with yesterday, I interviewed 17 prisoners from No. 2 Camp. Inspected 5 and 3 Camps and collected 6 bed boards. A medical board sat in the camp today and examined all outstanding cases.

Thursday 11th of June 1942
King's birthday today. Young **Zwinger** was transferred to Sarona today to join his father who left last week. Took office and recommended one TAW for dismissal for being asleep on duty. Inspector **Rubinstein** visited the camp today and had an interview with **Wentland**.

Friday 12th of June 1942
News came through this morning about the fall of a stronghold in Lybia. I am having trouble with wood supplies. I have been trying to get wood since yesterday. At 4.30 I had to phone up Mr **Parker** about it. A Greek office arrived at the camp to

interrogate one of the Greek internees. He then asked to see **Pasconoff** but I refused him this request. Mr **Witold Hulanicki**, a Pole, came to the camp with Inspector **Robinson** and interrogated **Joseph Wentland** about Polish affairs. 2nd Lieut **Kliarchos Dimitropoulos** was the officer mentioned above.

Monday 15th of June 1942
Mr **Grant** came to the camp about 10 am and at 11.30 the DIG Capt. **Ballintine** and the AIG CID Mr **Giles** came to the camp and interviewed a number of detainees and internees. They remained in camp 2 pm. At 4.30 I went to a tea party at the ADCs Mr **MacGilvery** and afterwards I attended an ARP Fire Fighting display at Acre.

Tuesday 16th of June 1942
Spent the day checking stores with Inspector **Strong**, In the afternoon Major **Kendall** came and interviewed Captain **Dragor**, a Romanian Sea Captain. Spoke with **Craig** from Beityam who informed me that the camp was not ready to receive the 16 Italians until the 24th.

Wednesday 17th of June 1942
Orders for the release of 16 Arabs was received from Gaza and the Bersheeba area. Sent a party to the Advisory Committee and received in German A from Jerusalem. Took afternoon parade - 46 present.

Thursday 18th of June 1942
Inspected all camps this morning. No 4 Camp was not up to standard. I returned a load of wood which had not been chopped up sufficiently. The Cpl saw me this morning about attending the usual weekly parade. I visited the sentries and guards at 4 am (Friday).

Friday 19th June 1942
Mr **Gee** ASP CP Jerusalem acting for Mr Scott inspected the whole of the camp today. He left the camp at 2 pm. A rough sea blew up in the late morning and this carried on throughout the rest of the day. **Aria Goldstein** was released from camp today and **Anton Azzam** who is on hunger strike was transferred to Acre Prison Hospital.

Saturday 20th May 1942
Escort to Athlit Clearance Camp to bring back one internee.

Monday 22nd of June 1942
Fall of Tobruk announced this morning. My back is still bad and I can only just get about. I took the parade in the afternoon and after inspection I dismissed it as the weather had become bad.

Tuesday the 23rd of June 1942
My back is still bad, but slightly better than yesterday. Two Romanians were released from the camp this morning. The Polish pay officer arrived with money for the Polish internees.

Wednesday the 24th of June 1942
Hans John Oldman was handed over to the CID Acre today on the first step of his deportation to the UK. Fourteen Italians were transferred to Beityam camp by order of the DIG CID. I tried a case of theft by a detainee and sentenced him to 7 days solitary confinement to Acre Prison.

Tamam as at 12 noon today:

Camp		
	1	106
	2	133
	3	105
	4	107
	5	29
	6	17
	Total	497

Thursday the 25th of June 1942
Went to Haifa to collect the children from school but did not get away until about 3 pm. Mr **Catling** CID visited the camp and saw one of the Stern Group. A mosquito specialist visited the camp and found millions of them in the cess-pit at the back of No. 1 Camp.

Friday the 26th of June 1942
Mr **Grant** visited the camp today with six members of the Stern Group. They went to Camp 4. One Pole released and handed over to the Polish Army.

Saturday 27th of June 1942
Mr **Grant** visited the camp today and inspected 1, 2 & 3 compounds. Searched a number of convicted prisoners and found them in possession of cigarettes.

Sunday 28th of June 1942
Day off duty. **Brown** of No 1 Camp was admitted to hospital at 4 pm.

Monday 29th of June 1942
Went to Acre to collect the pay and spent the rest of the day paying out. No 2 Camp is very uneasy and the fall of Messamatru has made them very nervous. They are asking what the Government policy is in regard to their position.

Tuesday 30th of June 1942
Mr **Grant** came to camp and investigated a case against BI **Strong**. I went to Acre to collect ration money for B/Ps. An Air Raid Alarm over Haifa at 4.30 pm. No bombs dropped.

Wednesday 1st of July 1942
At 2 am sharp an air raid over Haifa. It lasted about 30 minutes. No bombs dropped. Camp defences are working well. Ten prisoners from Gaza discharged today. **Cowell** resumed duty and **McGovern** started his month's leave.

Today's Tamam:

Camp		
	1	106
	2	129
	3	99
	4	114
	5	23
	6	20
Total		491

Thursday 2nd July 1942
Heavy rain fell during the early morning. I spent all morning making inquiries into an incident which took place in No. 3 Camp. I recorded a number of statements. An Air Raid Alarm was sounded in Haifa about 4.30 pm but it did not last long.

Friday 3rd July 1942

Got in contact with Mr **Charlton** regarding money for the Germans. Tried **Ezra Levy** a detainee from No 4 Camp who was a bit funny at the Tamam yesterday evening. I sent him to the solitary confinement cells. **Billy** returned from Sarona after convalescence. **Brosman** went sick and got excused duty for three days. His foot is bad and he will be off duty for some time. I have ordered that **McGovern** be recalled from leave for the present.

Saturday 4th of July 1942

Received LP20 from Polish officer for the Polish internees. **Roym-Romske** a Pole was released from camp today warned the ration contractor about the filth of his truck in which he carries the rations.

Monday 6th of July 1942

Major **Thilhowan** visited the camp and saw **Mahmood Kharsim**. Mr **Gee** and Mr **Grant** also visited the camp and saw **Gillile Nason** and **Segal** about a letter which had been sent by **Gallatin** about conditions in Acre Prison Hospital twelve months ago. I took the parade in the afternoon and explained the regulations regarding enemy aliens.

Tuesday 7th of July 1942

The air raid alarm sounded at 8.30 am. The all-clear sounded 20 minutes later. Took the afternoon parade and read over the F.O. regarding enemy agents.

Wednesday the 8th of July 1942

Out early morning. Guards and sentries all alert and regular. A large life boat was washed ashore in the south west of the camp. The name of the boat was *Hero*. She was badly damaged. Mr **Miller** of the YMCA called and brought some books. He also saw a number of internees.

Today's Tamam:

Camp	1	107
	2	135
	3	98
	4	116
	5	22
	6	18

Thursday 9th of July 1942
Father **Lamb** and **Edmondson** called in at the camp in the afternoon. Mr **Grant** arrived for inspection and stayed until 5 pm. Wireless message received from Sgt **Frugarde** "The IG directs that the **Homse** brothers be released immediately". They were released at 2 pm. Visited all sentries in the camp at 1030 pm. All alert and regular - visibility good.

Friday 10th of July 1942
Went to Barclays bank, Haifa and withdrew some of the prisoners' deposits. Called at the traffic office and got my car tested. Arrived back in Acre at 1.30 pm.

Saturday 11th of July 1942
Went to the bank and got the allowances for the Palestine Police. Mr **Grant** called accompanied by Mr **McGillvery** and discussed the ARP exercise which was carried out during the afternoon.

Sunday 12th of July 1942
Visited sentries and guards at 4.15 am. All alert and regular. Air Raid alarm in the morning and again in the evening. No bombs were dropped. **Darky Goult** came with his family and stayed a few hours. I met **Pike** in the canteen and spoke to him about **Grunsyer's** message to him.

Monday 13th of July 1942
Busy morning in the office. One internee to Haifa for an X-Ray examination. Lieut. **O'Sullivan** called and informed me that an officer dealing with Romanian affairs would call at the camp shortly. **V. Rotting** returned from Zen Zanie today. He refused to go into No. 1 camp. Eventually he was persuaded to go there. Spoke to Mr. **Grant** about the hunger strikers. I suggested that they be sent to Acre Prison.
   Today's Tamam:

Camp	1	109
	2	133
	3	96
	4	117
	5	22

6	18
Total	495

Tuesday 14th of July 1942
Von Rottick on hunger strike. Mr **Scott** CID called and brought **Buster** with him. He did not see anybody. One Greek handed over to the Military Authorities.

Wednesday 15th of July 1942
Four Jews from No. 4 released and 3 Jews transferred from Camp 5 to Camp 4. Went to Acre and saw the store keeper regarding books. Nine British convicted came from Acre today. Spanish Consul came and visited the camp. The usual crowd came to see him. **Max Brown** made a complaint about his treatment in Haifa Hospital. He left the camp at 6.10 pm.

Thursday 16th of July 1942
Went around all the camp and counted the forms and tables. **Kamam Abu Khadra** was sent to Jerusalem for interrogation. **Goldstein** was admitted to Athlit Hospital after waiting 4 days for a bed. Nine British Police came in from Jerusalem for refusing to obey orders. I put them in camp 6 and cleared out the Jews from the Cook House.

Friday 17th of July 1942
Mr **Catling** called in at the camp and interviewed Mr **Costing** (a Romanian). **Mariel Covel** to PHD (Public Health Department) Haifa for treatment. I found a number of internees in camp 2 under the influence of drink. **Colin Wade** came from Haifa with clothing for internees and detainees. Had a walk around the camp before midnight. Everything in order.

Saturday 18th of July 1942
Inspected the bake house with a view to fixing up a new kitchen for B/Ps. I will have to get PWD to do a bit of work on this. Dr **Luck Tuck** came to camp and ordered that **Rottick** and other Romanians be sent to Acre Prison Hospital until they finish their hunger strike.
    Tamam:
    Compound 1   109

2	134
3	94
4	114
5	21
6 (Nat.)	18
6 (Brits)	16
Total	506

A British convicted arrived from Acre.

Sunday 19th of July 1942
Had a day off duty. Went to the camp church with the children. In the afternoon there was a fight in No 3 Compound and **Turfin Abdul Khadh Maniss** was beaten up and admitted to the Sick Bay. He was afterwards seen by the doctor. The accused in this case are:
Mohd Kiswani
Mohd Sha'ar
Issu Silhab
Aubli Bayoume
Izzat Zulawi
Ahmed Bashia Bedor

Monday 20th of July 1942
My insurance is due today. **Anatol Eisenstein** came back from Acre Prison Hospital today on a stretcher. He is on hunger strike and was returned from Athlit Hospital. The three **Kassims** were sent to Acre today. I got a letter from home to say that my father had died on April the 10th.

Mr **Parkhouse** came to the camp and interviewed a number of internees, the young **Grants** and the **Sedergreens** came out swimming. Rations did not arrive in camp until 2.30 pm today the excuse given was that he got a puncture and had no spare wheel.

Tuesday 21st of July 1942
Camp 1 & 2 getting photographs taken today. Mr **Syer** arrived to take statements from 4 Arabs who alleged before the Advisory Committee that they were badly beaten by the Police before their internment. Mr **Grant** came to the camp at 10.30

am and remained until 1.30 pm. Rations did not arrive until 1.30 pm today. Today's excuse that he could not find a driver. He bought shamam to camp but I refuse them for I had ordered grapes.

Wednesday 22nd of July 1942
An attempt was made in the early hours of the morning to get away from 3 Camp by 3 Arabs:
   Mohd She'ar
   Khalil Mesuumi
   Ishud Selhab
Dr **Luck-Tuck** visited the camp today. The first visit since Saturday. One Arab admitted to Haifa Hospital, suspected appendicitis case. The victim of the case of violence was sent to Acre Prison Hospital. The 5 accused were taken to Acre Prison awaiting trial for assault. Major **E. C. Masterson** G.S.I.J. Pal. Base Jerusalem came and saw a few of the Romanians.

Thursday 23rd of July 1942
Inspected the whole camp. In the evening **Snearson** came from Haifa Hospital in a bad state. I sent for Dr Luck Tuck but I could not get him to come out. At Tamam No. 4 Camp refused to go to their huts until such time as I saw **Snearson**. I went to the camp and he told me that he was removed from the Hospital by force against the doctor's wishes and that he was removed on the orders of the CID.

Friday 24th of July 1942
Phoned up Dr Luck Tuck this morning about **Snearson.** I also spoke to Mr **Grant** about him. Mr **Grant** said that he was sent from the hospital on the orders of Dr **Hamyre** the MO i/c, as he was making a nuisance of himself. The doctor ordered that he be sent to Acre Hospital. **Snearson** went to hospital at 5 pm. There was a bit of a scene in the camp, but the lad is really ill. I phoned his wife in Haifa and told her that he was being transferred to CP Acre. I received information today that there are about 69 individuals leaving my camp at short notice. Sgt **Freeguard** called at 9.10 pm and brought the lists of the persons leaving the camp. The list consisted of 96 individuals.

Saturday 25th of July 1942
Went to the bank and then had to go to Haifa to get deposits from the safe. There were a number of protests against what they called 'deportation', in particular from persons who had their wives and children in the country. A captain came to interrogate some of the Greeks. At 9 pm **George Horia** a Romanian journalist attempted suicide by cutting his wrist pretty badly. I sent him to hospital at Haifa and I informed the duty officer CID.

Sunday 26th of July 1942
Everybody to work early. All kit out and searched. On football field CID instructed that **George Horia** would travel with party and that his wife would go with him. Transport arrived on time. Mr **Hood** was i/c and was assisted by **McLeod**. There were no incidents and the affair went off satisfactorily. There was a bit of a mix up over the transport. Both Haifa and Nazareth supplied. Mr **Grant** was present. 65 persons left the camp. Today Tamam is as follows:

Camp No. 1   96
         2   88
         3   82
         4   113
         5   18
         6   34

Monday 27th of July 1942
I attended a memorial mass for my father in the camp. A great number of people, including many detainees and internees, turned up for it. **Beliski**, a Pole; one Arab and one Jew were released today. Went around the camp during the afternoon and found two members of the No. 4 Camp having a stroll between the wires. Spoke to Mr **Grant** at the S.W. Gate when he came to collect the kids. The auditors visited the camp in the afternoon.

Tuesday 28th of July 1942
The Government Auditors arrived and started to check up my books. Two detainees in from Lydda area sent to Camp No. 5. **Billy** and one other sent out to Government Hospital for X-Ray.

Wednesday 29th of July 1942
The Government Auditors into the camp at 9 am. Went to Acre at 11 am for pay and paid out in the afternoon. Went out for a swim at 5 pm. Afterwards did my rounds of the camp. Everything in order. Received orders of habeas corpus in respect of three detainees who left this camp on Sunday.

Thursday 30th of July 1942
Auditors still in camp. Checking accounts today. A Captain of the British Intelligence (**Foglan**) was in the camp all day. He is investigating the Greek affair. The auditors did not leave until 8 pm.

Friday 31st of July 1942
Auditors still in camp. Went to the bank and cashed the messing cheque. Called in at Acre Prison and saw **Parker** who is still on his seat and his leg is still in plaster of Paris.

Saturday 1st of August 1942
The Assistant Paymaster together with a representative of the Accountant General's Office arrived at 7.30 am and checked through the accounts. They left at 1 pm. **Hamonde** on the telephone regarding **Pearlman's** eyesight. Sgt **Hoskins** left on transfer to Central Prison Jerusalem. Sgt **Rogan** arrived on transfer from Jerusalem.

Sunday 2nd of August 1942
The solicitor General arrived in the camp and saw a member of the anti-Nazi group, mostly Finns and Romanians. A Naval officer came to see the wreck. He may arrange to take it away during the week, if not we can have it for fire-wood.

Monday 3rd of August 1942
A quiet day in camp. **Snearson** went to Haifa hospital for a medical board. They sent the ambulance for him. I inspected all the camp, and, with the exception of Camp 3 which had dirty tables, everything was in order. I made an application for 10 days leave.

Tuesday 4th of August 1942
I went to CP Acre to see Mr **Grant**. Later he inspected the camp and remained here until 2 pm. About 15 people visited No 5 camp today.

Wednesday 5th of August 1942
Went to Acre and made a statement regarding the boat affair. Orders of release came through for 6 persons - 5 Arabs and one other. Haifa ablaze with search-lights. There were no interviews with any members of Camp 2 today.

Thursday 6th of August 1942
Called **Gallali** to the office and confiscated his primus stove from him. He had it blazing away in his hut during Tuesday's inspection by Mr **Grant**. Returned a number of Ga Helmets to ARP Acre today. Today's Tamam is as follows:

Camp	
1	94
2	88
3	84
4	113
5	21

Took office at 12.30. A number of cases of absence from parade dealt with.

Friday 7th of August 1942
I was expecting Dr **M McQueen** at 10 am but he did not arrive until 5.50. Dr **Bigger** was with him. They inspected BP (*British Police*) quarters and my quarters with a view to making this a convalescence camp later.

Saturday 8th of August 1942
Dr **McQueen** again visited the camp and had a look at it 'from his wife's point of view'. Mr **Grant** came and gave me some information regarding our move to Latrun. He informed me that I was to be officer in charge.

Monday 10th of August 1942
Left camp at 6.30 am for Latrun, but the coil box of the car went flat at the petrol pump and after playing about with if for an hour I had to run for it. I arrived in Latrun at 12.15, three quarters of an hour late. Mr **Scott**, **Gee** and **Dudley Higg** were also inspecting the camp. I visited the compounds and offices etc., and then went on the Latrun Police Station to see my quarters and to have a cup of tea. I then went to Tel-Aviv at 6 pm. I saw **Lou Downing** and his wife and went to the pictures. I got back at 12.30.

Tuesday 11th of August 1942
Left Tel-Aviv at 10 am and arrived in Haifa 12.30. Saw **Tubby** and Inspector Q and asked him to phone **Downing** about his nephew who is on HMS Destroyer. Returned to Acre at 2 pm. Phoned Mr **Grant** and **Kiel**. Later went to Acre to pick up my car which was being repaired.

Wednesday 12th of August 1942
Arrived at office to clear outstanding work.

Thursday 13th of August 1942
Went to Haifa in connection with internees' property and returned home at 1 pm. The camp played football against the Royal Artillery and got beaten 6 - 0. Went around the camp at 10 pm and found everything in order.

Friday 14th of August 1942
Sent Sgt **Haslem** on transfer to Athlit. Also **Marcel Covel** to Haifa Hospital for X-Ray examination. **Von Rottack** and **Garbasky** returned from Athlit Hospital. **Major Blackmore** A.I.F. and left a parcel for **Cosmatis**. Went into No 2 Compound and saw **Dr Kutten** who was having a birthday party.

Saturday 15th of August 1942
Mr **Scott** visited the camp and made a complete inspection of the whole camp, He was pleased with everything he saw with the exception with the ex-British Police who were not working at their tasks. Air Raid alarm during the night. It did not last long.

Sunday 16th of August 1942
Day off duty. Persons out in No 4 compound in the early hours of the morning.

Monday 17th of August 1942
Key of safe not working. Air Raid alert at 10 am. AA guns opened up. No bombs dropped. Six British convicted into Camp 6. I had a good look around No 4 Camp and gave instructions that the Cpl must not go in alone but must bring someone from Baracanda with him and they must carry pick pick-handles with them.

Tuesday 18th of August 1942
Mr **Homsie** called in at the camp to see me. A Polish Intelligence Officer called and paid in the money for the nine Poles Acre Prison played the RA and got beaten 4 - 0. A good hard match. The MO and the Adjutant from the OTC came and asked permission to use the swimming pool in the afternoon.

Wednesday 19th of August 1942
Had a number of interviews - mostly Greeks, Phoned PWD about my safe, but nothing has happened. Checked through the accounts and as a result closed No 2 Camp account until further notice. Mr **Grant** visited the camp.

Thursday 20th of August 1942
Went to Central Prison and discussed stores with **Mohd Sariff**. Had the children inoculated in the afternoon.

Friday 21st of August 1942
Mr **Parkhouse** called in the morning and remained about one hour. At 10.30 inspected 1 - 2 - 4 - 5 - 6 camps. Air Raid alarm in the afternoon in Haifa. AA guns went into action. All clear went at midnight. The government supplied glasses to all personnel in need of them.

Saturday 22nd of August 1942
Willie Winkler admitted to Haifa Hospital. **Strong** went to see MO Haifa. ARP exercises carried out in compounds 1 & 2. Everything in order. Everybody knows where to go and what to do when the alarm is sounded.

Sunday 23rd August 1942
Went to Latrun and Wilhelma. Left camp at 6.45 am and arrived in Latrun at 10 am - 161 kms. I had a look around the new camp and it looks a lot better than it did on my first visit. Got back to camp at 6 pm.

Monday 24th of August 1942
Sent six people to Haifa to a Medical Board. **Cosmato** was one of them. A fire started in the dry grass on the north end of the camp. It stated at Sidney Smith Barracks and came along to the camp. No damage done to the wire supports. Issuing

out identity discs which arrived from Acre today. Two British convicted in from Bisam Striking Force. Walked around the camp after 10 pm. All sentries alert. 1 Jewish detainee admitted to Haifa Hospital. Sgt **Covell** escorting.

Today's Tamam:

Camp	No 1	93
Camp	No 2	93
Camp	No 3	85 + 2
Camp	No 4	112
Camp	No 5	22
Camp	No 6	33
	Total:	440

Tuesday 25th of August 1942
Ex-BC to see doctor with a very sore leg. I visited the sick bay and found some of the (beds buggy) straffed the hospital staff. ASP Mr. **Grant** called to the camp in the afternoon. I did not see him. **Strong** was on duty. Attended a football match in the afternoon - Prisons v AA Battery - draw 1-1.

Wednesday 26th of August 1942
3.30 am visited the sentries around the camp. All alert and regular. Very bright moonlit night. Sgt **Rogan** on duty. Telephone message from Jerusalem that 29 seamen, Romanians, Finns and Bulgarians are to be handed over to the military. Went to Acre and collected money, but the notice was too short and I could not go to Haifa to collect the safe deposits. I had to return the 29 seamen to their camps at 6 pm as no transport arrived for them. I 10 pm I had to send for Dr **Khairy** as **Snearson** took a bad turn. He was taken to hospital.

Thursday 27th of August 1942
Three Jewish detainees, one Arab internee and one mixed 'C' **Lesan** to Athlit Hospital for minor operation.   Internee **Segal** did not wish to go. He stated he was feeling sick. Mr **Martin** DSP Haifa came to see ex-BC (*British Constable*) **Liddel** who, it was announced, had won the MBE for his services in Syria. Arrangements were made to transport the seamen to Latrun Military Camp.

Friday 28th of August 1942
Two members of the International Red Cross*, Col. **Boc** and Dr, **P Descoludres** arrived here at 10 am. Mr **Parkhouse** and Sgt. **Freeguard** were with the party. They met the representatives of all the parties and discussed many subjects. **Zwilling**, for the Germans had a lot to say for himself and he did not create a good impression. One member visited the camp whilst the other carried on interviews with a number of people. There was a general complaint about the bread. Air Raid Yellow Warning over Haifa at 8 pm. Nothing happened.

* Delegate of the Committee of the Internal Red Cross, 16 Maleka Nagli, Cairo, Shepherd's Hotel.

Saturday 29th of August 1942
The trial started today in the Magistrates Court Acre of the five Arab detainees accused of assault.

Went to the bank and collected the pay. I spent the afternoon paying out at the camp.

Monday 31st of August 1942
Went to CP Acre about the theft of blankets yesterday. Called in and got my pay from **Hook**. Brigadier **Rodwell** visited the camp at 5,30 pm. He went around camp 1, visited the Baracanda and went into the living quarters. He left the camp at 6 pm. Mr **Grant** was also present. Investigated the case of the theft of blankets by two warders **T. Mustafa** and **Eissa Steman.**

Tuesday 1st of September 1942
Went to Acre Police and handed them a case of theft of blankets. **Ali Sayed Omar**, a warder at the camp, was found in possession of 3 camp blankets. Mr Grant inspected the camp and did not appear very satisfied with things.

Wednesday 2nd of September 1942
Ilzak Yesovnilyk Erza Levy Elehan Yelada[6] were not in their huts at morning *Tamam*. I was informed at 7.5 by B/Sgt Buckley. I went and examined the hut. The hut leader **Marcel Covel** gave me the names as **Jakoby** and **Hagahle**. I sent for the

---

6   Two names or three names?

supervisor and asked him to confirm the names. He went to the hut and asked then and they repeated the two names. Inspected hut wire fences all around. Sent warder and N.C.O[7]. to search vicinity of the camp. No trace. Mr Grant arrived later and carried out on inspection. Checked up names and later called the roll of the camp twice in order to ascertain who the absent men are. Mr Grant came to camp at 4 pm and carried on taking statements until 7 pm.

Thursday 3rd of September 1942
3.15 am Air Raid alarm sounded in Acre. Later bombs were dropped in the sea near the camp. Enemy planes remained around until 6 am. No 3, 4 & 5 compounds were allowed out into their trenches. Tightened up all round on No 4 and No 5. Spent the day in B camp. All internees and internees returned from the clearance camp, Athlit.

Friday 4th of September 1942
Arranged to send **Segal, Lesean, Rois** and **Galilie** to Acre Magistrates Court to sign an affidavit. I spent all morning going through the accounts and checking up the cash books. **Brosnan** admitted to Haifa Hospital. Sent for Dr **Khairy** in the evening to come and look at an internee in No 2 camp who had a bit of a temperature.

Saturday 5th of September 1942
Aman Kamal Hadad transferred to Jerusalem by order of AIG CID. Phoned up and ordered wood from **Sedergreen** but up to 2 o'clock I had no luck. Picked up what spare wood I could collect from around the camp and used it for the kitchens. At 6 pm I phoned Mr **Grant** and explained the situation to him and he promised to help. **Strong** rang up - he is spending the night in Haifa. Visited the sentries and guards at 10.30 pm. Sgt **McGovern** on duty. All alert and regular.

Monday 7th of September 1942
Visited camps - only 3, 4, 5 & 6. Father **Eugene** came to the camp to see me about the schooling of the children and we proposed sending them to St. Joseph's Jaffa. The wood problem is still acute and all efforts to get a supply have failed.

---

7   Non-commissioned officer

Tuesday 8th September 1942
Sent the prison van to Haifa to collect **Magolitu** from Hospital, BI **Strong** to hospital for X-Ray. Six Jewish visitors today. Had to check Inspector **Schwelly** for slackness - timing etc for visits. A number of books came in today. I will have them sent to CID for examination with the Advisory Committee party tomorrow.

Ration car came at 12 today - the excuse a driver could not be found. Two Polish officers came to the camp to pay out to Polish internees. The interrogated **Rozenblatt** and **Djick**. A Polish Intelligence Officer spoke to **Wentland** and (**Urgrain**) and he remained in the camp for many hours. Dr **Zakhariah** admitted to hospital,

Wednesday 9th of September 1942
A Yugoslav officer came and collected **Korkaska,** who is detained here for 13 months. **Tusai** left camp for Beit Yam, **Abu Khadra** and **Margolitu** left for the Advisory Committee Jerusalem.

Schnearson was released from detention today. He is crippled and cannot get about. Visited sentries around the camp at 10.30. All working well. **Buckley** i/c.

Thursday 10th of September 1942
Took office midday. **Sharat** remanded for Supervisor of Prisons. Asleep on the west post No 4 Compound. Mr **Grant** arrived in the afternoon and made further investigation into the escape of Jewish prisoners. I spoke to him about the Jewish Feast and he agreed to grant the same privileges as last year, but said that visits to Camp 5 should be strictly supervised.

Friday 11th of September 1942
Captain S. Lolic of the Jugoslav Mission came to collect **Panovic**, but I had no instructions from Headquarters and so I could not let him go. Mr **Catling** and BI **Wilkin** arrived to interrogate Camp 4. The Jewish Community of Haifa sent in eggs, wine, potatoes into the camp for their people. Dr **McQueen** arrived and I accompanied him around the camp. **Patchan** on No 3 was supposed to go to hospital today. When he was searched a sum of money on him LP6. When the money was confiscated he refused to go to hospital. Camp 4 & 5 Huts open until 10 pm. Lights on until midnight. No incidents.

Saturday 12th of September 1942
Jewish New Year. Six visitors came and I arranged the first visit for 10.15 am at north of Camp 3. They protested and asked to see Mr **Grant**. I spoke to Mr. **Grant** and he suggested the South side of Camp 2. When I sent for the party to be visited, they demanded unlimited time. This am not prepared to grant and I sent the visitors away. Deputation from 3 camp and asked for: Huts to be closed at 10 pm. Huts to be open 3 am - 4 am for morning meal. They also want light and water. Request passed to Mr **Grant**, who will ask Mr **Scott**. I spent the afternoon examining parcels for No 4 Camp. Visited the camp at 10 pm. Tamam taken in No 4 Camp. Everything correct.

Sunday 13th September 1942
Visited guard at 2 am. All correct. Interviewed supervisors 4 & 5, the latter requested his visit this morning. There were 17 visits in the morning and 4 in the afternoon. Mr **Grant** came in the afternoon and tried **Sharrat** for being asleep at his post. He was fined 7 days pay. The supervisor of Camp 3 saw him regarding privileges for Ramadan. He gave permission for the huts to be open until 8 pm and that primus stoves could be lit in the hut until 4 am. Searched a number of parcels for camp 4 and 5.

Monday 14th of September 1942
Sadik and **Yani**, two supervisors from No. 4 were transferred from the camp to Acre Prison this morning. **Gallalie, Segal** and crowd went to Jerusalem this afternoon for the High Court. **Ehrenblatt** was transferred to Acre Prison Hospital. Went to Acre Prison in the afternoon.

Tuesday 15th of September 1942
A spot of bother in Camp 3 this morning regarding some Moslems not observing Ramadan feast. Went down and managed to settle the affair. Tried a member of number 4 Camp on 2 charges and sentenced him to 7 days on each charge. Went to Acre in the evening after the 'all clear' went and returned at 5 pm. Checked up on the sentries. All in order. Visibility fairly good at pm.

Wednesday 16th of September 1942
Went to Haifa with the prison van and collected deposits from the safe for Dr **Zaharia**. Returned to camp at 12.30 pm. Then off to Latrun camp. No kosher meat

was brought in for the Jews. Mr **Parkhouse** came in the afternoon and interviewed 26 internees during the course of the afternoon. He left at 6 pm.

Thursday 17th of September 1942
Around the camp to make sure that everything was ready in anticipation of the Sup. P [*Supervisor - Prisons*] visit. Had two reports regarding the conduct of hut 4 and 3 of Camp 4. on the 14th of September and on the 16th. I stopped them from going to the canteen and froze their account until such time as they appoint a supervisor.

Mr **Scott** did not come to the camp today. He went back to Jerusalem. I went to Acre in the afternoon and saw Mr **Grant**. I walked around the camp before going to bed in order.

Friday 18th September 1942
Went to Acre to see **Bill** who had some information to give me. Rations came at 12 noon today. **Ghardour** to hospital and Dr **Zaharia** out. No 4 Camp have appointed a new supervisor **Nahman Deutsch** who promises full cooperation. I therefore lifted the canteen ban. The Jewish Community in Haifa sent some food for the camp for the Jewish internees and detainees. Dr **Zakharia** discharged from hospital in Haifa. He is now waiting to be collected by the Greek Military Authorities.

Saturday 19th of September 1942
Mr **Grant** came for his weekly inspection. He was not pleased with No 1 Camp, hut 1 & 2. He interviewed the supervisors of 5 and 4 camp regarding the Jewish Holiday. The military played football on our ground in the afternoon. Visited the camp during the early part of the night. All in order.

Sunday 20th of September 1942
Jewish Feast today. No movement in camp 5 and 4. An inspection by the Food Control. - they inspected the books. No incident occurred during the day. Had the contents of the FO No. 241/40 read out to the parade this evening. Walked around the camp at 10 pm. **Brosman** was taking the Tamam in both 4 and 5 Camps. The lights will be on in both camps until midnight.

Monday 21st of September 1942
Inspected 3, 4, 5 & 6 Camps. It is a job to get something to employ the British

Police as they are working on the football field today.

Rations came at 12.50; no meat was brought. When I phoned up Haifa I was informed that I would get 2 day's meat tomorrow, or alternatively I could get sardines and eggs tomorrow. This was unacceptable. I phoned Acre but Mr **Grant** was not there so I referred the matter to Mr **Scott**.

Tuesday 22nd of September 1942
Colonel **Kalioris** and Lieut, **Abalyouglou** into camp to interrogate three Greek internees. Rations came today at 12.30 and the contractor brought good meat. I find that David **Kipper**, an internee under 15b is known by 3 other names - **Zauberman**, **Talari** and **Israeli**. The Greek investigating officers left the camp at 6 pm. They only managed to see one of the three persons they wanted to interrogate.

Wednesday 23rd of September 1942
Saw the four Greeks who are on hunger strike in Camp 2. I could not persuade any of them to stop. I read over the contents of their warrants to **Gallalie, Laison, Rois** and **Segal**. Mr **Grant** called in on the camp in the afternoon with his family. Air Raid alarm sounded. All staff turned out. All-clear sounded at 11.55 pm. Guns did not open fire. No incident.

Thursday 24th of September 1942
Went and tried to persuade the hunger-strikers to break their fast but without success. The Greeks were in the camp today carrying out their investigations, Dr **Zakharia** was handed over to them before they left. He is to go the Greek Army in Egypt. Soap, toothpaste, 24 toothbrushes and 100 razor blades arrived today and were issued out immediately. I accorded the Jews the usual privileges for their feast - eg lights.

Friday 26th of September 1942
The Ear Specialist arrived in the camp and he saw about 20 of the inmates. The Greek Colonel also arrived and spent the day carrying out his investigations. In the evening I took him to see the four hunger-strikers and they spoke with other inmates of the Greek Barracks, Mr **Hogan**, Crown Solicitor, came saw the old Romanian monk and **Marino**.

Monday 28th of September 1942

Strong went to Jerusalem on the prison van to see about his uniform. Father **Lesian** was transferred to Jerusalem today. **Harry Segal** to Bet Yam and two others to the POW camp Latrun. A spot of bother in Camp No 3 again, and as a result of this I sent **Salim Abu Khalid** to CP Acre for seven days. Col **Callirou**, Greek Investigation Branch came to camp today and interrogated the third and last of his people. On his departure he asked me not to let this person get in touch the other Greeks, so I detained him for the night in Camp 6.

Tuesday 29th of September 1942

Colonel **Callirou** of Greek Intelligence in camp with his staff. I went to Acre to collect pay. I met Mr. **Parker** at the bank.

Wednesday 30th of September 1942

Major **Munro** came to the camp today and had a look over the huts with the hope of taking the camp over as a training depot. The MO reports that 2 of the Greeks are in bad health and it is dangerous for them to continue their hunger-strike. I spoke to these Greeks and they promised me that if the Counsel General **Sakeluriou** would visit them they would call off the strike. Sgt **Feeguard** phoned to say that somebody from the Greek Consulate would come to the camp this morning to see the hunger-strikers. Today the bread supplied was un-baked - also no potatoes and no oil received.

Thursday 1st October 1942

Went to Haifa with family who were on the way to Jaffa School. Collected money deposits from the bank. Returned to camp at 2 pm and found that the representative of the Greeks had called as promised. I phoned Jerusalem but could not find **Freeguard**. Visited sentries in camp at 11.15. All alert and regular.

Friday 2nd October 1942

The Greek Counsel General came to the camp this morning and as a result of his visit the 12 Greeks on hunger-strike broke the strike today. The contractor could not supply eggs, he will not supply cheese, he did not bring the bread which was supposed to replace the previous day's supply which he was forced to take back as it was condemned by the doctor. Ex-BP came to me and spoke to me about the rations. The bread which they had returned yesterday was not replaced. They made a general complaint about the rations.

Saturday 3rd of October 1942
Inspected all the camp. The drains of No 2 Camp which were blocked are still out of order and the frequent appeals to the PWD are of no avail. The ration contractor did not bring the bread that was short, neither did he bring anything in lieu of yesterday's eggs. I spoke to him and he produced some cheese.

Sunday 4th of October 1942
Day off. It rained most of the day. Real heavy showers. In the evening 2 Greeks from Camp 2 beat up two Italians who went into the camp to pump up a football. I make peace between them.

Monday 5th of October 1942
Another incident occurred this morning when an Italian struck a Greek. I have confined both camps to their compounds until further notice. PWD sent two men to fix the drains - at last.

Tuesday 6th of October 1942
Mr **Grant** came to inspect the camp. He was not pleased with No 4. The reason for the poor standard seems to be a general shortage of brushes, both floor and scrubbing. The drains are still chocked up and the PWD did not do much to improve things. I reported the matter to Haifa but without any result. Played bridge at night and visited sentries and guards at 10.45 pm.

Wednesday 7th of October 1942
Interviewed 4 persons from Camp 2. PWD are on the job this morning and I hope it will be finished today, In the meantime I had the camp drained. I tried a detainee from 4 Camp - destroying government property ie one pair of bed feet. I sentenced him to 7 days in Acre. Brushes, etc. arrived from stores today. PWD worked all day on the drains but without any success. There is still a river in camp 2. Captain **Fogaline** arrived in camp at 5.40. Walked around the camo at 10 pm. All alert,

Thursday 8th of October 1942
Issued brushes to all camps as I had received 12 hard and 12 soft. Tried 1 detainee

from Camp 5 and sentenced him to 7 days sc in Acre. The supervisor appealed to me to squash the sentence, as he thought it was very severe and that I had taken only the Arab warder's word for the incident.

Friday 9th of October 1942
Margaleto and **Khadra** were released this morning. I phoned Mr **Grant** again. He promised he would see the PWD foreman. I warned the supervisor of the ex-BP that I am going to tighten things up. The drain pipe was cleared at 4 pm today after a week of smells. The commandant of the OTU (*Officer Training Unit*) came and asked when I was clearing out of the camp.

Saturday 10th of October 1942
Rations were good today. Eggs and potatoes at last. Admonished 2 ex-British Police constables for leaving their task without permission. The eye specialist and the dentist visited the camp today. Five prisoners from Acre came to see the eye specialist.

Sunday 11th of October 1942
Start of Arab Feast *Eud el Fether*. We had many visitors even though these were contrary to regulations. Captain **Lefogouli**, intelligence officer, arrived with BC **Duffy** escorting a Greek bint **Anna Argyraki** from Beit Yam for the purpose of identification by **Katseks**. It was a miserable day - a real khamseen.

Monday 12th of October 1942
Many visitors today for the 2nd day of the Moslem Festival. Ex-BC **Murphy** released today from detention. Issuing clothing to 3 Camp this afternoon. **Panovic** came to me today. Something is worrying him and he can't get it off his chest. **Steward** to Haifa hospital to see Dr. **Thompson** regarding his hand. Around the camp at 11 pm - all sentries working well. It rained during the night, Visibility bad.

Tuesday 13th of October 1942
Eleven ex-British Constables are on hunger strike this morning as a protest against their sentence. Mr **Grant** came and interviewed them. They submitted a form of protest to the IG. A captain from the field security came and interviewed **Abu Laban** regarding the kit that was lost.

Wednesday 14th of October 1942
Polish officers into camp to interview **Wentland** and **Kanokoski** (a Czech). Sent two Arabs **Sabli Bayoum** and **Ahmed Rashid Bader** to Acre for 14 days for fighting in the camp. Rations today short - no onions, no potatoes or sardines and no Kosher supplies for the Jews. The camp MO says that the contractor should supply either 1 tin of sardines or 2 eggs each. The 11 ex-BP are still carrying out their hunger-strike.

Thursday 15th of October 1942
Zedka Koniakowski and **Jan Hartman** are on hunger strike today. I informed the ex-BPs on hunger strike that they are committing a breech of prison regulations. The MO saw them today.

Friday 16th of October 1942
The eleven ex-British Police and the three Czechs are on hunger strike today. Heavy rain fell this morning and a real cold wind blowing. **Costin** was released. We are glad to get rid of him. He is practically an invalid - very hard to deal with in a camp of this kind. More trouble in camp 3. The supervisor resigned. I have stopped their canteen and recreation until such time as another supervisor is appointed. **Hoare** refused to take UK letter because he could not get his local mail. **Abu Jab** is appointed supervisor of Camp 3. As a consequence of this I have removed the ban I had imposed on the compound. Around the camp at 11.30 pm. Guards and sentries working well.

Saturday 17th of October 1942
Furious rain storms during the night which continued throughout the day. The eleven British constables were fed today. They drank the milk that the doctor had given them. They were issued with an extra blanket each as they complained of the cold.

Sunday 18th of October 1942
Visited the guards and sentries at 12. 45 am. Some heavy rainstorms and a half gale blowing. The visibility is poor and the sentries on the west side of the camp have a hard time of it. The doctor came to feed the ex-BPs. Mr **Grant** came to look on. Phone message from Mr **Scott,** IG would consider their cases only if they went off their hunger strike. At 1 pm they ended their hunger strike on the condition that no action be taken against them for refusing food. They were informed that no action

would be taken regarding their food. On the whole the day was not bad. There were occasional showers, but they did not last long. Issued clothing to **Kolback**.

Monday 19th of October 1942
A cold clear morning. Occasional showers throughout the day. Rations came early but no potatoes. I received a complaint from No. 1 regarding rations. I sent it on to Jerusalem. I called in on the AA Battery to see about the warders coming in and out for duty through their camp.

Tuesday 20th of October 1942
Czech Consul came and bought money and books for the inmates. **Hans Masyeck** got the opportunity to see him as instructed in the IG letter. The three that were on hunger strike ended it today at 11 am, when the consul saw them. I have nobody on hunger strike now. Acre B/Sgt **Montgomery** came and collected **David Kipper**, a 15b detainee, and took him to Nahariah for investigation. He returned him to camp at 3 pm. **A Gronberg** No 4 Camp admitted to prison hospital, Acre.

No eggs or egg substitute brought by the contractor today. So the ex-B/P in the camp have got to go hungry. They have no supper. Captain **Biedmead** in with a Greek **Mavroyanu** from Aleppo. **Bartl** in from CP Acre. Went around the camp after midnight. Sentries all alert.

Wednesday 21st of October
A bright cool day. Inspected "B" Camp. Saw **Abu Khalid** regarding information he got about a **Helma Pasha**. Meat was received for today's ration but nothing yet for yesterday. The ration car is at present stuck in the mud between the camp and Acre. Three persons out to advisory committee, Four persons in from Clearance Camp, Athlit. No meat or a substitute came for the Jews yesterday. Mr **Grant** spoke on the phone last night and said that Mr **Scott** and himself met **Haz Karaman** and discussed the general policy for feeding the camp,

Thursday 22nd of October 1942
Awaiting Mr **Scott**'s arrival for inspection. Sent the children's ration cards to Jaffa. A35 25 75 121328 A27 A28. There was 32 kilos of milk short today, but it was later sent together with 1500 eggs, 200 kilos soap and 3 drums of gaz. Went to the NAAFI concert party at the cadet school.

Friday 23rd of October 1942
Mr **Scott** visited the camp at 9 am. He went into the question of rations and pointed out the difficulties which the contractor was experiencing. He left the camp at 1 pm.
[C]Saturday the 24th of October
The rations arrived early. Received both potatoes and macaroni. Sent 160 eggs to CP Acre on request. **Zedka** went to Ajanit Acre for a rest cure, His nerves are getting bad.

Monday 26th of October 1942
A bright clear day. 588 BC **Coyle** arrived on transfer from Athlit. Mr **Grant** came from Acre regarding enquiries into discipline cases, Mr **Scott** phoned about rations, Rations today were good. **Sherman Shiber** transferred from 5 to 4 compound - Stern Group.

Tuesday 27th of October 1942
Looks much like rain this morning. Rations today - eggs instead of meat, fruit, tomatoes, grapes, 4 boxes of sardines, Mr **Grant** called in this afternoon and enquired about an ex-BC **Waterhouse** who while he was detained here was refused the services of an advocate. **A Grinsberg** - Camp 4 - came from hospital. It rained during the night.

Wednesday 28th of October 1942
A dull day. Interviewed Mr **Kusijanes** who requests to see a military intelligence officer who speaks Greek, but not Capt. **Lefogouli**. A petition by ex-British Police forwarded to ASP CP Acre. Signed by 9 of them. **Dryden** and **Dawkins** did not sign. Petitions to IG. They wish to be informed how their case now stands since the ended their hunger strike. Weighed ex-BPs and completed their record cards.

Thursday 29th of October 1942
Some showers during the day. Went to Acre to get pay at 11 am. The Spanish Consul with Mr **Hadad** called and interviewed a number of persons from Camp No. 1. Paid out during the afternoon. Had a walk around at midnight - all alert.

Wednesday 28th of October 1942
A dull day. Interviewed Mr **Kusijanes** who requests to see a military intelligence officer who speaks Greek, but not Capt. **Lefogouli**. A petition by ex-British Police forwarded to ASP CP Acre. Signed by 9 of them. **Dryden** and **Dawkins** did not

sign. Petitions to IG. They wish to be informed how their case now stands since the ended their hunger strike. Weighed ex-BPs and completed their record cards.

Thursday 29th of October 1942
Some showers during the day. Went to Acre to get pay at 11 am. The Spanish Consul with Mr **Hadad** called and interviewed a number of persons from Camp No. 1. Paid out during the afternoon. Had a walk around at midnight - all alert.

Friday the 30th of October 1942
Cold morning with signs of rain. (Zol) who has been absent for 5 days, came to the camp for his pay. The supervisor of Camp 5 released together with ex-BC **Bryant**. **Marcel Covel** to Haifa for medical treatment. No eggs received in today's rations. I issued a half a tine of sardines to each sick person. Potatoes arrived, but no eggs and no cheese.

Six Arabs arrived in from Syria. They were brought in by an escort from the Coldstream Guards, they arrived here at 6 pm and were sent to 3 compound.

Saturday 31st October 1942
Spoke to Mr **Grant** about the ration question. He states that there will be a difficulty with oil.

Rations: no macaroni received today for issue; no potatoes received for issue but tomatoes came instead.42 kilos of milk short - they will bring extra tomorrow. Eggs 120 for the sick only.

Mr **Grant** phoned up and gave me instructions regarding future disciplinary action against British Police and TAP who are now under Military Law.

Sunday 1st of November 1942
Schwilly away to Jerusalem on 2 days leave.

Rations today - 10 kilos of milk short, no macaroni. **Arboud** finishes his hunger strike (4 days)

Nikon Psaltis the Greek monk is on hunger strike today (5th day). **Hassan Samadi** and **Abdul Rahman Assef** were taken into campo at 4.23 pm. They were taken over from Acre Police.

Monday 2nd of November 1942
No doctor. Twelve arrived in from Clearance Camp at 11.30 am by prison van.

One Arab 17/1 to Haifa Hospital with **Brown** as escort. He was later returned and advised to go tomorrow for an X-Ray. Seventeen ex-refugees transferred here from Athlit Camp. I also received two arabs from Syria

Abdul Aziz Halash and **Wajpe Halash**,Rations: no potatoes and no macaroni. The Apostolic Delegate came to the camp and saw all the RC personnel in the Camp One. He remained for about an hour. He gave LP10 to the camp fund.

Tuesday 3rd of November 1942
No doctor. Mr **Grant** came and inspected the camp. Milk tested and found to be deficient of 5% fats.

Drains in No 3 out of order. Boiler also out of order. Attempts to solve the drain problem not successful. PWD informed.

Wednesday 4th of November 1942
No doctor. Had a number of interviews with new arrivals from Athlit. **Panovic** was in bad form today. He came out of his compound already dressed up and said that he was leaving camp. I spent over half an hour with him but to no avail. I asked a PC to escort him back to his hut, but he resisted. I was forced to send him to Acre for 14 days. Rations - fish and sweet potatoes, Milk had 100% fat deficiency today. Drains and boiler still out of order.

Thursday 5th of November 1942
No doctor. Good news from Egypt today. Inspector **Motram** came today and issued out ration cards for B.Ps.

Rations good - macaroni, sweet potatoes and meat. I had to return the milk - deprived of all its fat - unfit for human consumption.

Drains and boiler still out of order. Spoke to **Newman** PWD about the situation and he promised to do something tomorrow morning,

Friday 6th of November 1942
Good news coming from Egypt. Phoned **Newman** but he states that he can do nothing about drains and boiler today.

Rations: oranges, mandarins and sweet potatoes. Milk good for a change.

Mr **Millar** Jerusalem YMCA visited the camp and spoke with some of the internees. He left some books.

Saturday 7th of November 1942
Inspection of all camps. Rations today were good, but the usual Saturday shortage of milk - 36 kilos. Capt. **Churchill** came to the camp and spoke to me about the supervision of the two Maltese who were taken to the camp some days previously - **Attilio Renna** and **John Charles Cortez**. I have given instructions that they are not allowed out of their compound without my permission.

Sunday 8th of November 1942
I distributed some cigarettes around the camps from the LP10 that the Apostolic Delegate had given me. Rations very good - but 36 Kilos of milk outstanding. Rained very heavily during the night.

Monday 8th of November 1942
Fairly clear after the night of heavy rain. Polish officers came to the camp and paid LP2.5 for each of their subjects. Rations today - milk 94 Kilos short. Issued tinned milk at the rate of 1 tin per litre. This does not seem to please the contractor. Vegetable figle returned because the contractor would not agree to cut tops off.

I handed Capt. **Panovic** over to an escort of the Jugoslav Army on his release. Life won't be the same without him. It rained again during the night.

Tuesday 10th of November 1942
Rations: eggs, potatoes. tomatoes in lieu of cheese, beityan (the Arabic word for Aubergine/egg plant,) Milk appears good. I did an inspection of the camp at 1.20 am. All sentries alert and regular. Some of the TAW are complaining of the cold and that they were not issued with cardigan jackets.

Wednesday 11th November 1942
Rations: eggs, beityan; a shortage of milk. General shortage of wood. Mrs **Grant** came to the camp to sell poppies. She sold out. One Jugoslav in from the Military in Syria, Outbreak of diphtheria at Sidney Smith Barracks. **Bill Black** into camp to interrogate No 1 in connection with a fight in Acre.

Thursday 12th of November 1942
A nice dry day, Mr **Grant** came here to inspect the camp. Mr **Scott** CID arrived here for investigations. Contractor failed to bring eggs for the ex-BPs.

Friday 13th November 1942

I got instructions that **Murse** is struck off our strength on 15.11.42. I dealt with 7 disciplinary cases, **Haim Roth** is the new supervisor in No 4. He will be OK. The previous supervisor got a further extension to his warrant and he wants to study. I think **Roth** will turn out to be good. **Arboud** had a visit from the Secretary of the Belgian Consul. One detainee had a visit on the IG's permission. I informed the ex-BPs that the IG states that their case is under active consideration and that a further communication will be issued soon. Ex-BC **Home** would not accept an air-graph letter handed to him. This is the second time that he has refused his letter on the grounds that if he is unable to receive his local mail he will not receive any,

Saturday 14th of November 1942

Got information that **Huslak** and **von Rottak** are preparing for an escape. Both are in Camp 2, Hut 5. Mr **Grant** came and saw **Dawkins** concerning a letter sent by Mr **Scott** saying that **Turner** and **Dawkins** were sending out letters. **Dawkins** wrote and asked that this letter be returned to him, but Mr **Grant** assured him that the letter did not exist. **Dawkins** was sent to hospital with instructions to Dr **Thompson** that he was to be admitted into the British Police ward and not the prison ward of the hospital.

Rations: milk short, 21 eggs short.
Tamam: 451

Dawkins returned from Haifa. Dr **Thompson** states that the operation required is performed at the Jerusalem Government Hospital.

Sunday 15th of November 1942

Had a day off, but I remained in camp. Capt **Churchill** called and interviewed **Morrison**.

Monday 16th of November 1942

A very wet day. Mr **Grant** informed me that ex-BCs would be sent to Jerusalem to Depot tomorrow, He would give me further particulars. They are now going by train from Haifa.

Heavy rain during the day. Went around the camp at 9.30 pm. Sentries all alert and regular.

Tuesday 17th of November 1942
Mr **Grant** came to camp at 11.15 and informed the ex-BCs that the High Commissioner had remitted all their sentences. They were going to Depot on half pay until they were repatriated. All deposits and property handed over to them. Good riddance.

It rained very heavily during the afternoon. **Balty** to hospital with a suspected broken ankle.

Rations: No macaroni, 92 eggs short, 136 kilos of milk.

Wednesday 18th of November 1942
Raining again today. Major **Vladeta Bogdanovic** interviewed me today. He handed me two letters, one for AIG CID and one for the High Commissioner. Received a wire from Jerusalem that ten persons from Syria were to be handed over to the Military on the arrival of transport. This order was later cancelled.

Freeguard spoke from Jerusalem and confirmed that the party of Arabs, whose hand over for today had been cancelled, would leave tomorrow. A member of Mr **Scott's** staff 853 **Akram Kawar** came to interrogate **Mohd Scarfic**, **Ibrahim Ottman** and four Syrians.

Thursday 19th of November 1942
Went to Acre Bank and got LP280 to pay out 10 persons leaving the camp who are to be handed over to the Military at Haifa. **Akram Kawar** is still here in the camp carrying out his investigations. Transport arrived from Haifa at 10.30.

The rations van broke down on the way here. The prison van had to be sent out to rescue the rations. Went to Acre in the afternoon for a walk and met Col. **Rice** late AIG at **Bill Black's**. Visited the camp at midnight, everything OK, visibility good, sentries working well,

Friday 20th of November 1942
Raining heavily all morning. Later a wind blew up. Rations: milk 110 kilos. eggs 102.

Heavy rain throughout the afternoon and night. **Strong** to Acre for a board of survey.

Saturday 21st of November 1942
Heavy rain this morning. Mr **Grant** came to camp and made enquiries regarding ex-BC **Sweeney** who had spent one month here last year.
    Informed officially that the camp starts to move on 1. 12. 1942. Something wrong with the lights. I phoned PWD and PE Coy.

Sunday 22nd of November 1942
Day off. Four warders arrived from Acre to make up the establishment. Went for a walk along the see-shore in the evening.

Monday 23rd of November 1942
Heavy rain again. **Haim, Masarik** and **WIS** for Magistrate's Court Acre to swear an affidavit. A party of officers came from OTU to inspect the A Camp as they are intending to take it over on the 7th. Mr **Grant** came to camp to show them over.

Tuesday 24th of November 1942
A dry cold day. Issued orders to camps regarding the move. Visited the camp with Insp, **Schwilly** before midnight. All sentries alert and challenged well. Visibility very good.

Wednesday 25th of November 1942
A cold dry day. Greek Intelligence Officer to the camp at 8 pm to interrogate two of the Greek internees. Tender from Acre to collect the old boat. **Russel** sawed it through and got it on the tender.

Thursday 26th of November 1942
BI **Strong** to Latrun. Three lorries from VRD reported at 7 1m. I got them away by 8 am. The tables and forms are bulky and difficult to pack. Mr **Scott** came in the afternoon and went into details about the move. He left at 6 pm.

Friday 27th of November 1942
B/Sgt **Rogan** to Latrun. Three truck loads out at 8.10 am. Some more tables left over. They are very awkward to pack in. Someone from GHQ to interview **Stilisen** regarding his debts.

Saturday 28th of November 1942

Three trucks and a small tender pulling out at 8.30 for Latrun. B/Sgt **Covell** i/c of convoy. Rations were good. I had the milk tested by Mr **Haddad** in the camp here. The Ear, Throat and Nose Specialist arrived in camp today to examine 24 persons.

Sunday 29th of November 1942

Mahmoud Pachacha was handed over today to the Military at 8.30 am. There are two of his suitcases at Latrun and about LP28 to go from this office. A Sgt **Drimmer** from the recruiting office came to enlist some of the Polish Jewish internees with the object of recruiting them for the army. As I had received no instructions from the CID about this visit I took no action.

Monday 30th November 1942

Brown, **Marshall**, **Coyle** & five Palestinian warders

Three trucks loaded and away to Latrun at 8.15 am. Went to Acre to collect the pay. Pay sheet numbers: 47/11; 45/11; B4/11; B269/11; 16/11; 335/11, together with LP56 and 3 chits books handed over to Insp **Schwilly** for payment at Latrun camp.

[*signed: S. D. S. Schwilly*]

Walked around the camp with some army officers who were looking at the accommodation of A camp.

Tuesday 1st of December 1942

Inspector **Schwilly**, Sgt **Abboud** and BC **Walsh** + 5 Palestinian warders.

Two trucks and 3 buses arrived on time. All left camp at 8.10 am. Nr **Grant** was present during the search. One tender left at 10 am. To Acre with tender withdrawing stores. Metre reading on this date: 3493.

Wednesday 2nd December 1942

B/Sgt **McGovern**, BC **Jones**, BC **Belham**. 2 Cpls and 16 warders.

Convoy left at 7.45. **Von Rottick** went handcuffed. He did not want to go without **Huslak**. **Rois** would not turn out, because he was late with his packing. I put him on the bus.

Tamam:	Camp 2	34
	Camp 3	81
	Camp 4	111

Camp	5	17
Camp	6	15
Total		259

Thursday 3rd December 1942
BI **Strong**, B/C **Steward**, + BS, 2 warders **Mohd Abdul** and **Fattah Mohd Affari**
Received 1 frig on loan to Inspector **Higgins** and 1 radio set HMV on loan to BC **Steward**
[*signed pp T.S. Bauhagy*]
Party left at 7.45. The buses appear good, **Strong** i/c party.

Tamam	Camp 3	62
	Camp 4	81
	Camp 6	6
	Total	169
	Working party	10 constables
	Total	179

Friday 4th of December 1942
B/Cs **Sykes**, **Longden**, **Goodrick**, **Young, Lynch** + 10 G. guns
Stern Group left at 8.10 am. All were ready at 7.45 but could not go due to A.C. flat tyre. **Mohed Shariff** out with stores fixing things up.

Tamam	Camp 3	18 internees
		16 convicted

Some olive wood confiscated from one of the camps.

Saturday 5th of December 1942
All B/Ps with the exception of **Covell** on transfer. Sgt **Rushdi**, 2 Cpls and 8 warders left to guard camp.
Got all of 3 Camp ready to move, when the rain poured down. Everything was soaking wet, mainly due to bad packing. All will be cleared out tomorrow. Phoned **Dudley Higg** regarding the discharge of No 18 today.

Sunday 6th of December 1942
Sgt **Covell, Rushdi, Clerk**
Three trucks moved away at 9.10 am. All office and hospital furniture. Mr **Grant**

came to camp at 9.20 am PWD taking over. Final check of all rooms.

Monday 7th of December 1942
Left camp at 10 am and went to CP Acre to collect cheque for S.A. Ramle. Left for Latrun at 10.20 am and arrived at 1.45. Did not go to camp as I spent the evening settling in.

Tuesday 8th of December 1942
To camp at 9 am.

Wednesday 9th of December 1942
Phoned up Jerusalem about internee deposits and got authority to open up an account. Saw Post Master regarding mail. Returned from Ramle at 1 pm. Went to POW camp to see Lieut. Col. **Bingham** but he was away in Jerusalem. Called in at the monastery and arranged milk delivery to house. A Persian general received as an internee.

Thursday 10th of December 1942
Out at 8 am. Met two persons from Tel-Aviv who came out to see the arrangement of oil burners for boilers. Went to POW camp to see Lieut. Col.**Bingham** and discussed the training of 8 of his personnel as warders. Met the ration contractor and complained about the late arrival of the rations. In the afternoon Col **Bingham** came to see me and have a look around the camp.

Friday 11th of December 1942
Met the area commander at Amwas Monastery. He was down to inspect the building with a view to taking it over as prison for 17A people. It rained all day and the camp was miserable.

Saturday 12th of December 1942
A fairly dry day. Discussed the detail of guards and sentries. Spoke to Mr **Scott** about various problems, including about my leave which had been turned down. Some Jews were on the road shouting to people in the camp I had one of them arrested.

Monday 14th of December 1942
To camp early and went into the question of security. B/Sgts must do more work in compound. I am not satisfied that they are doing sufficient. Spoke to Mr **Scott** about pillows, etc which are required. Rations came today at noon.

Tuesday 15th of December 1942
Went to Haifa by the 7 am train and closed up with Barclays Bank. Returned by the evening train.

Wednesday 16th of December 1942
Mr **Scott** visited the camp with a Major **Victor** who was looking over the camp. He was due to take over a prison camp in Lybia. Returned to camp after lunch when an order came through to release 7 Polish Jews for the army. It was 7 pm before I got them clear. When I arrived home there was an alarm in the camp. I turned out and took tamam. I could not find the reason for the alarm.

Thursday 17th of December 1942
Dudley Higg was transferred to Jerusalem

Friday 18th of December 1942
Tried Cpl **Abdulla Jayoussu** for refusing to do duty and remanded him for Mr **Scott** with the recommendation that he be reduced to the rank of warder Cpl. Phoned Jerusalem twice about the wood. I had to accept a load on Wednesday which was rather too big. I returned a truck load yesterday. Went into all the camps and had a good look around. Arab Feast day today and there were a good number of visitors.

Saturday 19th of December 1942
A lot of visitors in camp today. Spoke to Mr **Scott** about the wood.

Monday 21st December 1942
I tried 4 persons for getting away out of their Barakanda through the wire and warned them. **Chisther** would not take any notice of my warning so I sentenced him to seven days s.c.. During the evening he asked for knife to cut his bread and he cut his wrist with it. The doctor dressed the wound and sent him back to the c.c. Went to the mess kitchen and saw the lunch which I considered to be very good. Rations are satisfactory.

Tuesday 22nd of December 1942
Went into 1 & 2 compounds and pulled down all the clothes lines, etc. Mr **Millar** YMCA called and left some games for 1 & 2 camps. Col **Bingham** from POW camp called regarding the transfer of 29 17A people to his camp. The 8 soldiers who were here for duty went back to their unit at 2 pm. At 4 pm I informed the supervisors that the 29 persons would be ready by 10 am tomorrow. Inspected the lunch - drab but satisfactory.

Wednesday 23rd of December 1942
Handed over the 29 persons held under 17A to the Military and completed the procedure at 12.30 pm. **Pakaros**, a Greek, released. One Italian transferred to Jerusalem. Mr **Parkhouse** arrived in the afternoon and I took him around Camp 1. He was very pleased with all he saw. Mr **Hadod** from the Spanish Consulate arrived and he stayed until quite late. A Polish chaplain came and saw his Poles.

Thursday 24th of December 1942
The Polish Delegate for Polish Refugees arrived and paid LP5 to each of the internees. Went to the military camp and paid LE 29 and LP 10 (30) for the Major and LP5 for **Rozenblatt** to the adjutant.

Went to midnight mass at the Trappist Monastery and did not get home until 2 am.

Friday 25th of December 1942
Christmas Day. Came to the camp and went round the whole place. Went to the British mess and saw all the staff seated for lunch. In the afternoon went for a walk with the family and then early to bed.

Saturday 26th of December 1942
To camp and had a look around. Everything in order. Went to Amwas and had lunch with the Muktar. Afterwards returned to camp and worked until 5 pm.

Sunday 27th of December 1942
Mass at the Trappist Monastery at Latrun. There is a strong wind today but the camp is standing well up to it. I made a complete inspection of all the camp. There is a door off its hinges in the ablution room, and several of the window hinges are out.

Tuesday 29th of December 1942
Fourteen persons attended fire frill given by me with the assistance of Sgt **Rushdi**. An escort came from Ramle to bring 6 of the Stern group to the Magistrates Court in Ramle, but on arrival it was discovered that the men in question were all in CP Acre. However they did take one person from here. I saw **Isaac Lurdeche** and reprimanded him for making an improper remark to a BC.

Visited the compounds and was not satisfied with the state of No 2. The supervisor will give the names of the persons responsible for cleaning to the B/Sgt and action will be taken if the duty is not carried out. Two from No 3 camp were put in the cooler for not turning out on Tamam roll call.

Wednesday 30th of December 1942
I am informed by the Sgt that No 3 do not wish to come for rations today. I interviewed some people from No 3 camp and they asked that the two persons put in the cooler yesterday be released. The ration contractor brought no meat or other substitute today. Had a message from Jerusalem that **Willy Winkler** an internee working in the BC mess was arrested outside the camp. I came to the camp immediately and opened up an enquiry. I did not get home until 10 pm.

Thursday 31st of December 1942
I had a big office today and did not get away to lunch until 2.15 pm. **Dibbins** came out from Ramle to finish the payment of the warders. Returned to the camp after lunch. I was informed that 10 10 pm that there was trouble in Camp 1 between Bulgarian and Italian internees, One Italian **Dordic Amedeo** was stabbed in the throat. He was taken to hospital in the late hours of the morning. **Nikola Ivanoff** is in solitary confinement cells ad he is accused of striking **Amedeo Dordic.** B/Sgt **McGovern** escorted **Dordic** to hospital and reports that the doctor does not have much hope for him. **McGovern** had a statement recorded from **Dordic**. This statement is in Arabic and so I handed it over to the police.

....

So, ends the Mazra'a Camp Diary for 1942. I have not amended in in any way except add a few explanatory notes. I am grateful to Martin Higgins for allowing me to reproduce his father's unique diary and for patiently bearing with my numerous questions.

MICHAEL HIGGINS

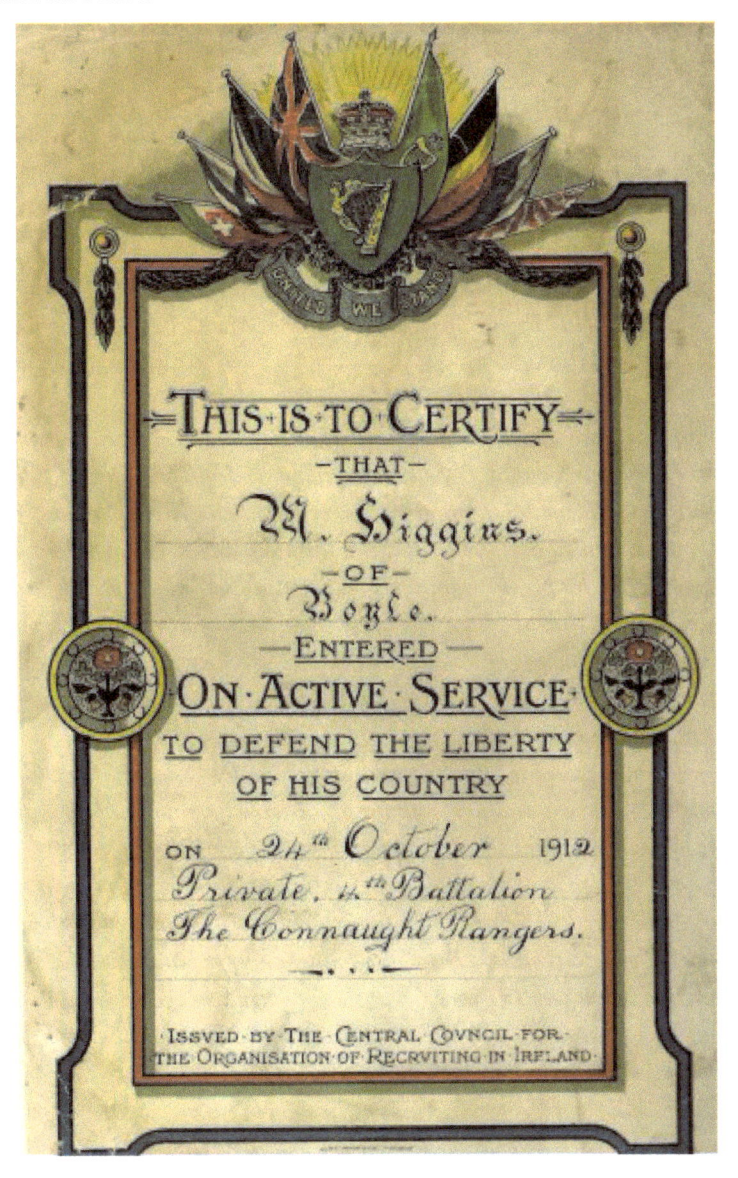

Sarafand New Recruits Connaught Rangers Michael 2nd from left

Michael Francis Higgins was born on 1st April 1898 In Boyle County Roscommon, at the foot of the Curlew mountains in Southern Ireland. He enlisted in the 4th Battalion (Special Reserve) Connaught Rangers at the end of 1912. His Service Number 4645 giving his profession as 'labourer' and his age as seventeen and eleven months in he added two years on to his age, he was in fact fourteen and seven months. He was a fresh complexioned youth with blue eyes and fair hair described in the military notes as 'respectable.' The Connaught Rangers created in 1881 were an Infantry Regiment that mainly recruited from the west of Ireland. They were disbanded in 1922 on the establishment of the Irish Free State.

The brothers were posted to Crosshaven, County Cork for basic training with the 4th Battalion, then weapons training with the 3rd Reserve Battalion in preparation for deployment in France. Training was complete by late August 1915.

Michael and Patrick were mobilised with 'C' Company the 5th Connaught Rangers in Salonika 6th November 1915. The 5th Battalion had lost 50% of its strength fighting in Gallipoli thirty-five replacements were sent to France and five hundred to Gallipoli. By the time they arrived September 1915 the Gallipoli campaign was over. Michael was serving on the Front Line in Macedonia in the autumn of 1915. He was still in the field when his brother Patrick was killed in action on Tuesday 7th December 1915. The brothers had enlisted in the Connaught Rangers at the same time, both lying about their ages, Patrick was a year older, so fifteen on enlistment. Corporal Patrick Higgins 4354 was killed in action while serving with the 5th Battalion in Salonika, in the north of Greece near the Macedonian Border. He was eighteen years old.

On 25th June 1916 Michael was appointed as an unpaid Lance Corporal. He was deprived of his stripe by the OC on 13th June 1917 for failing to salute an officer. He embarked on HM Briton at Salonika 10th September 1917, arriving in Egypt at Alexandria when he disembarked six days later on 16th September. On 25th May 1918 he embarked aboard 'Ormonde' arriving in France at Marseilles. He was invalided to hospital then home possibly in Juneto-September 1918 before being sent to a Military Hospital in Boyle 23rd October 1918.

Michael was demobilized Special Class 'Z' Reserve 7th January 1919. Special Class Z Reserve was a contingent of the British Army of previously enlisted now discharged army personnel. First authorized by the Army in December 1918 to ensure combat readiness in the event of a re-breakout of hostilities, it was abolished 21st March 1920 so Michael was discharged at that time.

His military career now behind him Michael served for two years with the Royal Irish Constabulary, then in March 1922 he joined the British Gendarmerie in Palestine. He transferred as a corporal to the Palestine Police 1926 after the Gendarmerie disbanded. Michael married in Palestine and his three children were born and raised there until their evacuation under 'Operation Polly' in 1947.

In 1942 when he was the Commandant of Mazra'a Detention Centre his rank was British Inspector the insignia was one pip on the shoulder. In 1948 he was awarded the Colonial Police Medal for long service, that same year he retired to the place he was born in Southern Ireland and took up farming on a small scale.

He died at home 31 Marian Road, Boyle, after a period of ill health on 20th March 1967 and was buried on 23rd March after a Requiem Mass at St Joseph's church. He left a widow, two sons and a daughter.

NOTES

Yitzhak Shamir, 7th Prime Minister of Israel, 22nd October 1915 - 30th June 2012
Joined the Irgun Zvai Leumi Zionist Paramilitary group opposed to British control in Palestine. The Irgun split on 1940 when Irgun adopted the Haganah policy of aiding the British against the Nazi's. Shamir joined the more extremist faction, Lehi better known to the British as the Stern Gang after their leader, Avraham Stern. Stern was killed by the British 12th February 1942. Shamir had been imprisoned by the British in 1941, in 1942 he was in Mazra'a Camp. Several months after Stern was killed Shamir and a

fellow prisoner Eliyahu Giladi hid under a stack of mattresses until nightfall in one of the camp warehouses before escaping through the barbed wire fences.
PS: The only escape mentioned in the diary is on 2nd September when it appears two prisoners were unaccounted for.

THE BALKAN CAMPAIGN - THE SALONIKA FRONT
Early in October 1915 Allied British and French troops were part of an Expeditionary Force landing in Northern Greece to aid Serbia. According to the Great War 1914-1918 – Connaught Association Boyle on 6th October1915 a combined German and Austrian Army launched a full- scale invasion of Serbia from the North. Two days later a Bulgarian Army attacked from the East. The Serbian Army were in full retreat. Neutral Greece allowed the Allies to use Salonika (now Thessaloniki) as their base to prepare operations into Serbia.

The Re-enforced Connaught Rangers arrived at Salonika 10th October 1915 training in atrocious weather conditions and crossing into Southern Serbia's snow- covered mountains.

On 7th December a huge army of Bulgarian troops overran the frozen trenches occupied by the 10th Irish Division, near the village of Kosturino, the main thrust of the attack was the part of the line held by the Connaugh Rangers. In the fierce battle that followed the Rangers suffered massive losses and were forced to retreat back into Greece. Patrick Higgins was one of the one hundred and thirty- eight officers and men of the Rangers who were killed that day. A further one hundred and thirty men were taken prisoner.

The 5th Battalion remained in Salonika for two more years. Michael Higgings left Salonika for Egypt on 10th September 1917 when the Rangers were transferred to the Egypt/Palestine Front disembarking on 16th in Alexandria. They took part in the Allies third attempt to take the fortified towns of Gaza and Beersheba which protected the entrance to Palestine across the Sinai Gaza fell 31st October and Jerusalem 6th December 1917. The combined Turkish and German Army retreated north the offensive came to a halt and the Rangers spent two months on the Front-Line north- west of Jerusalem before going int action against the enemy held village of Neby Saleh. As the Germans broke through on the Western Front in France offensive operations on the Palestine Front came to an end in April and the Egyptian Expeditionary Force in Palestine were ordered to send troops to France. Michael is with the 5th Battalion Connaught Rangers when they embarked at Port Said for France on 25th May 1918 and on 1st June 1918 when they reach Marseilles. The records are now unclear, we know between June and September 1918 he was invalided to hospital and that on 23rd October 1918 he was sent to a military Hospital in Boyle.

PALESTINE 1917- 1948
Palestine Gendarmerie

The Mandate Gendarmerie in Palestine was recruited chiefly from among constabulary and auxiliaries who had served in Ireland. In 1922, British authorities put out a request for unmarried men under the age of 30 to join this new force but found that the soon to be disbanded Black and Tan constabulary from Ireland provided a large and willing group to recruit from.

This force was assembled in Plymouth to undergo training before being despatched by Steamer to Haifa where they vigorously pursued bandits or brigands through the deserts and mountains of the Mandate on their Model T Fords or by horseback.

The force was unusual in that it was entirely British manned with no local recruitment. This also meant that they were relatively expensive for a colonial gendarmerie and so were disbanded in 1926 and effectively merged into the Palestine Police Force which included Arabs and Jews in addition to British officers. The majority of the Palestine Gendarmerie transferred to this force, but a significant number transferred to the Trans-Jordan Frontier Force or the Imperial Mesopotamian Police Force in Iraq.

CHAPTER 5

With The 2nd East York's on D Day   1944
Lionel Roebuck

Private Lionel Roebuck

WATERLOOVILLE

On arrival at Shorne we checked into the transport staging camp as the driver has been instructed. This was because he also had to pick up some other things at that camp on his way. It was easy to get a meal, but there did not seem to any overnight sleeping arrangements for us. It was most fortunate, because of my knowledge of the area, for us to be able to find a nice dry place in the woods and to be able to settle down with a ground sheet and a blanket for the night. The next day we travelled back all the way we had come on the very congested roads south of London and on towards Southampton. There to join up with old friends and mates in a new tented woodland camp near to Cowplain and Waterlooville.

The camp was close to the main Portsmouth road and we were still in bell-tents for sleeping, but, with many larger ones for group instruction and recreation. It was well hidden away, under the mature trees in the woodland, as were most of the other camps around the area. From the camp it was easy to get into the towns of Havant, Emsworth and Cosham in the evenings, and at weekends there were twenty-four hour leave passes for trips up to London. I was quick to take advantage of this and soon had my leave pass and then traveled by electric powered train from Havant station to the city, arriving at Waterloo station.

My trip to London, on my own and not really planned without any thoughts on what to do or where to go, proved to be a real waste of effort. The opportunity was taken to look at a few of the sites that were near Waterloo station, walk over the bridge and along the Embankment, and look up at Big Ben. It was possible for me to stay at the YMCA near the station for one night and return to the camp the next day. Not quite the kind of leave expected on what had been my first visit to London, but an enjoyable release from the routine of camp life.

On Monday 22nd of May 1944 all the troops were marched out of the camp to line up in single file, along the nearby country lanes, to be reviewed by the King. Together with senior officers he walked slowly along the in front of his assembled troops, stopping every so often to speak to one of them. Arthur, my old school friend was one of those to whom he spoke and gave a personal greeting to. the King, really small in stature, wished him good fortune in the coming conflict.

On Friday following the King's visit the camp was sealed, and no one was allowed out. In the briefing-tents, large relief model maps, with code names for towns and places to maintain security, were displayed, showing an exact replica of the terrain and defences which we were going to attack. these were studied very carefully as was the manner in which it was hoped the attacks on them would be carried out. On these maps (of the Normandy Coast) each of the strong- point defences had a printed code name and all relevant features of the pill boxes, wire, mines and guns were portrayed. All were encouraged to learn, and carry in our minds, as much detail as possible of the features shown.

The 2nd Battalion of the East Yorkshires had to attack on the extreme left of Sword Beach. 'Queen Red!' 'A' and 'B' Companies, supported by specially designed swimming tanks, were to break through the beach obstacles. 'A' Company together with 'C' Company of the 1st Battalion South Lancashire's, which was to land on our right, would then attack and eliminate the strong-point, COD, a defence feature which covered a wide area along the beach frontage. 'B' Company would simultaneously then advance across the open ground, to attack the first inland strong-point, SOLE. They would be supported by 'C' Company which would be following up closely behind them and eliminate it. The next task would be then to advance further inland to the Strong-point DAIMLER, (a massive complex of defence works with strong obstacles, a most formidable objective) then attack it and put it and out of action in order to stop the four 75-mm guns positioned there, from shelling the beach. This task was to be mainly the responsibility of 'C' Company. All of us were encouraged to visit the briefing-tent for group instruction, or to go there on our own, to really absorb all of the details and get to know exactly what was required of us after the landing.

FRANCE, BUT WHERE?

Confined as we were in the sealed camp, despite some six months absence from 'C' Company, my old friendships were quickly renewed. All the training activities were concentrated on our weapons and kit readiness, and parades were held with this feature mainly in mind. weapon training was long over, only the readiness and ability to use them effectively in action against the enemy now mattered.

The last pay day before leaving camp each man was given two-hundred French Francs mostly in five Franc notes. These were blue-green in colour, square and had a picture of the French Flag on the reverse side. In addition, we were given a tin of Taverner and Rutledge quality boiled sweets and two F'L's (condoms.) Some were used to protect rifle barrels from the ingress of sand and sea water during the landing and others as waterproof containers for watches and other valuables.

Although the game of Housey- Housey run by the NCO's, who were on to a good thing, was the only officially allowed gambling game, there were many others. These were the usual ones on the result of card games, using a mixture of French money and English money. Pitch-and-Toss, using any flat secluded area to toss up two half-pennies also seemed very popular.

Daily visits to the briefing-tents continued and a French language phrase book issued, but with no indication of exactly where the landing would be. Personal precautions were given out, along with dire warnings against drinking milk or untreated water. This included the issuing of water sterilising tablets. (Blue ones were to sterilise, yellow to make it palatable.) Lectures were given to us on the correct behaviour and attitude towards French civilians. Also, unofficially, the problems of taking too many prisoners! With all the training completed D-Day, the real test, to prove whether we were right or wrong.

The next step was for us to move from the camp to the dispersal area, then to the boats or to small camps adjacent to harbours where the assault-boats were moored. Due to re-joining my unit so late, and obviously finding myself an odd man out, allocation of all the places in the L.C.A. (Landing Craft Assault) assault craft had been made. Each one held a platoon of around thirty- two or so men together with their weapons. In consequence of this I could not join the L.S.I. "Glenearn," the mother ship with the L.C.A.'s in the davits for lowering some seven miles out from the shore. Instead, together with second's in command, at various levels in the battalion, I went to a dispersal area camp close to the port of Newhaven. This was where our L.C.I. (Landing Craft Infantry) (L), a larger assault craft was waiting with others in the harbour.

It was still a sealed camp, with military police guards, set out within a part of the grounds of a large private estate. This was Firle Place, close to the village of West Firle in the South Downs. The usual cluster of Nissen huts and tents served for accommodation for the few more days of waiting for the word to go.   Without parades or other duties gambling with cards or Pitch-and-Toss was soon started up again, anything to speed up the time of waiting!

On the afternoon of the 4th June the order came to get ready to leave the camp, we formed up in the road outside the main entrance gate. After a short time, we were dismissed. Next day, again, mid-afternoon, the same thing occurred. This time the entire group started off on the slow journey, down the long-curved valley, into Newhaven. We went over the level crossing then turned towards the railway terminal station adjacent to the quay and the harbour. There we could remove our heavy loads for a break. Local ladies served tea and cakes, but not for me, my English money had been gambled away. I was never a clever or a successful gambler, there was not even threepence for a 'char and a wad!' However, my new issue of two-hundred French francs in square notes was still intact.

We were soon marching along the quay to where the three L.C.I. (L) and L.C.T.(R) 's (Landing Craft Tank Rocket - rocket firing craft) all with the 3rd Division emblems painted on their sides, were tied up. In the way we had practiced in training for so long, we were dismissed, broke ranks and boarded our assault craft.

ACTIVE SERVICE IN FRANCE D-DAY JUNE 6TH 1944
Assault Boat Crossing and Landing
After boarding we made our way down the steep ladder stairway to the below-deck bunk-area. The bulkhead door with sealing flanges and locking handles at the entrance was viewed with some trepidation. Once there I put my equipment on the first bottom bunk to the right of the stairway, considering it best to be as near the escape hatch as possible. It was fairly obvious that when underway, holing would like as not be contained by shutting off individual compartments. This was not a pleasant thought to start off a long sea voyage!

The bunks had a wire- mesh base and were packed in tightly, so with the large amount of equipment carried there was not much room to move about. Having got rid of my heavy load and weapons I remounted the stairway and returned to the fresh evening air, away from the sickening stench of fuel oil in the hold. The cooks were busy with the evening meal with the petrol pressure burners roaring away in an enclosed well along the midsection of the ship. The spuds needed to be peeled, so making myself scarce, I went forward and away from the centre well of the ship's deck to watch some of the happenings along the quay side.

Two big Red Caps, the military police, hurried along a couple of chaps (AWOL'S) absent without leave. Probably they had been laid in the 'clink' until the last possible opportunity, but they were not going to be allowed to miss out on tomorrows big event. The two of them looked pretty miserable and the hair on their heads had been cropped short. they passed by and climbed aboard another L.C.I. (L) further along the dock side.

When ready the meal was mainly thick meaty stew with potatoes, and strong tea. Most of the ingredients from fourteen man 'Compo' ration packs, served up to the

THROUGH FIRE, SHOT AND SHELL

hungry crowd of soldiers lined up with their mess tins and brown enamel mugs at the ready.

As dusk fell the L.C.L. (L) 'S cast off to follow the L.C.T. (R)'s. These were for rocket launching and they had been moored alongside away from the harbour wall. The decks were a mass of tubes, all inclined forward. As the crafty moved slowly out towards the harbour entrance, a group of local residents waved and cheered from the right-hand side of the harbour, acknowledged in turn by the ship's hooter. Then, out through the entrance to the rougher water. Initially the effect was not too bad, soon however, the shallow-bottomed craft were rolling and pitching. It was only a short time before these effects took hold and then the uneasy feeling of seasickness welled inside many of us!

Despite the conditions I took to my wire-mesh bunk and was asleep for most of the trip across the Channel. I was also much troubled by dreaming of switching boats part way, to join with school pal Arthur and other soldiers who had the initial and most dangerous part of the landing to do. They were to land from the much smaller L.C.A.'s after being lowered on to the rough sea many miles out from the hostile coast of France from the mother-ship, 'Glenearn.'

The chocolate from the fourteen-man packs must have lain heavy on my stomach, for on waking seasickness from the movements of the ship made me feel really awful. I struggled from my bunk and pulled myself up the stairway to reach the deck intending to reach over the side of the craft, not quite making it. That wasn't all; my head was swimming, I was giddy and I still felt pretty poorly. Looking up, a few of my mates were laughing at my predicament but I was certainly not on my own. There were a few who did not suffer from the effects of seasickness on the crossing. Some, in a far worse condition than me, lay green and immobile on their bunks. The cooks were busy on deck with their petrol pressure stoves roaring away in the centre well of the ship. Breakfast was greasy bacon and sausages out of tins with fried bread but few had any appetite. A mug of tea made me feel better. Able then to retrieve my gear and weapons from below I started to take interest in what was happening in the Channel and on our landing craft.

THE BEACH

Having pulled myself together and taken my bearings, I watched as the greyish dawn was just breaking through. In a dim grey light, a sight that would not be seen again met my eyes. As far as the eye could see here was an assortment of ships of every type size and description. Lamps flashed messages in morse, also semaphore and loud hailers were used. Ships with Barrage balloons anchored to them sailed along over to the left. All were moving steadily with common purpose, sailing along through the smoky haze towards a shore just coming into view to meet with that fearful threat of the unknown.

One of my soldier mates, Mickey Riley, was at the rear of the L.C.I. and he was looking at the map. It wasn't like the ones we had seen in the camp; the correct names were given of places on the coast we were fast approaching. Lion-sur Mer showed up as a line of white buildings over to our right, it was just disappearing in the smoke and lit up by flashes of explosions as our guns set their shells shore-wards. The rocket firing ships alongside us let out salvo after salvo, these swept upwards in an arc towards the shore, adding to the smoke and din as so very slowly the hostile shore of France came ever nearer.

All too soon the heavy shells from the German positions were exploding around the ships with huge waterspouts, the shrapnel from them splattering against the sides. There was no direct hit on our craft nevertheless we all felt an increasing urgency to get off the craft as at almost a snail's pace it relentlessly progressed slowly towards the shore.

As a result of the rough crossing and the disabling effect of seasickness it had been a difficult task to get some of the soldiers up on deck. At last they were all there, wearing their webbing, carrying their weapons equipment and formed up in lines. From that position we were ready to disembark from the ladder type stairway exits on each side of the craft's bow. My own position was well forward on the right- hand side of the boat. the ship then ran hard and high up on to the beach! We got down the steep stairways into the water as quickly as we could then made for the beach, taking our chance in the midst of the lethal barrage which was raining down all around!

We had been lucky, the water came barely up to our knees, but all around was a scene of utter destruction. Wrecked boats lay broadside on, our dead comrades floated face down in the tide, others lay in grotesque positions on the beach. Exploding shells fell as we raced towards the gap in the defence wire. It was being made wider by the brave stalwart men of the Royal Engineers who swept the sands with their mine detectors and then lad out white tapes to mark the safe track through. The sand dragged at our feet and slowed our progress. All was seen just as if in a flash- a sight never to be forgotten!

The gap was to the left of strong-point COD, which was in the process of being put out of action by 'A' Company of East York's and 'C' Company of South Lancs. On a sloping grass mound which covered a huge bunker, there were three dead Germans. They were immaculate in their grey overcoats and uniforms, caught as they had run away, they lay, two of them face down, in a neat line. The track led away from the beach going towards the lateral road. All was as remembered from the large-scale relief model maps we had poured over at the briefing- tent sessions at Waterlooville.

On reaching the road which had a railway rack on its landward side, those of us who had to join up with 'C' Company went off to the right. The traffic was heavy, with everyone making for their planned assembly points. We turned off along the first track going inland. The enemy shelling, which had been so intense when on the beach and the track leading off it, had by then slackened considerably, only a few shells and mortars were falling near us. Many empty cases that had held mortar bombs and shells were strewn all around. The dead, wounded, wreckage and litter of war, the destructive effects of the intense pre-invasion bombardment lay everywhere for all of us to see.

MOVE TO CONTACT

The ground on each side of the track was soft and boggy for the first half a mile, too treacherous even for foot soldiers let alone tracked vehicles. There was also many mine warning signs, - Skull and Crossbones 'Achtung Minen' put there by German troops, which conveniently for the British due to the surprise of the attack they had not had time to remove.

After advancing a few hundred yards my group stopped to try and determine the best way forward to join up with the main force 'C' Company. A runner was sent on ahead to try and make contact, it was thought prudent to dig (the first of many) slit trenches for protection from shells and mortars. There was a convenient hedgerow to the left of the track and we dug along its line as best we could with the small entrenching tools we carried. These were soon to be replaced by proper picks and shovels. We had made little progress with our digging when the order was given to move forward again. We were a little way off the correct line, (near to the present war cemetery) so we had to veer away to the left across some orchards where only stumps of trees remained, all the branches having been torn off by the shell and rocket bombardment.

Dead farm animals, hit by splinters, lay as they had fallen with their legs stuck out like fence posts and bodies fat and bloated. The smell of death was horrible, even in their dying, the gas from the fermenting gas inside them could be heard escaping in farts and belching.

As we moved forward we had to pass a burnt-out Bren-carrier from the earlier wave. There were two blackened bodies of soldiers trapped inside. It has been hit by a shell or Mortar and was still smoking. Another Bren-carrier, a 'maid of all work' passed by only to get stuck when the broken branches became entangled in its tracks, after help it went on its way. The officer who was in the carrier, Lieutenant Dunne of 8th Brigade H.Q. recognised me and we gave a wave to each other as the carrier was driving away. The Bren- carrier must have been seen by the enemy, shells and mortar bombs rained down, their firing ranged in on it causing a few flesh wounds and nicks but nothing serious.

The party was smaller than when we left the ship and we still had not contacted the main force. In a lower -lying small field surrounded by trees, there were more horses and cows which had sought shelter in vain. They were all dead and swollen- a tragic outcome to the intense barrage. Further along the track joined the road from the beach to Colleville, the route taken by the main force of 'C' Company. On the left-hand side of the road lay a dead Commando, his face a grey and greenish hue, fixed in the wax-like serenity of death. A few Teller plate-mines had been lifted and piled in a heap nearby, the Commandos had passed through Colleville whilst taking the most direct way to reach the Airborne Force at the canal bridges at Benouville (Pegasus *Bridge*) bypassing the strong-point defences which were the 2nd Battalion East York's 'B' and 'C' Companies specific D Day objectives.

A middle-aged woman in drab dark clothes in a long black skirt stood close by in the doorway of a house with a small child beside her. These were the first civilians that my group had seen, a surprise in the midst of all the noise and danger of war! She watched us pass with no sign or greeting, quite obviously saddened by what was happening in their lives.

It had taken us quite some time to reach the main axis of the East York's advance from the beach. Our progress had been slower than intended expected on account of the amount of enemy fire of shells and mortars and then deviating from the most direct route. We had gone over less open ground so our progress had been easier and less costly in casualties. The earlier force had travelled the most direct route from the beach over open ground, they had been pinned down and had lost many men from heavy machine gun fire as they approached strong-point SOLE, the first inland objective.

Pegasus Bridge in a museum

Utah Beach Memorial

D Day landing craft

CLOSE UP TO THE OBJECTIVES

Attacks on pockets of the enemy in progress. we'd moved up, were being consolidated. There had been some resistance and East York's losses, but they had been overrun and put out of action with help from the beach area, given by the initial artillery support from the guns of the 76th Field Regiment and troop of Self-Propelled Guns plus tanks of the 13th/18th Hussars. The prisoners were filing out readily and were being taken back to the beach under escort. One escort 'Tabby' Barker, returned looking disturbed, he had run into a group of French Commandos who had relieved him of his catch of prisoners and sent him back. He was somewhat upset having reason to be apprehensive about their fate.

As each pocket of resistance was taken, it meant less firing targeted towards the beach and was yielding many prisoners. Further along the road Arthur and Winterbottom, a thin pale looking soldier, called out to me and my group from behind a wall, then climbed over to join us, warning of a sniper who was firing from a high building on our right. Arthur talked about their landing and their losses on the beach and on the move forward from it. Cliff Milnes, the boxer, has been badly wounded - gunned down when trying to cross over the open ground. He had shouted to Arthur to rescue him, but all had been in vain. Both his legs had been badly shattered, and he died later from his wounds. Sergeant Arthur Thompson, who had led those left out of the beleaguered and decimated 'D' Company off the beach had found him. Surprised when Cliff, normally a non-smoker had said "Give us a cig Tommy." He had lit up one for him to smoke and supported him on his shattered legs for a while.

Mortar bombs were falling at intervals and seemed to be directed towards our track, so we took shelter near a bunker into which Mickey threw a Mills (36) grenade in case it had been overlooked. A few more mortar bombs dropped close to us as we were moving up to where the rest of 'C' Company were reforming in preparation for taking SOLE and DAIMLER strong-points.

Two small German planes flew overhead going towards Lion-sur Mer, and not a Spitfire in sight! A few moments later they were on their way back with Spitfires in hot pursuit. A burst of firing was heard over to the right and, with its tail shot off, one of the German planes crashed to the ground. More wounded came along the track on their way to the Field Dressing Station (FDS), mainly flesh wounds from mortar bomb or shell splinters.

On reaching a big open square by a big farmhouse, which had a huge gable end without any windows in the yellow stonework, we found some of our dispersed 'C' Company. They were gathering in the shelter given from the farmhouse. The CO Colonel C. F. Hutchinson DSO and Major D. de Symons Barrow MC, the 'C.' Company Commander, were planning their next move in the attack. They decided to attack on the strong-points from the rear after moving the Company up to it along paths through woodlands. The objectives lay between us and the beach so we moved along the narrow track through the woods. Mortar bombs were still falling nearby, this made me a trifle fed up having to throw myself down continually. The back of my head was getting sore with being hit with my big pack every time. Only later did the realisation strike me, of the futility of this action, for, by the time the noise of the explosion had been heard it was already too late to take cover from the lethal spread of shrapnel.

Another clutch of mortar bomb landed across the track as the CO, with two other officers had been in the process of scrambling up the bank on the track side to try and locate the position the mortar bombs were being fired. Splinters from exploding bombs caught the CO wounding him in his arm and side. Although I was in the ditch on the opposite side of the track, some bits of shrapnel thwacked my pack, without causing me any harm. We went along the track and then on the path, arriving at a junction where we took the right-hand fork. We realised we were going the wrong way so we retraced our steps and took the left fork. This brought us out of the wood onto a wide track that served as a service road leading to the strong-point where we joined up with a few more of the Company who, by using another route had arrived at the assembly point a short while before us.

THE ATTACK
From the fringe of the wood we could see the perimeter defences of the pillboxes and wire of the strongly fortified position. From relief models and maps in the briefing-tent, we knew, that behind the wire fence there was a complex system of interlocking and overlapping cross-fire machine gun positions. Also, a deep open trench network linked all the pillboxes and, partly below ground-level blockhouses with a central domed shelter and an ammunition store bunker. There, four 75-mm guns were housed, standing on a large concrete base together with a stack of shells. These were capable of traversing in all directions, with their fire directed towards the beach and the vital crossing from it. This was until attacking forces could knock them out. It was also believed extensive minefields covered all approaches of the strong- point

defence system.

Those that were left from the original complement of 'C' Company were assembled, plus a few from a Signals unit and other non-infantry soldiers. There were no more than half of those for a full company, but all were needed to make up the numbers. Suddenly the guns on the beach opened up with a stonk right on target, although the promised artillery support from a cruiser was missing it did not matter. The 76th Field Regiment's guns along with Self- Propelled Guns and the tanks of the 13th/18th Hussars more than made up for it as they bombarded the position with a good twenty-minute spell of heavy shelling.

As the guns laid down their High Explosive shells to good effect, our small force of assault troops started to organise ready to attack across the open field. We lightened our loads by stacking large packs and any surplus near by the track, hopefully for picking up later and crept forward, nearer to our goal until we were about fifty yards from the wire fence, waiting for the end of our supporting fire. There was a wide, sloping dug-out pit (a feature used by the Germans, to protect and house their vehicles.) For some, including myself, it made an ideal place to take temporary cover. Others stood watching from a gateway, curiously tempting providence, as bits of spent shrapnel from exploding shells, screaming and singing, winged over towards us. A piece hit one of the officers hard on his chest, giving him quite a shock and slightly winding him. He quickly picked off the hot piece of metal to throw it away with no apparent harm done to him.

Bren Gunners were positioned to give covering fire along each side of the line of the attack. As the shelling finished, the rest of us in the company, with rifles and fixed bayonets at the ready, started out on our advance towards the outer wire and pillboxes. We were in a single line abreast, in what could have been seen as a futile gesture, it fate had decreed it, for there was every possibility of the German machine-gunners opening up their fire from the pillboxes long before even the wire had been reached. Miraculously for us, the attacking force, nothing happened and we all reached the wire unscathed.

THROUGH FIRE, SHOT AND SHELL

Sword Beach

Atlantic Wall Battery

Horsa Glider

Normandy defences

It was a simple style of double- apron fence, which spread over a three or four-foot base, at about the same height, not appearing to be a serious obstacle. Even so, in attempting to step through the wire- my trouser leg was caught on the barbs -not the best spot to be caught in, so close to the possibility of being blasted by fire from German machine-guns. Quickly tearing myself free I dashed straight for the nearest pillbox on my right with a Mills (36) grenade in my hand and the pin out and ready to throw into the slotted opening.

The luck of the East York's at SOLE and DAIMLER wasn't repeated for the Suffolk's at an identical strong-point, HILLMAN. They suffered heavy casualties at the hands of more resolute and determined enemy forces before it fell to them.

INSIDE THE FORT

The Germans made no attempt to return to their defence positions as we pushed on with our attack, getting well through them before there was any chance of this happening. This boded well for most of us in 'C' Company and meant a really successful outcome to our attack. Once inside the wire fence we had been told to spread out, then make for the main central area. So, moving forward on my own, I followed the line of the open trench over the surface of the ground until reaching the blockhouse, which was built so it was partly below ground level, the trench ran up to this before continuing on beyond it. The grenade, initially intended for the pillbox, was dispatched through the blockhouse entrance from the trench. When it exploded I jumped down into the trench, with rifle and bayonet at the ready, following it into the blockhouse, to find myself in a small furnished office-like room with chairs and a desk. A framed picture of Hitler gazed down at me from the wall. Without hesitation, and in acute anger, I smashed the glass with a blow from my rifle butt. Looking around, there were two fountain pens on the desk, and these went into my pocket. There were bunk-type beds and blankets up against the wall opposite the desk. The exploding grenade had ignited one of the blankets and smoke was already building up from the fire. There had been no one in the blockhouse, so it was possible for me to leave by the other exit into the continuation of the trench system.

This was just as, over to the left, Lieutenant Dickson, 13 Platoon Commander, a Commonwealth volunteer from Rhodesia, fell down wounded. He had fallen over on his left side with his back arched up, he was writhing, straining and twisting to try and ease away from the pain. The wound appeared to be near his right buttock for he was reaching back with his right arm to the spot and was in severe pain. Even so, when I reached him he insisted he would be alright and that I should leave him to help in continuing the attack. Remembering the blankets, I went back into the blockhouse for one of them. Returning with it to make him feel easier before going on my way.

The next move was toward an Ack-Ack position on a low mound. The gun, lighter than a Bofors, had a magazine of shells fixed above the barrel, with two huge shoulder pads and hand grips for directing aim. It was in a small emplacement, surrounded by a low sandbag wall with just a gap through to enter. I took hold of the gun and swung it around, then aimed it in the direction of the large domed shelter entrance just behind the 75-mm guns and shells which were standing close to them. While making every effort, although the magazine was fully loaded, the mechanism was beyond me, I couldn't get the gun to fire. Suddenly, coming from my left, I saw a small German fighter plane, so, quickly redirecting the gun to aim at it I followed it round, keeping it in the sights as it flew towards the beach. It was very slow moving as it circled to the left and flew back again. If only I could have managed to fire the gun, and been able to shoot it down. Mickey Riley shouted at me to leave the gun, warning it might be booby trapped, so together we continued towards where the big guns stood. Mickey had gone some way when he fell. There hadn't seemed to be much in the way of firing or shell bursts, but on reaching close up to him, he was still and appeared to be dead.

Meanwhile, the rest of the force, who were well spread out, converged on the 75-mm guns and the shelter behind them. Captain Crauford was the first to approach, he went up the sloping ramp, firing his Sten gun into the entrance. C.S.M Pullen was just behind him, waving his revolver. The captain's batman Morris Bouldridge, with misjudged enthusiasm, dropped a Mills (36) grenade down one of the ventilation openings. This happened just as the captain had gone inside to persuade the Germans to come out, giving him quite a shock and a close shave. Another of the chaps, a big tough type character, whose last name was King, stood upon top of the domed shelter, threatening the occupants with a Sten gun ready and apparently quite prepared to shoot them as they emerged.

PRISONERS GALORE

After a moment of hesitation, the Germans started to come out of their bunker shelter with their hands raised. One said in English "Only a raid, Hey?" to which came the instant the chorus: "This is the Invasion!" Another who produced a set of his prized pornographic photos, showed them around in an effort to please his captors. A third had tried to conceal a small pistol in his hand, about .02 calibre, had second thoughts and handed it over. They were a mixed bag of Poles and men from other occupied countries. Probably pressed into service in the German Army., in no way the enthusiastic cream of it. Some seventy prisoners were taken. The whole complex was honeycombed with underground living quarter and the procession out of it seemed never ending.

While routing out the Germans their messing area had been discovered and, in taking advantage of this, a few of the victors were soon seen carrying out cases of wine and beer from the store place. Things could easily have got out of hand, until CSM Pullen decided they had gone quite far enough and threatened to shoot the next one he caught looting. However, when he saw what they had got he relented a little. Although it had been an easy victory, he knew that this was neither the time nor the place, in which to play about and celebrate with a drunken orgy. So, as tanks and S.P. guns rolled up to give cover to the area of the strong-points we took out leave, victorious and somewhat relieved to go back the way we had come. Apart from the few who were casualties we were able to retrieve our packs from the track where we had left them.

My share of the booty was a bottle of red wine, very dry and not at all to my taste, but the day had been hot, making me thirsty. So, I took a drink and saved the rest for later. By following the paths through the woods and fields, steadily by ascending, we reached the higher ground, close to St Aubin-d'Arqtenay overlooking Ouistreham. On the first fields were a series of vertical posts spaced out at intervals, (Rommel's Asparagus) supposedly proof against glider landings. It was there that we dug in once more along a line of hedgerow, with the beach assault, and taking the strong-point objectives, the 2nd Battalion of the East York's had achieved all the had been set to do. It was a weary group of troops who dug in, some of us with thoughts of a possible enemy counter- attacks on our position. at least those were my secret thoughts as I settled into my trench and started to finish off the last of my German wine.

The reason for the tiring toil up to the high ground was soon to unfold. We were thrilled and relieved at the sight of a mass of gliders and their tow-planes as they came in over the sea and beaches which had been won that day at such great cost. The fact that the area where they were going to land was clear of the enemy was much to their advantage. They flew in, circling low, backed by a reddish-blue glow in the sky as the sun sunk lower." To land on a free part of France!"

THROUGH FIRE, SHOT AND SHELL

As the aircraft let go their towlines, the gliders swooped down to land in the fields all around us, with an assurance of a friendly reception. Some had heavy landings, others had their wings chopped off as they hit the vertical posts, but whether they crashed or nor didn't seem to matter, like a speeded-up film, men, materials, light vehicles and guns were all quickly disgorged from out of the gliders tail-end doors. Everyone seemed to know what to do and where to go. They didn't seem to notice that other troops were around, so absorbed were the Airborne troops in getting themselves established quickly.

The Airborne troops, fresh and fit from their English bases only an hour before, were there to keep rolling the action that had been so successfully started by the assault force of ground troops earlier in the day. (All units had not had the same success; or maybe too much had been expected of them!)

With barely enough time to finish off my looted wine we were ordered to line up as if on parade then marched westward into the dusk of the night.

REST AFTER THE STORM
It was fully dark by the time the troops of 'C' Company stopped again, to dig in once more, on a more peaceful hillside. This time along the edge of a partly ploughed field. It had been a long weary march back and at times they had not been sure of the correct way. After going through a small village on a rough track they came to an elevated position. This, as morning dawned, was to provide a marvellous panoramic view of Sword Beach, fronting Colleville, Hermanville and Lion-sur-Mer- the beach we had landed on the day before.

So, finished our first day of action, for too many, also their last one!

With the coming of day-break, from my (safe) slit trench overlooking Sword Beach (in particular Queen, White and Red beaches of the Sword sector) the scene was a fever of activity, the unloading of men, machines and stores which went on all day. The larger supply ships had to lay off shore and then smaller craft ferried the stores and equipment to the beach. The still larger warships were positioned well away from the shore, and from time to time fired their big guns at targets well inland which were far beyond the immediate horizon.

My first thoughts on waking was about improving and enlarging my slit trench, (still my own but amongst a group of many similar trenches) and then to make a small recessed shelf into one side of the trench on which to place my 'Tommy Cooker'(a small tin- plate collapsible , three- legged stand on which a block of white solid fuel could be placed, when ignited it was used to heat up water in a mess tin.) When in use we had sugar lump sized cubes, which were a compressed combination of tea, sugar and dried milk, and made a kind of substitute for tea. Along with the tea, my first breakfast in France was hard-tack biscuits, a slice of corned beef, some chocolate and boiled sweets.

Later in the day some parachutes were seen to drop over to the east. Eventually, after some trepidation it was realised that they would be those of parachute reinforcements and supplies for men dropped the day before. These were the troops who were to the east of the river Orne, not yet easy enough to risk suppling by other means.

While the British appeared to have command of the air, hardly any German planes were able to get through, a couple did manage to come in on a low-level bombing raid over the beach and some bombs fell, with disastrous effect, on the build- up of stores which were piled up there. For a few days after this this pile of stores burned with a huge column of smoke.

During the landing and the moves inland from the beach, some of 'C' Company's soldiers had become separated from their unit, mainly due to being pinned down or holed up during shelling, and been unable to catch up again and re-join it. Such a party of stragglers wearily reported in, having been lost for a couple of days. To even up the sections, Sergeant 'Topper' Brown, ordered me to vacate the trench on which so much of my time and effort had been spent to make it comfortable. This was so that two of the group who had just caught up with us, could be placed with their regular section.

The order made me pretty livid, particularly as no offer was made by the new arrivals to help me in digging a new one. Admittedly they had been lost and wandering around trying to find their unit, and were very tired, but that was no consolation to me. I just picked up my gear, annoyed and grumbling, moving some thirty yards away to join another section and made a start digging my new trench. The two ex-India regulars, Dixie Dunbar and Jock Anderson, just threw off their gear and joyfully took possession of my well-made dug-out, delighted with what they thought was their luck. On my own, I kept on with my digging!

DEATH IN THE AFTERNOON

How the 'hands of fate' can be so cruel for some, and for other so kind, that day, was well and truly demonstrated. It was no more than a few minutes later, five at the most, when a lone ranging shell landed directly in the trench I had just vacated.

This instantly killed Dixie and Jock! Len Brown, one of their mates who had been standing by the trench chatting to them, caught the shrapnel blast from the explosion full on his legs and the lower part of his body. It lacerated the flesh and ripped off the legs of his trousers. I rushed over to them, not really appreciating at the time, that had it happened a few minutes earlier it could easily have been me lying there instead. CSM Pullen was immediately on the spot and asking Len "Who had been in the trench?" Such was the appalling havoc of broken bodies from the explosion. Although he was so badly wounded, Len was able to tell him. This was before he was put on a stretcher and taken to the Field Dressing Station for the attention he so badly needed.

Dixie's and Jock's earthly remains were wrapped in their own ant-gas capes and were buried later in the afternoon, this was at the place in the field near the boundaries near the ploughed and the unploughed ground. A Church of England and a Roman Catholic Padre together performed the solemn committal service as their bodies were laid to rest, temporarily, in just one grave. Before taking their leave, one of the padres took the compass bearings from the grave on to fixed points. Possibly, one of those used was the twin spires of the church at Douvres-la-Selivrande, which could be seen to the west of the position.

"That there's some corner of a foreign field that is forever England."

These were my thoughts and also the thoughts of any of us, as the two close friends, in death as in life, were laid to rest. Their grave was covered over and a rough wooden cross placed in position at the head of the grave. That was the only time I witnesses such ceremony (in the field) and, in the circumstances, it has held a lasting memory for me, as did most of the events of that time. Only later did the real significance of that incident, and of my own closeness to death, that day, strike home. The lone shell was going to hit that trench and it was going to kill or maim whoever was in it. Being killed or injured had not crossed my mind. That only happened to others!

It was the next day, 9-6-44 that we left the hillside of such tragic memories to go back to the rough sunken track. Waiting on the road were a line of T.C.V.'s (Troop Carrying Vehicles) As each one was filled with troops, it quickly went on its way. with the high four-wheel drive vehicle's gears singing away with its very distinctive note. Their destination was via the coastal road, (the direct one, over and across a ridge, under enemy observation,) to a small village which was shown on the military map as 'Cazelle', but for many, myself including, years passed before the correct name of the village of 'Mathieu, became known to us.

THROUGH FIRE, SHOT AND SHELL

Sword Beach Memorial

POSTSCRIPT

LIEUTENANT ANDREW DICKSON 299273 OF BULAWAYO, SOUTHERN RHODESIA DIED 7ᵀᴴ JUNE 1944 AGED 24

It had been my every intention to return to see to the needs of Lieutenant Dickson, also Riley, although without doubt Riley was dead. This was to make sure they were receiving the attention they required. Instead, after our successful attack, there was no alternative but to go forward with the rest of the company. It was normal practice to leave wounded to be looked after by the Regimental Stretcher-Bearers (RAMC – Royal Army Medical Corps) and to get on with pursuing the main objectives of the attack. I was not too concerned about the seriousness of the wound suffered by my platoon commander Lieutenant Dickson which, although it appeared to be very painful, was not in a vital spot.

My own preoccupation with things that followed, the minor wounds towards the end of June followed by subsequent serious wounding in February 1945, five months after re-joining my unit, left me out of touch with anything to do with the Army or the 2nd East York's. Invalided out and with a civilian career to make good in, it was only on my first return to Normandy in 1970, that the shocking discovery was made of finding the grave of Lieutenant Dickson in the Hermanville War Cemetery. It had immediately crossed my mind had I been guilty of some neglect after the battle, being the one who knew he had been wounded and where he had been left covered over with a German blanket? On reflection, although my doubts still lingered, surely, he must have been found by medics and taken to Field Dressing Station on the beach. On every return to his grave it was not possible for me to find out the explanation for him being there.

OI the fortieth anniversary of the D Day invasion, a chance meeting with an ex-2nd East York's soldier, from a company other than my own, led me to contact an ex- "C" Company, 13 Platoon comrade. This was Len Beevers and, during our correspondence he sent me an old newspaper cutting which referred to the way Lieutenant Dickson died so many years ago. In fact, he HAD been picked up and for a while lay on a door by a wall, until taken by stretcher to the FDS. There he had his wounds attended to and then was put aboard the boat for evacuation to England. The same level bombing raid over the beach, seen from the viewpoint overlooking the beaches, had hit the boat and he had been killed in that attack. My unease at his fate had been for nought!

The newspaper item which had been received, while referring to the incident, was concerned with Lieutenant Dickson's parent's decision to allow Gladys Erskine, his fiancé in Nairn, to take over their business in Rhodesia, which, but for his death, he would have inherited.

LEN BROWN

It was over forty years later that Len Brown and I were reunited. This was at his home on a farm at North Cave near Beverley, the Regimental home of the East York's. When at a Regimental Reunion we made a visit. Len was able to tell me how he had fared after being so badly wounded. Although he had taken a long time to recover, he had eventually been able to take up farming again.

His legs had been a real mess, the emission of shrapnel from the shell ripping the flesh away right down to the bone on both of them. By the time the boat on which he was evacuated, had reached England, the congealed blood had stuck him to his blanket and the stretcher. It had been a difficult and painful process to get him free. He had been in and out of hospital for many years and had countless pieces of shrapnel removed from his legs. Len told me that there were still bit left in.

It was obvious he would never be able to forget about the incident, nor the tragic deaths of Dixie and Jock, also of the way in which my own death had been narrowly avoided. This was when ordered by Sergeant 'Topper' Brown to leave my trench as I did, and giving it up to the two who had been killed.

LIONEL ROEBUCK 2ND BATTALION EAST YORKSHIRE REGIMENT
Private Lionel Roebuck joined as a general service recruit from October 1942 to February 1945 when he was injured. He was wounded in Germany on 27th February 1945 as he was last into a trench after taking a call of nature when a direct hit into the dugout from an exploding shell sent shrapnel into his head through his steel helmet. Seventy-three years later some fragments still remained.

When he left the Army, he spent time at a rehabilitation and government training centre in Oxfordshire. He was in St Hugh's Combined Services Military Hospital and then convalescence at Tusmore Park until March 1946. Re-entering the workforce proved difficult, many employers thought he would not be able to work successfully. In March 1947 he returned to his old employers, 'Brook Motors Limited' initially working as a 'Jig and Tool fitter' then a draughtsman and finally as a Mechanical Design Engineer. He left his employment in 1977.

Lionel had suffered paralysis down his right side but due to dogged determination he managed to regain his mobility. He began to use a walking stick in the 1960's and only went into a wheelchair after he broke his hip when he was eighty, a lot of the time he would uses elbow sticks. In the last four or five years of his life he became more wheelchair bound. Lionel died aged ninety-four on 1st September 2018.

SOURCES:
David Delius
Janet Brown

NOTES:
St Hugh's Military Hospital (Head Injuries) 1940-1945
Despite being open for only five years, St Hugh's Military Hospital (Head Injuries) has a seminal place in the history of neurology, neurosurgery and rehabilitation medicine. At its peak, during the Normandy campaign of 1944, it provided 430 beds for the treatment of service personnel. Between 1940 and 1945, 13,000 patients were referred to St Hugh's

providing a unique opportunity for ground-breaking research into the management of head injuries. The doctors at St Hugh's collaborated with research scientists at Oxford University in many areas of fundamental research including the treatment of infection, the mechanics of brain injury, brain surgery, neuropsychiatry and rehabilitation, and the use of electroencephalograms.

D DAY OBJECTIVES:
    Strong points - numbered Wn German abbreviation 'Wiederatandnest'- resistance nest.
    Stutzpunkt - abbreviation Stp translation Strong point/ outpost/base.
    DAIMLER Wn12 South of Ouistreham 4th Battalion 716 Artillery Regiment
    SOLE Wn 14 Southwest of Ouistreham Command Post 736 Infantry Regiment
    COD Wn /Stp 20 Hermanville la Breche Command Post 10th Battalion 736 Regiment.
    HILLMAN Wn 17   Colleville Command Post Coastal Defences- ATLANTIC WALL

Private Norman 'Dixie' Dunbar 4343010 aged 31 and **Harold 'Jock' Anderson 4342985** aged 29 died on 8th June 1944. Harold Anderson from Howden le Wear in County Durham left a wife Eva. Like Lieutenant Dickson they are buried in Hermanville Commonwealth War Grave Cemetery that contains 1,003 burials, 103 of whom are unidentified.

Hermanville June 2007. Lionel and Lady Anne-Marie Harris (born and raised in Normandy.) Lady Harris is the widow of Lieutenant-General Sir Tommy Harris who commanded the 2nd Battalion Royal Ulster Rifles as a Lieutenant Colonel on D Day.

Grave of Lieutenant Dickson

*Hermanville Commonwealth War Grave Cemetery.
Both photos Courtesy of the War Graves Photographic Project in association with the Commonwealth War Graves Commission*

CHAPTER 6

Post War National Service   Egypt 1946 -1949
Peter Butler

When I returned to England with my brother after the Second World War, sometime in February 1946, I wanted to start a career as a Quantity Surveyor, having met one through my father in Burma. At the time I was seventeen and a half years old and reliant on my family in this country, as my parents were still in Burma. Consequently, my father's eldest brother, Uncle Percy, took me under his wing and did some research to obtain meetings with suitable companies in London. In addition, he spoke to my cousin, Roy Robinson, who was with a prominent firm of Architects in London, and he was able to arrange at least one appointment for us to get advice. We met Mr. Mills, a partner with Davis, Belfield and Everest, Chartered Quantity Surveyors in the West End, who was very kind and firm when he heard my age. His immediate recommendation to me was to get my National Service over and done with and return to him after completing this obligatory task. I thought at the time that his advice got out of having to employ me to satisfy a friendship.

My uncle and I were quite disappointed but left London not having achieved anything. However, I took extensive private French lessons with a tutor and then joined a Pitman's course in Eastbourne to fill in time, as I would not be eligible for National Service until September of that year. Apart from shorthand and typing, I spent most of my time sketching the young ladies in my class, sometimes in the nude as I imagined them. this had to stop when I was caught by one of the girls!

I spent the rest of my time cycling around the countryside surrounding Eastbourne, as I lived with my married sister, whose husband was in the Regular Army serving in Germany. My companion on my cycling jaunts was a boy I had last seen in 1940, we had attended the same school from the age of eight.

Finally, in October 1946 I received my calling- papers and a rail warrant to travel from Eastbourne to Colchester, where I would be met off the train. I travelled up with another old friend from before the War, more in apprehension than excitement, and we were both taken to the same barracks in Colchester. There our ways were split and I didn't see him again for quite some time. I joined a mixed bunch of young men, all round bout eighteen years of age. I was eighteen years and three weeks old. We were designated an Army number and given a demobilization code which should give me an idea when I would be discharged from the Army. My number was 19087120 and my code was 77, which meant little to me at the time.

Our "square bashing" started almost immediately, after collecting our kit and uniforms, and the men who had not experienced boarding school found it very difficult to adjust to the life. Indeed, many of them cried themselves to sleep and had to be shown how to iron shirts, polish shoes or boots, sew buttons on uniforms and darn socks. They were a pathetic lot! Along with those public schoolboys who had boarded, I found it less onerous than many. It was the boots that proved difficult, as we had to burnish them to a high gloss, using a hot spoon on the toecaps to get that finish. Of course, we all realised that the War was over and it was extremely unlikely that we would fire a gun in anger.

The first week in Colchester was deadly, we ran everywhere, and if we weren't running we were quick marching or slow marching. Inevitably, most of us caught the eye of the training staff, who were corporals or sergeants, and were suitably punished for transgressing the laws of the Army. It was always an early to start in the mornings and usually a late bedtime thanks to the need to clean and smarten up equipment. Many of us were not sorry at the end of the week, as we were put on lorries with all out kit and taken to the station to catch a train to Reading. There, we were taken by lorry to Brock Barracks in the centre of the town, and started the next phase of our training, which wasn't much different to the first week. The only light-hearted occurrence was the introduction of twin corporals named Pluck, who took over responsibility of our training, they proved to be human but disciplinarians.

We were kept there for two weeks than some thirty of us were moved again to a Nissen hutted camp at Bulford near Salisbury. The accommodation bore the marks of bullet holes in the ceiling, the camp having been used by Commando's during the War where privates were woken up each morning by gunfire. It was at this camp we learned we were not allowed out of camp for at least six weeks, as we were considered to be Privates in the General Service Corps, not part of a Regular Army unit. It was only at the end of our training that we would be moved to a recognised unit and become a regular private of the Army, paid at the rate of £3 a week, which included the King's shilling.

I was given weekend leave at the end of my training and posted to No. 3 Royal Engineers Training regiment at Cove, near Farnborough and Aldershot. There, we were subjected to three more months of specialist training, such as Bailey Bridge building, land mine laying, use of explosives, use of knots, and lashings of road building etc. It included a visit to the firing range to learn how to use a standard 0.303 rifle and Bren gun, the latter becoming a favour with me which earned me a proficiency badge and extra pay.

All this was carried out during one of the most severe winters in 1946/47, which ended in March 1947 with severe flooding throughout Kent and Sussex after the snow melted. It was so cold, we put on more clothing than we took off at night. Our accommodation was in wooden huts which froze internally, including the washroom areas, which caused difficulties trying to keep some 1,500 men hygienically clean.

At the end of our training we "passed out", as the saying goes, and I was put in a special squad for Officer Cadet training, which took a further six weeks. By then the weather was much improved and considerably warmer. I was able to get home to Eastbourne on fairly regular weekends, staying with my sister who was waiting passage to Germany. I decided that, rather than go through Officer Cadet training for some six months, I might as well join the Regular Army, but only if I passed the tests to go to Sandhurst. In due course I was sent to Knepp Castle near Horsham, for four days of tests, which was fun, but sad to say, I was well out of my depth and failed the tests miserably. The General interviewing me thought I was a nice man but not cut out to be an Officer in the Regular Army!

Consequently, I was sent back to Cove Camp where there did not appear to be a job for me in any other unit. After much wasting of time, I was eventually told to be the Tannoy man, principally waking up the camp at 6.30 or 7 am on the camp Tannoy system. I was housed in a cell in the Guard House, along with a large piece of machinery that was, effectively, the radio transmitter on which I would play the BBC or 78 records or, indeed, hear my own voice making announcements as required by the departments of the camp. After a shaky start, I began to give book readings at set times of the day and ran a 'Family Favourites' programmes, inviting camp personnel to write in to me asking for their favourite record to be played over the Tannoy system. This was partially successful, as it was intermittently busy, sometimes not having more than a handful of requests which I couldn't fill the hour I had allocated to the programme. I collected records from the camp library, who seemed to have an endless supply available. As you can imagine the requests were very lowbrow, very few classical pieces being requested.

This easy lifestyle I found very dull and boring, only offset on days of good weather when I could stroll the camp and visit the NAAFI for something to eat and drink. I was left to my own devices, even the sergeant-major left me in peace. The officers thought it was quite hilarious that I should be broadcasting on the Tannoy system and also left me alone.

The summer of 1947 was very pleasant and during that time my parents came back to England on leave, making their headquarters the flat in Blackwater Road in Eastbourne which had been originally rented by my sister. They hired a car and spent some time travelling around, visiting friends and relatives throughout England and taking my brother and I (when I had leave) with them.

One weekend I was put on fire guard along with six or eight other "squaddies" and we were delegated to sleep in the fire hut so we were close to the firefighting appliances which were housed near the front gate of the camp. We all dutifully went to bed at about 10.30pm, all of us changing into pyjamas as we didn't expect problems overnight. How mistaken we were! At about 2o'clock in the morning we were rudely awakened by the Duty Guard Officer, who was a keen young man, and shouted at us to get the fire tender mobile and run out the hoses. This, we duly did, and connected up the hoses to the fire hydrant, which we then turned on. Unfortunately, someone had attached a 'Y' junction to the hose but only ran out a hose from one branch, so when the water was turned on, no water appeared at the "business" end of the hose. We looked round in bewilderment, not understanding what had happened until someone shouted that their feet were getting very wet. Naturally enough the water was charging down the hose to the 'Y' junction and then out of the unconnected branch. The Officer was not best pleased and we all found ourselves on special duty the following day, doing things like cleaning the parade ground, cleaning out the toilet blocks, etc.

As the end of 1947 loomed, I decided this was too boring for words and applied to be sent abroad, giving three preferred options, the first as Germany (where I might see my sister and her husband), the second as Northern Ireland and the third as Malaya (not Malaysia, where I hoped to take some leave to see my parents in Burma). Needless to say, the War Office (now the Ministry of Defence) in their wisdom, posted me to the Suez Canal Zone in Egypt I was not entirely displeased, except for the fact that at the time we were taking a pasting from the Jews and the Arabs in Palestine, so I hoped to stay in Egypt. Before leaving Cove Camp I was promoted to Lance Corporal for some reason, which puzzled me.

So, in early 1948 we boarded the 'Empress of Scotland,' an old Canadian Pacific Line Ship that had been commandeered by the War Office as a troopship. Two weeks later we arrived in Port Said, Egypt, having called at Malta to off-load passengers and goods. We didn't go ashore, mores the pity, but did get a good look at Valetta from the ship.

At the transit camp in Port Said we were sent off to various Army units throughout the Suez Canal Zone and I found myself in a Royal Engineers accommodation camp right out in the desert, with a workshop camp about five miles away where plant of all shapes and sizes, from cranes to bulldozers and diggers of all sorts, were repaired and dispatched back to their work units.

The actual accommodation consisted of corrugated iron steel framed sheds and plastered block offices, to the workshop camp and tents over sunken rooms in the sand, with plastered block offices and other facilities to the accommodation camp. Sleep was frequently difficult, due to the heat and the occasional sand storm. There were a number of marked out pitches for football, hockey, rugby, cricket and tennis, all of the well- used especially at weekends. There was nothing else to do and no female company at all. A fairly limited library helped us relax, but there was no swimming pool for us to cool off on particularly hot days.

I was in my element, I loved the heat, the sand, and the open-air type of living. But the start was crucial as I had been posted to a Palestinian unit which was still in Palestine, not what I wanted as it had become even more dangerous there. Luckily soon after joining, the unit was posted out of Palestine to our camp in Egypt where it was disbanded and re-formed to go to Kenya. That was more like it! I was one of a small party to collect the kit for use in Kenya and I chose the best 'Bush' hat available. However, it transpired that I did not have long enough to serve and it would be a waste of resources if I only went down for six to eight months. Little did we know at the time that we would all have an extra three months added to our time in the Army, owing to the Berlin Airlift problems in Europe.

My special hat went to someone else and I was left with two or three others to spend days carrying out maintenance work around the accommodation camp. Very boring and soul destroying! If we could we spent the time playing snooker at the NAAFI or lying on our beds in the heat of the day, whilst all the other troops were taken by lorry to the workshop camp five miles away. Then one day we got caught by the sergeant- major and were immediately put in the Guard House as Regimental Policemen, another boring job! One day the sergeant-major caught me talking in a very friendly to some new officers who had arrived and were old friends of mine from training days. He was impressed (anything would impress him, he was quite unbelievably thick) so he decided he would make life easy for me and put me into the Officers Mess running the bar. I hated it, having to serve my friend, so after a week I asked for a transfer.

This time I was put into the Administration Offices, joining several clerks who were sappers, lance- corporals and corporals with a sergeant in charge. We worked in an air-conditioned office which was nice, because the temperature outside was hovering around 40 degrees Celsius, plunging to 10 degrees Celsius at night. It was busy in that office, especially filling in returns and dealing with other official documents. Soon after I arrived the sergeant was sent back to England and I was given the unenviable task of running the office. I was promoted to full Corporal, with additional pay, arriving at work at 7am and leaving about 6 pm, while the remaining troops took the afternoon off. The volume of work began to get me down so I sought an upgrading in rank to compensate for the extra duties I was performing. It was turned down as there were already too many sergeants on pay list.

Finally, after four to five months, I asked for some leave and went to a holiday camp at Port Sudan with a corporal friend of mine who was called Corporal Sergeant! We had a brilliant two weeks on the beach, eating, drinking, reading, sunbathing and swimming in the sea with porpoises, a very happy time. The friend was a shortish man with very blonde hair and an effeminate appearance, which I had not really taken in, being very naïve. Two Royal Marine Commando's shared our tent and they asked me one day if the friend was my special friend, which I could not work out at all, so they explained, much to my horror and embarrassment. I spent less time with him back at base camp! I was only nineteen years old!

In my absence, another corporal had taken over from me in the office. He lasted six weeks before they had to replace him. Meanwhile I was given the job of second-in-command of a workshop repairing cranes and diggers. My boss was a staff-sergeant and all the workmen were Egyptians as well as Italian prisoners-of-war who were billeted at a camp about five miles across the desert known as Base Laundry. The workmen were sometimes very difficult, especially the Egyptians who had to be watched constantly. Both types of worker were searched when they entered the camp and again on leaving. I found it particularly interesting to find Italian prisoners-of-war still in existence in 1948, three years after the War. They were still there when I left permanently in February 1949.

My duties were not onerous, spending most of the day preparing request forms for spare parts to the machinery being repaired and then going across to the main stores to collect them. I taught myself to drive on heavy lorries in the evening and small trucks during the day. When I could borrow a caterpillar tractor, a D7, I would drive around at three miles an hour which was top speed. One day, this proved to be a disaster, as I lost control while entering the main workshop and hit a concrete column full on, bending it dangerously and making the workers run for their lives. I was not popular with my boss and was banned from using the tractor forthwith. Pity, as it was an exciting vehicle to drive.

I was called upon to appear as an armed guard one evening every six weeks at the workshop camp, commanding some eight or ten sappers for the evening. We manned a large searchlight with two Egyptian operators on a tall tower in the centre of the camp. We took turns patrolling the perimeter wire which was about five to seven miles long, either walking sections or driving around in an open truck, taking our fully loaded rifles with us. That is, until early one morning I was driving around with a young sapper, neither of us carrying our rifles, when we came across several Egyptians who had broken into camp and were stealing parts from vehicles parked in the vast area well away from the workshops. I tore back to the guardhouse to collect our rifles and returned to the parking area to see the thieves beating a hasty retreat across the desert. They were about two—hundred yards away when we reached the perimeter fence, so I lifted my rifle, took aim at the fleeing figures and fired one shot. One of the figures staggered but continued on his way, I assumed they had been frightened enough by the shot, so we continued our patrol, meeting up with a platoon of Sudanese kaffirs who had heard the shot, and were investigating, a bit late! The Sudanese were employed as guards at the parking end of the camp but were not a very effective group of soldiers. In fact, we were under the assumption that they were in the pay of the Egyptians to turn a blind eye to the blatant thieving that took place.

One Sunday morning we were all preparing for a long weekend of relaxation, when there was a tremendous explosion and a visible column of smoke and flames coming from one of the smaller workshops. Apparently, the workshop was a special vehicles place, staffed by Maltese engineers. One of the Maltese had disregarded the regulations that smoking should not occur in that particular workshop and lit up a cigarette near stored fuel. The fumes from the fuel caught fire, thus causing the explosion and the poor Maltese engineer also caught fire. When I arrived on the scene to assist in putting out the flames, I saw the charred body lying on the ground. Still moving from shock, he was bundled onto a canvas sheet, lifted to be put into the vehicle to take him to hospital, but he was so hot he burnt a hole in the canvas and fell back onto the ground. Needless to say, he did not survive many minutes after that catastrophe, a pointless disaster that not only took a life but ruined the workshop and the vehicles in it. I don't think the Maltese engineers smoked in confined spaces after that episode!

Eventually in February 1949 my time in the Army came to an end, I was detailed to join a train, along with six others from my camp to be transported back to Port Said to return to England. There were a number of Military Policemen surrounding us as we boarded the train because there were a considerable number of local Egyptians who had turned up for the occasion with the express intension of robbing us whilst we struggled with our kitbags and suitcases. The weight of my kit bag was particularly great because I had decided to take home with about 5 kg of rice, which had been in short supply when I left England in early 1948, and this was stuffed in the bottom of my kit bag. I have to say I was terrified by the occasion and only too glad to arrive at the Base Camp at Port Said several hours later, safely under the protection of the Military Police. Those of us who were joining a ship were only too pleased to get on board and we very happily bade farewell to Egypt without any regrets at leaving the God forsaken country.

Finally, we joined an old Marshall Plan ship, the 'Empire Helford', size about 8,000 tons, rusty, dirty and uncomfortable, not at all like the 'luxury' liner 'The Empress of Scotland,' that we came out on. It was part cargo ship but mainly a troopship, and we occupied the main holds where we stowed our hammocks for the night, slung over tables of twelve soldiers of varying ranks (except, of course, the officers!) I found it quite comfortable sleeping in a hammock, always providing I could get into it! At my table I was given the task, together with a colleague, of collecting rations for the twelve of us from the kitchens and delivering it to the table for consumption.

The Mediterranean Sea was not particularly calm; indeed, it was very choppy for the week that we travelled from Port Said to Gibraltar. It gave my colleague and myself the opportunity to announce on arrival with the meal that it was nice and greasy and would be ideal for those feeling seasick. This cruelty was designed to get other troops at our table to offer their share of food for us to consume, as it was plainly inedible for them with such a rough sea running! We ate like Kings as both of us were not prone to seasickness. Most of those who suffered spent the day up on deck, regardless of the weather conditions.

We didn't call at Malta on the way home and only berthed briefly at Gibraltar to pick up additional passengers. No chance to go ashore but none of us worried, we were going back to Blighty. finally, after some two or three weeks we docked in Liverpool and were transported by Troop Train to Aldershot, our final destination ion the Army. A night in barracks and the following day we were civilians again, handing in to the Regimental Stores the remains of our kit that we didn't want (or they wanted) and being given a sports coat, grey flannel trousers, a shirt, tie, socks and a pair of black shoes to finish it off, and a rail warrant to pay for our train ticket home.

So, ended my life in the Army, never again was it necessary for me to don a uniform (not quite true, as when I was working in Hong Kong I joined the Royal Hong Kong Marine Police which required the wearing of a uniform.) I was discharged from the Army as a Z-Class Reservist which, I was pleased to know, did not require me to be called up with other reservists during the Suez Canal Conflict in 1956.

Was my two and a half years in the Army a waste of time? I really didn't learn anything useful for my later civilian life, but I quite enjoyed it. However, it did give me a certain confidence and I became less naïve. Those are assets that many today cling to as arguments for the re-introduction of National Service. I'm not so sure, I think it would be pointless learning, only suitable for those who wish to become regular members of the Armed Forces.

PETER BUTLER

Peter's father Wilfred ran a building construction company in Rangoon, Burma, having met and married his mother Gladys in India whilst in the army during the Great War. On demobilization he found a job in Calcutta before moving over to Burma in the early 1920's. They had four children, a daughter born in Calcutta and three sons born in Rangoon. There were no suitable schools in Burma for British children, only those for Burmese, Indian, Anglo-Indian and Anglo Burmese children. Teaching was in either

Hindi or Burmese with some lessons in English so the two older children were sent to a boarding school in Eastbourne, his sister from the age of seven and his brother from five years old.

Audrey, Norman, Peter and Tony Butler

In 1935 his parents returned to England with Peter and his younger brother briefly settling in Bournemouth before finally finding a house in Eastbourne. During this period all the children attended day school. After about eighteen months his father returned to Rangoon on his own, his mother not following him until 1938. That same year Peter's elder brother joined the Merchant Navy, the two younger boys, their sister and their Burmese nanny were left in the charge of their mother's older sister, a widow who lived in Hove. War broke out in September 1939, after the Fall of France and the evacuation of the British Expeditionary Force at Dunkirk in 1940 an Invasion was expected. The Far East was far safer than Europe so in July the children and their nanny set sail from Liverpool in a convoy of about seventy ships to return home. Fifteen months after arriving in Rangoon the Japanese bombed Pearl Harbour and the War in the Pacific began. The family spent the rest of the war in India.

In January 1946 Peter and his brother Tony sailed aboard the troopship 'Empress of Australia', which was carrying mainly troops but some civilians, out of Bombay bound for Liverpool So, ended a chequered childhood, Peter was at the age of seventeen and a half, ready for the next part of his life in the Army and beyond.

The story of Peter's Colonial childhood is told in *Over the Hills and O'er the Main* published Brown Dog Books 2017.

CHAPTER 7

Insigency in the Holy Land   Palestine 1946 -1947
John Bosley

John Bosley, 1944

One of the youngest paratroopers with the 11th Battalion the Parachute Regiment to go into Arnhem on 18th September 1944, wounded, captured and imprisoned in Prisoner of War Camps in Germany, John Bosley survived the starvation and the conditions. Early in 1945 he was sent to a small work camp near Leipzig, Stalag 4G in a small town called Borna. He worked ten hours a day on an open cast coal face surface on just a bowl of soup and a slice of bread a day.

Early in April 1945 orders were given to evacuate the camp and march to Bavaria to be held as hostages. John knew he would not survive the march so he hid in the camp hospital until the camp was abandoned. When he came out of hiding he discovered three or four other prisoners who had hidden in a mine shaft. Four days later the Americans arrived and he was free. He normally weighted twelve and a half stone, he was now just eight stone, full of ulcers and boils and very weak- but still alive. A week later he was sent home on double rations.

Three months later he was issued jungle kit in preparation to fight the Japanese in the Pacific Theatre of Operations, however circumstances, the bombing of Hiroshima and Nagasaki intervened.

In February 1946 John was deployed to the 6th Airborne Division to Palestine. The young paratroopers were excited, oblivious to the trouble between the Jews and the Arabs they thought they were about to have a holiday in the sun.

In February 1946 there were five terrorist attacks, numerous aircraft were destroyed on RAF airfields; Mount Carmel the RAF Radar Station that monitored ships bringing illegal immigrants into the country was targeted and one soldier killed; an officer and a private from the Kings African Rifles were killed in an attack near Holon; seven Arabs selling cows were killed in Tel Aviv; eight days later a market in Ramle was bombed killing twelve Arabs and wounding forty-three more.

The 6th Airborne were sent to a camp in Egypt for several days to get acclimatised then taken by train to the Gaza Strip to Camp 21 at Nathanya where they spent several months living six men to a tent. The food seems to have been unappetising, no bacon or eggs, porridge for breakfast, some meat but mostly sausages with potatoes and greens for dinner. Lots of fruit though, large grapefruits and a never-ending supply of oranges.

Their role involved stopping and searching vehicles looking for illegal weapons and guarding ammunition dumps and railways as the Jewish Resistance had a habit of targeting the citrus trains on their way to the ports. On one occasion while in Camp 21 2 Para were attacked by mortars from Jewish insurgents outside the camp. There were no casualties and the attackers disappeared before they could be apprehended.

There was no socialising between the soldiers and the population. John remembers that the Jews were uncooperative and that it was impossible to tell the European Jews from the Sabras- those Jews born in Palestine/Israeli territory. The soldiers were confined to camp, swimming was the only recreation available to them, they were taken in groups with armed guards to protect them.

The Arabs that John came in contact with were reasonably friendly, though he recalls they would steal anything they came across given the opportunity. He was unaware that the Arabs killed any British soldiers.

The violence continued to escalate- on April 25th seven young paratroopers were murdered in a Tel Aviv car park by the Stern Gang. On June 16th a Staff Sergeant and a driver were lynched by Arabs in Gaza. That same evening the Haganah carried out attacks on road and rail bridges on the Palestinian frontier. They destroyed four road and four rail bridges. One road bridge across the Jordan was destroyed by a delayed action mine while twenty year- old Lieutenant Roy Allen of the 42 Field Company Royal Engineers was attempting to remove the charge.

On the 18th June five British officers and an RAF service man were kidnapped, one of the officers viciously clubbed. All the men were eventually released, the last three chloroformed and dumped unconscious in Tel Aviv. Passers- by took no notice!

On 22nd July 1946 the King David Hotel was bombed by the Irgun killing ninety-one people and injuring forty-six others. Captain Alexander Mackintosh died the next day of wounds sustained when he surprised the terrorists stacking explosives into milk churns in the basement of the hotel.

On 29th July twenty-three-year-old Cpl Leonard Cranwell of 2nd Ox and Bucks Light Infantry was killed by a sniper on the Bethlehem Road, Jerusalem. On 30th July Pte Colin Murray of 5 Para aged nineteen was killed by a sniper in Tel Aviv.

After the King David Hotel bombing wholesale searches were instigated. All the men of the 6th Airborne with troops of the 1st Infantry Division spent four days (28th August – 2nd September) on Operation 'Shark' searching every house and building in Tel Aviv and Jaffa, an area with 100,000 people. All inhabitants were screened and suspects detained. Amounts of arms and ammunition were found and confiscated. Village searches were easier as the soldiers would put a cordon around the village before going into action.

On 9th September a taxi containing four Jews dressed as soldiers stopped outside the Food Control Office near the Jaffa-Tel Aviv border. They approached the Temporary Arab Constable (TAC) guard and fired several bursts killing him. A second taxi drew up and four more men emerged. The taxis drove off. Major John Doran the Area Security Officer Jaffa engaged them from the balcony of the house and was wounded in the shoulder. DSP Cohen arrived at the Scene to investigate the shooting and was also wounded in the shoulder.

Some of the terrorists entered ASO's quarters which housed his office and records, and placed charges in position. There was a large explosion and the greater part of the house was demolished. Major Doran died later as a result of multiple injuries, his wife was seriously injured and another officer was slightly injured. That same day near Petah Tiqva Sgt Ernest Lambert with 7 Para was killed. September 13th saw a drive by shooting of Palestinian Arabs after a bank raid, a week later Haifa Railway Station was bombed. On 22nd a 20 year- old corporal with 224 Para Field Ambulance was killed in Tel Aviv by a sniper.

At about 2345 hours on 31st September Quarter Master Sergeant Instructor Leslie Lemon from London serving with HQ 1 Para Brigade was returning to Nathanya from Lydda on his motorcycle. He stopped when he saw a 'Mines' notice a road junction. As he pulled up he was attacked with automatic fire from a car which drew level with him. He was wounded in the chest, stomach and legs, and in spite of an operation the following morning he died in Hasssah Hospital in Tel Aviv at 18.30 hours. The mines on the road were dummies!

October proved another bad month. On 6th two airmen were shot in the 'Street of the Prophets' in Jerusalem. one died the other was seriously injured. The Stern Gang were the most likely perpetrators, though unusually they did not claim responsibility. On the 8th two young privates were killed, two other ranks and a Lt. Col. were seriously wounded when their 15cw British Army truck overturned and caught fire when was blown up by an electrically detonated prepared charge of considerable size on the Jerusalem-Jaffa Road. On the 17th British Inspector William Bruce a member of the Palestine Police aged 34 was shot as he left a café in the Jaffa Road, Jerusalem with three other police officers. Two of the accompanying police officers took him to hospital where he died of his wounds. On 20th a 19-year-old Coldstream Guardsman was killed in Jaffa by a vehicle mine.

24th October a corporal in the Sutherland Highlanders was killed and six others wounded, one fatally by mines hidden in dustbins and a shop shutter. On 25th a 19-year-old private from Wigan was killed by a mine in Jerusalem. 30th two British guards were killed in an attack on Jerusalem Railway station and two members of 1st Royal Ulster Rifles were killed shortly before 6am in an attack in the Sheikh Jarrah Quarter of Jerusalem. Charges placed in the parapet of a road culvert were electronically detonated at the moment two military vehicles laden with British troops and an Arab civilian truck were passing the spot. At the same time automatic fire was opened on the vehicles from positions north and south of the culvert. South of Petah Tiqva on the Main North Road on 31st October a 15-cwt truck of 195 Para Field Ambulance was travelling southward at speed when an explosion caused the driver to lose control, the truck travelled on for thirty yards, turned around and turned over into a ditch on the west side, the same side of the road as the mines. It caught fire and completely burned out. Two men were trapped inside and both died. That same day the British Embassy in Rome was badly damaged by a terrorist bomb.

After nine or ten months in Camp 21 the 6th Airborne moved north to the coastal city of Nahariya close to the Lebanese border. From here they were sent to Haifa to the docks to wait for the illegal immigrant ships. On arrival the troops would board the vessels, round up the occupants, put them on buses to holding camps, eventually they would be taken to camps in Cyprus. When the soldiers arrived on the dock they would be pelted by tins of bully beef from the deck. They collected the tins to take them back to camp.

Tel Litwinski, November 1946. Guard of Honour for Major General E. L. Bols Commander of the 6th Division. John Bosley in the centre.

November 9th three British Constables in the Palestine Police were killed responding to an anonymous call to a booby-trapped house in Moshe Street, Jerusalem. On 13th two more British police constables were killed by bombs. On 17th an unexploded contact mine was discovered by the railway line 2 kilometres south of Ras El Ain. Capt. John Newton of the Royal Engineers was killed by the anti-lifting device during disposal when attempting to move the mine. Another Royal Engineer was killed together with three British Police when the Police Mobile Force (PMF) vehicle he was driving was destroyed by an electrically detonated mine.

On 18th at Kefar Sirkin a pressure types mine found on the railway line exploded. A Royal Engineer party from 2 Para Brigade had undertaken the disposal, Capt. Stanley Adamson was seriously injured and died later. On 20th The Jewish Income Tax offices were bombed: one Jewish worker was killed and there were numerous other casualties.

December and the season of goodwill began but the killings continued. On 2nd six young men, the eldest just twenty-two were murdered. A 21-year-old gunner was killed by a mine on the Jaffa Road, another vehicle was blown up near Hadera killing a 22-year-old corporal serving with the Royal Army Service Corps. The third vehicle mine exploded beneath a jeep on its way to Jerusalem killing two Airborne gunners and two privates from the Air Formation Signals who were hitchhiking. Two Jewish insurgents were seen escaping in a taxi towards Jerusalem.

Between 3rd and the 8th December five more men were killed by vehicle mines, two of them as a result of a time mine being placed in a vehicle in front of Sarfand Military Headquarters. A sixth soldier died as a result of a terrorist attack. On the 18th a Palestine Police Sergeant was killed on duty.

According to 'Events 1947- British Forces in Palestine' on New Year's Day 1947 'Operation Lobster' cordon and search of Karton Quarter in Tel Aviv by 1st Para screened two thousand, two hundred and forty-two people and detained forty-seven.

2nd January 1947 the Irgun attack a military car park in Tiberias with flame throwers. 'Operation Mackerel' 3 Para cordon and search the Yemenite Quarter of Rehovoth nine Jews are detained. A lieutenant from 2/East Surrey Regiment travelling in a Bren Carrier is killed by a mine.

3rd January sixty-four Jews are detained when the Montefiore and Hatikva Quarters of Tel Aviv are searched. 5th twenty Jews are detained when an Arms Cache is found in Petah Tiqva. On 8th twelve members of Irgun are arrested by the military and police in Rishon le Zion. One hundred and nine Jews are detained between 8th – 17th across Palestinian Jewish areas during 'Operation Octopus.'

An attack by the Stern Gang on the Headquarters of the District Police in Haifa on January 12th resulted in the deaths of two British Constables and two Temporary Arab Constables in what is believed to be the world's first car bombing. A 2.5-ton RAF truck was stolen the previous day and was driven into the police compound and parked by the police canteen by a man wearing a police uniform. The bomb was discovered when one of the guards saw a burning fuse, a few minutes later the bomb exploded. In addition to the four fatalities nine more British constables were seriously injured, two with life threatening injuries. Fifty TAC's and many Jewish and Arab civilians were injured in a blast that caused wide spread damage. According to the Palestine Police report everyone on site when the bomb exploded was deafened so verbal orders could not be heard, visual signals were hampered by the dust and smoke from the resulting fire.

On 26th a retired major was kidnapped from his girlfriend's home in Jerusalem, beaten and chloroformed. He was release three days later but died from the chloroform. The next day a judge was kidnapped from his courtroom in Tel Aviv. He was released, unharmed on 28th.

The Irgun initiated a mortar attack Ein Shemer airfield. On February 28th there is a terrorist attack on Barclays Bank in Haifa, one British civilian and two Jews are killed, a British soldier, an Arab Legionnaire and a Naval rating are injured.

On 31 January 1947, following escalating political unrest, all non-essential civilians (women, children and men in non-essential civilian jobs) were ordered to be evacuated from Palestine. The scheme was code named 'Operation Polly.' On February 2nd the exodus began, with the evacuation of British women and children to Sarafand camp. Handley Page Halifax A9 transport aircraft of 113 Squadron evacuated a total of five hundred and eight passengers to Egypt within in two days.

On 1st March in the middle of the afternoon there was a terrorist attack on the Goldsmith's Officer's Club in Jerusalem. A vehicle entered from the street through barbed wire and a package was placed in the building that resulted in a small explosion which set a tent alight. Simultaneously the sentries were fired upon with automatic weapons. Several men dressed in army uniforms dismounted the truck and ran away, there was a heavy explosion which caused massive damage to the building. A police vehicle had been caught up in the crossfire, killing one British Clerical Officer and injuring another together with a British constable. At least twelve people died and more were injured in the attack.

That same day two young Royal Dragoons were killed when their scout car hit land mine on the Haifa- Jaffa road and in Tel Aviv an eighteen-year-old Sherwood Forester died in a vehicle mine explosion. On 2nd March a twenty-year-old guardsman was killed by a vehicle mine at Hedera while at Mount Carmel three Lance Corporals were killed when a landmine disguised as a kilo stone detonated as their vehicle passed.

Between 8th and 31st March six soldiers were killed and nine were seriously injured in terrorist attacks on six different days, three British Constables were killed on duty and a single private with the Royal Hampshire's was killed in a mine explosion on the Caifo- Haifa train.

Sergeant George Becket was an Irishman from County Armagh who joined the Royal Air Force in January 1935. In 1940 he was evacuated from France then served in Canada until he was posted to Egypt in 1944. He was awarded The George Cross for heroism and conspicuous courage in circumstances of extreme danger for his actions at Ein Shemer Air Headquarters.

"On the night of 28 March 1947 at Ein Shemer Air Headquarters in the Levant, Sergeant Beckett was the driver of a refuelling vehicle which was refuelling a Lancaster of No. 38 Sqdn. Suddenly, a violent fire broke out in the vehicle's pumping compartment; flames enveloped Sergeant Beckett and set alight the front of the Lancaster's fuselage. Another airman beat out the flames on Sergeant Beckett but not before the latter had sustained very severe burns on the hands and face.
There was a grave danger that the main tank of the refuelling vehicle would explode, killing or seriously injuring personnel who were working in the vicinity and destroying the twenty or more aircraft in the park. Mindful of this danger and in considerable pain, Beckett got into the driver's seat of the blazing vehicle and drove it a distance of about four hundred yards to a point where it could do no further damage.

At this point Beckett collapsed and he was taken by ambulance to the Station's Sick Quarters in a dangerously ill condition. The fires in the Lancaster and in the vehicle were eventually brought under control and extinguished with no further damage to persons or property." John Beckett died of his injuries on 12 April 1947. Source: Wikipedia

Two British Constables in civilian clothes were shot in Jerusalem on 8th April, one died the other was slightly injured. On 18th April Pte. Alan Tomlinson, a member of Royal Army Medical Corp, was killed in a terrorist attack on the British Military Hospital at Nathanya. On 20th a Red Cross Depot was bombed and many British soldiers injured. On 22nd a Lance Corporal with the East Surreys was killed in a terror attack in Jerusalem.

On 22nd April there was an attack the Cairo- Haifa train. According to the eye witness account of Major Plowman of the Royal Army Pay Corps the first five coaches were reserved for military personnel. As the train was travelling slowly along an embankment at Rehovoth there was a huge explosion, the last two compartments of the third coach bore the brunt of the explosion and were completely destroyed. The fourth carriage was blown of the rails and down the embankment, the fifth car was undamaged but had been telescoped into the sixth car Initially there was there was intermittent sniper fire at the survivors.

Five soldiers were killed, in the attack, twenty- three were injured and there were seven civilian casualties.

The men who died were:

Cole, Roland J (20) from Berhamsted; Signalman 7 HQ Signals

Hunter, Cecil S (23) from Beverley; Signalman 7 HQ Signals

Hutchinson, Peter HS (21); Signalman 7 HQ Signals

Watkinson, Arthur (35) from Totteridge; Staff Sergeant 13 Anti-Tank Regiment, Royal Artillery

Wells, Thomas (19) from Great Yarmouth; Signalman 7 HQ Signals

The Police Orderly Room and Telephone Exchange at Sarona Camp was bombed in the late morning on 25th April when a van stolen from the Palestine Post and Telegraphs Tel Aviv was driven into the compound by a Jewish terrorist in uniform. One British Inspector and three British Constables were killed, five British Constables, one British Soldier and a Temporary Arab Constable were injured. On 26th April an Assistant Superintendent of Police was mortally wounded in Haifa when two men opened fire from a taxi on his stationary vehicle.

The Acre Prison escape in the afternoon of Sunday 4th May was an Irgun operation. They planned to free as many prisoners as they had safe houses to hide them hence forty-one prisoners, thirty Irgun and eleven Lehi. The Irgun had purchased civilian and military vehicles, painted the latter in British camouflage colours and had their hair cut British military style. Three men disguised themselves as Arabs while the rest dressed as Royal Engineers, boldly driving in a convoy to the prison gate. The operation commander Dov Cohen in the lead jeep was in the uniform of a Captain in the Royal Engineers. Men disguised as telephone technicians set charges to the prison wall near the Turkish Bath that had been identified as vulnerable.

At 4.22pm while the prisoners were in the yard exercising, the charges blew a huge hole in the wall. Selected prisoners had access to smuggled TNT which had been used to make hand grenades to cause confusion and two small bombs to blow up iron gates blocking their exit through to the wall.

Meanwhile a diversion party dressed as Arabs had mortared a British Army Post, they had also mined nearby roads to hamper the British pursuit. A group of prisoners had managed to set light to a flammable barricade which added to the general chaos. The prison held Jewish and Arab prisoners, the latter confused by the fire, smoke and explosions added to the pandemonium. The Arab guards began shooting into the crowds, contributing to the mayhem, during the confusion many Arabs managed to return to the general population through the wall.

At the time of the Acre attack it appears that the jail held four hundred Arabs, one hundred and sixty-one Jews, sixty were Irgun, twenty-two Lehi and five Haganah, the rest were made up of felons. The numbers of escapers vary from different sources- two hundred and fifty-one Jewish and Arab escapees in total; Two hundred and fourteen of the three hundred and ninety-four Arab prisoners; eight Jews killed and thirteen captured; twenty-eight Jewish Irgun and seven Lehi prisoners. I am using the figures from the Jewish Virtual Library which states twenty from Irgun and seven from Lehi. Nine fighters killed in clashes with the British Army; six escapees and three of the Fighting Force. Eight escapees, some of them injured recaptured and returned to jail. Five of the attackers were arrested and did not make it back to base. It gives the number of Arab prisoners who escaped at one hundred and eighty-two.

Three of the five Irgun members who had been part of the blocking squad were tried in a Military court for the capital offence carrying weapons and sentenced to death. The other two men were minors and so escaped the death penalty. Avshalom Haviv, Meir Nakar and Yaaskov Weiss were hung on in Acre Prison on 29th July.

In the early hours of 12th July the Irgun had kidnapped two young sergeants in Nethanya to hold as hostages. Clifford Martin and Mervyn Paice were twenty-one, both serving the Intelligence Corps 252 Field Security. They were bludgeoned and chloroformed, bundled in a car and taken to a sound proofed, airtight cell twelve square feet in size and less than six feet high beneath the floor of an old diamond factory. For seventeen days they had been confined without air, light or sound, with two oxygen cylinders that needed to be carefully regulated in order to keep them alive. After the executions in acre took place they were taken to a eucalyptus grove, hanged and their hooded bodies boobed trapped. Their bodies were discovered after a tip off on 31st July- the Royal Engineer Captain from 23rd Field Company was temporarily blinded when a mine in the bodies exploded as he cut them down.

Two British Constables in civilian clothes were shot and killed in Jerusalem on 12th May. On 15th two Lieutenants in the Royal Engineers died while dismantling a mine on a railway line between Beirut and Cairo at Qiryat Moskin (Kiryat Motzkin). This was a strategic location between busy deep-water port of Haifa and Western Galilee. On 16th a British Constable died in an explosion in Haifa while driving a CID car; on 31st May the Haifa oil refinery was blown up.

In the month John Bosley was to leave Palestine, an eighteen-year-old British Constable was killed while on duty in Sharon, Haifa; a twenty-eight-year-old Dane in the Royal Army Service Corps was shot at close range in Tel Aviv; five British officers were kidnapped then released in Jerusalem; two officers were wounded and another killed by a sniper in Tel Aviv; three British soldiers were killed and a fourth wounded after being fired at in Tel Aviv. And, a group of officers from 6th Airborne were dining in the Astoria restaurant when two terrorists opened fire with machine guns killing a Captain in the Royal Irish Fusiliers.

John Bosley was demobbed in In June 1947, he abandoned his khaki drill shorts that ensured he always had sunburnt knees, for a demob suit and civilian life. Prior to joining the Parachute Regiment in April 1944, he had worked in a seed merchants earning two pounds a week. In 1947 the average wage was two pounds and ten pence. Given his service background it was suggested that he might join the police force. John joined the Wiltshire Constabulary earning two hundred and fifty pounds a year. Twenty pound a week was certainly a princely sum however from his pay he had to pay National Insurance and contribute towards his pension. In addition, he was living in single men's quarters in Swindon Old Town at thirty shillings (one pound ten shillings) a week. He was paid fortnightly- alternately seven pounds or seven pounds ten.

According to Wikipedia the Division located 99 mortars,34 machine guns, 174 sub machine guns, 375 rifles, 391 pistols, 97 land mines, 2582 hand grenades and 302,530 rounds of ammunition during their searches of Jewish and Arab settlements.

DOV COHEN CODE NAME SHIMSON 25TH DECEMBER 1915 – 4TH MAY 1947

Dov Cohen was born 28th December 1915 in Poland possibly in Horodenka, an area disputed by Poland and Ukraine (presently in Western Ukraine.)   During WW

II apart from a few Jews who survived to join the partisans, the rest of the Jewish population, approximately half of the inhabitants, were murdered by the Nazi's. Some were shot and killed in a mass grave in the forest, others executed in the town square and the remainder sent to the concentration and extermination camp at Majdanek near Lublin.

Majdanek

According to 'The Book of Horodenka,' between 1919 and 1949 two hundred and fifty people from the town had moved to Palestine, Dov Cohen was one of them. He arrived, arrived, probably illegally, possibly through Syria to Eretz Ysrael (Land of Israel) in 1938. There he enrolled in the Hebrew University of Jerusalem and shortly afterwards he became a member of Irgun.

During WWII Dov volunteered for the British Army either in 1939 or early 1940, enlisting in 401 Company (AMPC) Auxiliary Military Pioneer Corps. The majority of the Company were Jews from eleven European countries, the remainder were Arabs from Palestine, Sudan, Iraq and Egypt.

The unit, under the command of Major H.J. Cator of the Royal Scots Greys, sailed for France 22nd February 1940. Their duties were constructing railways and roads around Rennes. On 17th June, after the Germans invaded they boarded two trawlers for England. On 6th August they sailed for Palestine, arriving on 15th September. Three Middle East Commando units, unconnected with Britain were raised, 50,51 and 52, they formed specifically for a raiding- operations in and around the Middle East. The best three-hundred men were selected from the AMPC for the new 51 Commando, Dov was one of the chosen designated 'Raiders.'

A period of intense training which included demolition skills began in Egypt. On 24th January 1942 51 Commando sailed for Port Sudan for three weeks acclimatisation before being attached to the 4th Indian Division who were fighting an Italian colonial army for Keren in Eritrea. 51 Commando were to patrol and ambush in support of the division. The fighting was fierce and unrelenting, over difficult terrain. The Commandos were constantly in action, whether in hand to hand fighting, infiltrating enemy positions, or, drawing the Italians fire and forces away from the division.

When Eritrea surrendered to the Allies the 'Raiders' were exhausted, after a rest period they moved on to Abyssinia at the end of April 1941- tasked with taking a steep hill during the battle of Amba Alagi, the Commandos took the unnamed peak which was christened Commandos Hill in their honour. If taking the hill was difficult, holding it proved even more so. The hill was observed by Italian artillery and all supplies, water and ammunition had to be manually hauled up.

The 'Abyssinian Campaign' also known as the 'East African Campaign' is less well known and widely documented than other campaigns in WWII- it began 10th June 1940 and ended with an Allied victory 9th November 1943. It was a brutal campaign in difficult terrain and the men who fought with 51 Commando acted with incredible bravery. They were physically strong, well disciplined, highly motivated and had courage to infiltrate enemy lines with light weapons and equipment. Sergeant Dov Cohen was decorated (Military Medal) for heroism in battle against the Italians in Abyssinia.

Men of 51 Middle East Commando at Sarafand Camp 20th December 1941
Dov Cohen, Philip Koeger and Dolph Zentner

After 51 Commando disbanded he joined the SIG (Special Interrogation Group) a small group of fluent German speaking Jews trained in desert navigation, unarmed combat and handling German weapons and explosives who went uncover in German lines with false identities. They captured German vehicles, set up road blocks, gathered intelligence and carried out acts of sabotage. When SIG disbanded he seems to transfer to the Buffs (The Royal East Kent Regiment.)

After demobilisation he became active in Irgun military operations, always at the head of his troops in battle. During the War Dov had developed a wide range of skills that were obviously of great use to the Irgun. He expanded the Irgun training programme and brought the rifle and Bren gun unto operational use.

He was appointed commander of Fighting Force in Petah Tikva, leading the attack on Lydda Military Airfield on 25th February 1946 when eleven military aircraft were destroyed. He was also the overall commander of the Irgun's largest operation involving one hundred participants on 2nd April 1946. The objective was to immobilise the whole of the rail network in the south. Dov Cohen led the Southern Force raid on the railway station and bridges at Ashod.

He was shot and killed shortly after the Acre Prison escape when a van with a group of escaped prisoners came across a group of British paratroopers who had been bathing in the sea close to the prison. The paratroopers hearing, the explosions of the prison break, grabbed their weapons and ran towards the sound. When they saw the van careering towards them they opened fire, as the driver attempted to get away the van overturned. Dove with two companions were nearby in his jeep, realising what was happening he shouted in English to the paratroopers to stop shooting. Seeing a Royal Engineer Captain coming towards them the British soldiers were hesitant to fire, however they became suspicious when they saw the officer was armed with a Bren gun. When Dov realised that the British soldiers recognised him as an imposter he shouted in Hebrew for his men to scatter and gave covering fire. There was an exchange of fire, and Dov was one of three Fighting Force members together with five escapees to die in the encounter. He was thirty- one years old.

Dov and the six other etzel (Irgun) fighters killed after the Acre prison break are buried in the Shavei Zion Cemetery, Naharya- Hatzafon Northern District. This is the cemetery of a moshav, a cooperative settlement of small farms. It is primarily used for local burials, it also contains graves that no other community would accept. Jewish custom is to bury a body within twenty- four hours of death. The British Authorities asked local communities in the area to bury the deceased but no other village would agree to bury the bodies.

The word ETZEL refers to pre - Israeli military or organisations considered extremist and was commonly used when referring to Irgun. (It is an acronym of the Hebrew initials or abbreviation of Irgun Zvai Leumi (IZL.)

NOTES:
Dov common name amongst East European Jews translation Hebrew 'bear' Yiddish 'Ber.' English 'Bernard.'

   Shimson translates from Hebrew to 'Bright Sun' shortened version Samson (Hebrew translation 'Sun')

Jewish Resistance Movements

The Haganah ('Defence.') Trained as a part-time National Army pre -World War II. After the war ended the Haganah prioritised bringing Jewish immigrants in from Europe. Gave prior notice of impending attacks to allow personnel in the area to be evacuated.

The Palmach ('Strike Force'): Formed by the Haganah as a full-time force to counter the threat from the Axis Forces to the Middle East.

The Irgun ('The ***National Military Organisation in the land of Israel')*** advocated terror tactics.

***The Lehi (Fighters for Freedom of Israel* ')** better known to the British as *The Stern Gang* had very few members. It was so named because it was founded in 1940 by Avraham Stern. Together with the Irgun they had declared war on Britain by the time John Bosley arrived in Palestine.

The literal translation of the Hebrew word Lehi is 'jawbone' referring to Samson using the jawbone of donkey to defeat 1,000 Philistine warriors.

Palestine Police Force

Many of the police officers had served in the British Army. When marking rank, the nationality/ race of the officer came first. For example:

BC British Constable

JC   Jewish Constable

TAC Temporary Arab Constable.

Martin Higgins MA of the British Palestine Police Association explained that during periods of emergency the police were augmented by temporary (special) locals.

During the period that John Bosley was in country discounting British, Jewish and Arab civilians killed and the ninety-one deaths in the King David Hotel bombing at least seventy-five soldiers and two airmen died as a result of terrorist activities. Between the beginning of 1946 and the end of June 1947 thirty members of the Palestine Police were killed on duty, twenty-three police officers died as the result of bomb explosions and seven were shot, the majority from ambush, one in an attack and one while attempting to make an arrest.

Sources

S King - Events British Forces in Palestine 1946 & MOD Roll of Honour Events British Forces in Palestine 1947

Roll of Honour British Police Palestine Association
Martin Higgins MA British Police Palestine Association
'Cordon and Search- With the 6th Airborne Division in Palestine' Major R.D. Wilson MBE MC
Wikipedia
'Book of Horodenka' edited sh. Meltzer

Information on Dov Cohen
Yoav Gelber
Martin Sugarman
Steve Rogers Commonwealth War Grave Photographic Project
Maurice 'Tiffen' Monju Tiefenbrunner
The Irgun web site
The Jewish Virtual Library

Information on the Acre Prison breakout
'Terror out of Zion' John Bowyer Bell
'In the Lion's Jaws' Itzhak Gurian
'Let my people go' Jerry A Grunor
'A Captains Mandate' Phillip Brutton

Information on 51 ME Commando in East Africa October 1941
Harry Fecitt MBE ex 68 Company, Royal Pioneer Corps

Recommended reading and viewing
The book 'Exodus' by Leon Uris and the 1960 film of the same name starring Paul Newman, Lee J. Cobb, Ralph Richardson, Sal Mineo and Eva Marie Saint.
'Tobruk' 1967 starring Rock Hudson and George Peppard. (*SIG*)
'The Promise' DVD starring Christian Cooke and Claire Foy

CHAPTER 8

AWOL in the Canal Zone   1952   Duncan Boyd

I was commissioned into The Royal Dragoons (The Royals) on 8th February 1952. King George VI had died on the 6th February and so our Passing Out Parade was cancelled. After the usual Young Officer Courses at the Royal Armoured Corps Centre at Bovington and Lulworth, I flew out to Fayid in the Canal Zone in May in a York from Blackbush Airfield.

The Egyptian abrogation of the Suez Canal Treaty had occurred six months earlier and the storming of the Caracol, the Egyptian Police HQ in Ismailia, and associated unrest, had taken place in early 1952. **(See Note below).**

At that time, the 2i/c and all squadron leaders, except one, had MCs. The exception had an MBE as did the QM. The Colonel had the DSO, MBE and MC, the RSM had a Croix de Guerre and the Provost Sgt a DCM.

On arrival, I was posted to B Squadron, which was out on squadron training at Bir Odieb south of Suez. Further south of Bir Odieb and also on the Gulf of Suez was Ain Sohkna – an ancient port and settlement some 4000 years ago, but now only a destination for intrepid scuba divers. Our training culminated in a squadron advance to contact up the Wadi Hagul and up to the Suez/Cairo road. After a couple of weeks, I was given command of 5th Troop, consisting of two Daimler Armoured Cars (DACs) and two Daimler Scout Cars (Dingoes or DSCs).

Duncan Boyd in a scout car - Daimler Armoured Car (DAC) in the desert of the Canal Zone Summer 1952

Sometime afterwards, the Colonel changed the troop organisation to one DAC, two DSCs and a larger armoured car, mounting a more powerful gun than the 2-pounder gun on the DAC known as an AEC, after the company that built it – based on a London bus chassis! It mounted a 75mm gun, which fired an enhanced performance armoured piercing round and also a very effective High Explosive (HE) round. At the same time, all DAC 2 pounder guns were modified with the Littlejohn squeeze bore attachment to enable them to fire the higher performance Armour Piercing Super Velocity (APSV) round. This meant that HE rounds could not be fired, but as they tended to premature that was no great disadvantage. This change of organisation presumably resulted from an updated assessment of the Egyptian Army's threat to British Forces in the Canal Zone, which at the time consisted of two divisions, 1st and 3rd, plus "Corps" troops.

We were once deployed to form a screen- fully bombed up - to protect Ismailia and Moascar, where there was a large British garrison, including HQ British Troops Egypt, when an Egyptian armoured brigade was moving from Gaza to Cairo. The move passed off without incident. Otherwise, there were frequent nightly cable patrols and we took part in major divisional exercises, one of which was in Sinai and took in the Mitla Pass – which was a key area much in the news in the Arab-Israeli War some years later.

Waterloo Day was celebrated by a Trooping the Guidon Parade, the first time this had been done on foot since the Regiment lost its horses in 1940. On the recreational side, there was an Officers Club on the shores of the Great Bitter Lake, where one could swim, and a Sailing Club next door, where we had a couple of boats and where much time at week- ends was spent on their maintenance. I learnt to sail there. There was also a flourishing Polo Club at Fayid and I learnt to play.

Dinner Nights, with the Band playing, occurred every Thursday. On one occasion, as the regimental march was being played, the Orderly Officer, who had been summoned to the telephone, came back with the news that King Farouk had been deposed and Op Rodeo Flail was to be implemented. This was an operation to send an infantry battalion group, with a troop of tanks and a troop of armoured cars, by Tank Landing Ship to Alexandria, to protect the European population in case of rioting by the Egyptians. Within a couple of hours, my troop was on its way to Port Said, fully bombed up and ready to go. We spent the next three weeks embarked, but never had to sail. We returned just in time for the visit of the Chief of the Imperial General Staff (CIGS), Field Marshal Sir John Harding.

The only place one could go for leave was Cyprus. After about a year in the Zone, Noel Matterson and I went on leave to Cyprus. As everyone did, we went to Kyrenia, which was a lovely change from Fayid. After a few days, we decided to fly to Istanbul. We had a very good time there, sightseeing and partying. Having clocked in to the Embassy, we met the Naval Attaché, who was most kind to us and had us to stay for several days. We met a British engineer working for Petter Engines, who asked us if we would like to drive down with him, through Anatolia and Syria to Beirut. Of course, we jumped at the idea and off we went. We spent nights in Ankara and in the Taurus Mountains of southern Turkey, having visited the 4000-year-old Hittite pyramid cave dwellings at Urgup. We arrived safely in Beirut and stayed at the St Georges Club, where we said good bye to our friend who had driven us down. Our plan was to get to Amman in Jordan and persuade the RAF there to fly us to Fayid. By this time, we were getting close to the end of our leave time, so we got the Military Attaché at the British Embassy to send a signal to the Regiment saying where we were and what our plans were.

Problem number one was that we were running out of money, which we were discussing over a coca cola. "No problem, said the Coca Cola Stall owner, "You are British Officers- you have English cheque book? No problem!" And so it was! So, next day we took a dolmus to Amman changing at Damascus, (A dolmus is a taxi doing a fixed route, but you pay for your seat only) All went well until we were going out of Damascus when we were stopped at a police check point and everyone had to get out. The taxi driver was suspected of smuggling gold, we were told! And lo and behold they found a bar of gold, wrapped in sacking, in the engine oil filler filter! The driver was carted off and never seen again and in due course a new dolmus came and took us to Amman.

Problem number two was that the RAF told us there were no flights to Fayid for three weeks! Consternation! So off we went to Jerusalem, where we booked a flight on BEA to Nicosia for the next day, which gave us time to do a bit of sightseeing and visiting the Church of The Holy Sepulchre. We arrived in Nicosia on a Friday, to be informed by RAF Movement Control that there were no flights to Fayid until Monday. So, it was off to Kyrenia for a pleasant weekend.

We got back to the Regiment to be told that the Adjutant wished to see us! We were wheeled in to see the Colonel – who wanted to hear what we had been up to and where we had been! Despite the fact that we were a week overdue our leave, I think he was quite pleased that we had not just sat on the beach at Kyrenia all the time! Anyway, he was very nice about it all – and we got off very lightly, each getting four extra orderly officers from the Adjutant!!

Duncan Boyd as Adjutant, riding behind the Commanding Officer (not in the picture,) at the head of the Regiment as the Royal Dragoons celebrated the Freedom of the City of London to mark their Tercentenary, by marching through the City with Swords drawn, Bayonets fixed, Drums beating and Guidon unfurled. 22nd October 1963.

DUNCAN BOYD
Was *commissioned into The Royal Dragoons (The Royals) in 1952. After 18 months in the Canal Zone in Egypt as an armoured car troop leader, he spent the next three years with the Regiment in the British Army of the Rhine (BAOR) at Wesendorf, close to the inter-zonal border between the British and Russian Zones. He later served with the Regiment in Aden, Malaya and Tidworth (where the Regiment converted to tanks) and twice more in BAOR. Soon after the Amalgamation of The Royals with The Royal Horse Guards (The Blues), he was appointed Second-in-Command of The Life Guards.*

He passed the Technical Staff Course at the Royal Military College of Science at Shrivenham, subsequently instructing at the Armour School and, later, on the Directing Staff at Shrivenham.

He commanded the Armoured Trials and Development Unit at Bovington and later served in the Ministry of Defence in Chieftain and Challenger Tank Project Management and then in Challenger Gun and Ammunition (CHARM) Project Management until his retirement. He was promoted to Colonel in 1981.

Squadron Leader of 'C' Squadron The Royals, leaving to go on Ex Queen Cobra in BOAR 1966

CO of the Armoured Trials Development Unit, talking to the German Director of Armour at the Royal Armoured Corps Centre at Bovington 1976

NOTES:

The Suez Canal, built in the 1860s, was a link in the lifeline to India, the Far East, Australia and also to the Persian Gulf, where three quarters of Britain's oil supplies came from. The security of free passage through the Canal was a key strategic issue. After World War 2 British troops had withdrawn from the rest of Egypt to the Canal Zone, which stretched from Port Said in the north to Suez in the south, thus reverting to the conditions of the pre-war Treaty with Egypt of 1936, which was agreed should be for 20 years. The only other town in the Zone was Ismailia, on the shores of Lake Timsah, north of the Great Bitter Lake. In 1952/53, the period covered by this article, due to the deteriorating security situation, Port Said, Suez and Ismailia were essentially out of bounds to British troops, as was the rest of Egypt.

Contiguous to Ismailia, was Moascar, where a large Garrison area was located.

The storming of the Caraco involved elements of A Squadron of The Royals and a troop of tanks of 4th Royal Tank Regiment from Shandur as well as the Parachute Regiment.

King Farouk had reigned over Egypt and the Sudan since 1936. He was overthrown by a military coup led by General Neguib. The monarchy was abolished on 18th June 1953 and Egypt became a republic. Neguib was forced to resign the presidency in 1954 following another coup led by Colonel Nasser.

The Canal Zone Base was evacuated by Britain at Egypt's request in 1956.

Ismailia: in North East Egypt known as 'The City of Beauty and Enchantment' lies on the shore of Lake Timsah and on the West Bank of the Suez Canal. During World War I the British had an air base there opened around 1916. During World War II RAF Ismalia was used as a military airfield by the British and the Americans during the North African Campaign.

EGYPT (BRITISH MILITARY ACTION, ISMAILIA)
HC Deb 31 January 1952 vol 495 cc362-5 362
Of which the occupants were almost all auxiliary police. This building had been substantially fortified since its occupation

Mr. Aneurin Bevan (by Private Notice) asked the Secretary of State for War whether, arising out of the statement by the Foreign Secretary on Tuesday, he is now in a position to give the House more details concerning the recent clash between British Forces and Egyptian auxiliary police in Ismailia. The Secretary of State for War (Mr. Antony Head)

Yes, Sir, I am arranging for a detailed account of the incidents in Ismailia on 25th January to be published today in the OFFICIAL REPORT.

Following is the statement:

General
On 16th October, 1951, the Egyptian police failed to control the riots which broke out in Ismailia and British troops had to restore order. After these 600 auxiliary police arrived from Cairo.

Egyptian terrorists had been and continued attacking our troops and convoys while the Egyptian police looked on. In some cases, the auxiliary police, alongside the terrorists, attacked our troops. On 17th, 18th and 19th November, 1951, the auxiliary police fired on our patrols in Ismailia. After this General Erskine arranged for the regular and auxiliary Egyptian police to remain in their barracks while our families evacuated the town. After this both regular and auxiliary police in Ismailia were replaced by fresh companies from Cairo. The normal role in Egypt of auxiliary police is to provide a reserve for riot duty armed with staves. Those sent to the Canal Zone on both occasions were armed with rifles.

After the changeover had taken place evidence increased that the new auxiliary police were taking part in attacks on our troops and installations. On 3rd and 4th December, 1951, auxiliary police opened fire on our troops near the water filtration plant outside Suez and killed 11. On 18th December, 1951, fire from the police station in Ismailia killed a British officer passing in a jeep.

Twenty auxiliary police and four terrorists in a lorry attacked a road block near Tel-El-Kebir. As a result of this and other attacks in the neighbourhood our troops cleared the area, finding, in the police station compound of El Hammada (a small village), senior police major-general and 116 armed police, as well as quantities of ammunition and other arms.

The steadily mounting casualties amongst our troops and the attacks upon them caused the Commander-in-Chief, at the end of November, 1951, to recommend the disarming of the auxiliary police. On 7th December, 1951, His Majesty's Government authorised the Commander-in-Chief to take this step if the situation demanded it.

On 23rd January, 1952, when our casualties had reached 33 killed and 69 wounded, the Commander-in-Chief told the Chiefs of Staff that, in view of the repeated evidence of attack by the auxiliary police, he considered that he must disarm those in Ismailia, and that he had ordered General Erskine to do so. His Majesty's Government approved this decision.

Narrative of Events
Location of Egyptian Police on morning of 25th January.
   The position in Ismailia on the morning of 25th January was:
   (a) About 400 Egyptian police, of whom about 60 were regulars, were in the Caracol, the normal regular Police Station and the Governor's Office.
   (b) Some 600 Egyptian police, almost all auxiliaries, were in the Bureau Sanitaire located about 400 yards distant from the Caracol. The Bureau Sanitaire is normally the health office but was taken over as temporary barracks for the additional auxiliary police.

Message to the Sub-Governor of Ismailia

The operation started with a message to the Sub-Governor of Ismailia to the effect that, since the auxiliary police had been firing on our troops as well as helping the terrorists, it was necessary to disarm them. He was therefore requested to order them to come out of their barracks without arms and told that arms would be restored to the regular police who would then be allowed to continue their duties.

Message to the Major-General Commanding the Police

A similar message was sent to the major-general commanding the police who was at his residence. He replied that both the regular and auxiliary police would resist in accordance with their orders from the Egyptian Government. In view of this statement the operations against the Caracol and the Bureau Sanitaire were put in train.

The Caracol

In operations against the Caracol Egyptian casualties did not exceed single figures and ours were none. The Egyptian police opened fire first and subsequently fired repeatedly. The buildings were not damaged.

The Bureau Sanitaire

The major operations took place against the Bureau Sanitaire auxiliary police.

At 0614 hours and continuing until 0640 hours broadcasts were made from loudspeaker vans calling upon the police to surrender. At 0656 hours firing by the police started from the Bureau Sanitaire and continued with increasing intensity until 0710 hours. We then retaliated by firing one round of blank from a 20-pounder tank gun as a warning. The police continued to fire.

At 0715 hours we returned the fire for the first time, six rounds of 20-pounder tank gun and a few rounds of two-pounder being fired as well as small arms. This produced a very heavy fusillade from the police.

A fresh broadcast was then made, followed by a pause to give them time to surrender. At 0815 hours fire was again opened by us on the same scale, followed by a broadcast with another pause for surrender. All this had no effect on the police and they continued to fire.

At 0900 hours two platoons of our infantry, supported by tanks, forced their way inside the walled compound of the Bureau Sanitaire which was used as barracks by the auxiliary police. Our infantry quickly suffered fourteen casualties and were withdrawn.

Final Surrender
At 1000 hours fire was opened again and at 1037 hours surrender started. We suffered three killed and 13 wounded. The Egyptian police casualties were 41 killed, 73 wounded, and 886 surrendered.

Weapons used by British Troops
The weapons used by our troops consisted of small arms, tanks from which 23 rounds of 20-pounder were fired, armoured cars which used a few rounds of two-pounder ammunition. No artillery, aircraft or mortars were used except for one round of 2 in. smoke.

Comments
The operation was planned with the object of avoiding bloodshed. The buildings were surrounded at dawn and every possible effort was then made to persuade the police to surrender, but the responsible officials refused to take any action and the police general in Ismailia steadfastly remained in his quarters throughout the whole proceedings.

The police in the Bureau Sanitaire were first called upon to surrender at 0614 hours, but it was not until 0715 hours that British troops opened fire in spite of the fact that they themselves had been under fire from the Egyptians since 0656 hours—nearly 20 minutes earlier.

The first serious attempt to enter the building was made by our infantry nearly two hours later after a series of broadcasts, and this attempt immediately resulted in fourteen casualties to our troops. In order to avoid much greater casualties on both sides it was essential to complete the operation as soon as possible and in any case in daylight.

There were no casualties to civilians. Transport was produced quickly after the surrender and prisoners were taken away for a meal, whilst our doctors gave immediate medical attention to the wounded, some of whom were taken to our hospital and the remainder to the Egyptian hospital.

If the Egyptian Government had maintained proper control over their police forces and, in particular, their auxiliaries, it would never have been necessary to carry out the operation at all.

••

King Farouk of Egypt and Sudan succeeded his father King (formerly Sultan) Fuad at the age of sixteen. His coronation was on 28th April 1936, his abdication on 26th July 1952 ended one hundred and fifty years of the Muhammad Ali Dynasty. Farouk had been forced to abdicate after a military coup by the Free Officers Movement led by Muhammad Naguib and Gamal Abdul Nasser. King Farouk fled Egypt after the coup living the rest of his life in Monaco and Italy.

The monarchy was abolished on 18th June 1953 and Egypt became a Republic. Muhammad Naguib became the first President of Egypt on 18th June 1953. A power struggle ensued between the two powerful men who had orchestrated the coup, with Nasser ultimately the victor. Naguib was forced to resign the Presidency on 14th November 1954 after Nasser accused him of supporting the recently outlawed Muslim Brotherhood. Nasser isolated Naguib in a suburb of Cairo, an isolation that lasted for eighteen years and only ended after Nasser's death. When Anwer Sadat came into power as the 3rd President 15th October 1970 Naguib was released.

From 14th November 1954 Egypt was governed by a military dictatorship with Nasser ruling with an iron hand as the Chairman of the Revolutionary Command Council. Nasser became the 2nd President of Egypt on 23rd June 1956 and held onto power until his death in the autumn of 1958.

King Farouk was poisoned in a restaurant in Rome on 11th March 1958, supposedly on the orders of Nasser. The poison was Aconite and the reputed assassin was Ibrahim Al Baghdady.

Gamal Nasser's unhealthy lifestyle and heavy smoking left him with diabetes, high blood pressure, and arteriosclerosis (hardening of the artery's). He suffered two heart attacks the first in 1966 and the second in 1969. He died in office aged fifty-three 28th September 1970.

Muhamad Naguib died of liver cirrhosis aged eighty- three on 28th August 1984.

Anwer Sadat was assassinated on 6th October 1981. He was at a Victory Parade in Cairo to commemorate the 8th anniversary if Egypt crossing the Suez Canal. The assassination squad led by Lieutenant Khalid Islambouli were concealed in one of the troop trucks towing artillery in the parade. They exited the vehicle and fired AK47 Assault Rifles into the crowd until their ammunition ran out, mortally wounding Sadat, killing eleven others and wounding twenty -eight more. The attack only lasted two minutes but it silenced forever one of the truly great statesmen in the region. Anwar Sadat had been the first Arab leader to recognise the State of Israel, working with Israeli Prime Minister Menachem Begin to a negotiated Peace Treaty that offered a tentative yet realistic hope for peace in the Middle East.

SOURCES:
    Military Action Ismailia - Hansard Parliamentary Debate 31st January 1952
    List of Presidents of Egypt –Wikipedia

CHAPTER 9

Taking the Queen's Shilling   1983 -1989   David North

Eighteen-year-old Private David North's introduction to Army life with his local Infantry Regiment-The 1st Battalion Devonshire and Dorset Regiment was less than auspicious. His first posting, on 4th October 1983 was a two- year tour of Northern Ireland as part of the residential Battalion based on the coast close to the Mountains of Morne in County Down. The weather was awful or to use his words 'pissing down with rain' the and his arrival coincided with the biggest prison escape in UK history. Thirty- eight members of the Irish Republican Army (the IRA) escaped from H Block 7 of Maze Prison after taking prison officers hostage. To the Irish the prison was known as Long Kesh, it was the Colditz of British prisons, maximum security and supposedly escape proof. 15-foot fences, surrounded by an 18-foot concrete wall topped with barbed wire, and solid steel electronically operated gates.

The following day the Guardian reported:

'Twenty-seven IRA prisoners were being hunted last night after 38 broke out of the Maze prison near Belfast. One prison officer was fatally stabbed and six were wounded during the escape.

One prison officer was believed to be in a critical condition with gunshot wounds to the head, and at least one recaptured prisoner was in hospital. The nature of his injuries and his condition were not known, but according to one report he was shot when he refused surrender.

Late last night army helicopters carrying powerful searchlights flew over the countryside around the prison. But most of the escapers were thought to have covered substantial distances before the full cordon of road blocks was in place.

According to a spokesman for the Northern Ireland Office the prisoners, from a segregated Republican block, produced firearms and knives, and overpowered the staff taking some of the prison officers' uniforms and putting them on.

When a food lorry arrived from the prison kitchens it was stolen and the prisoners drove to the main gate of the prison. Where they again produced firearms and knives.

A quick-thinking prison officer blocked the gate with his own car and the prisoners made off on foot after a scuffle during which during which the fatal stabbing happened and shots were fired.

Police said that there were scenes of "total bedlam" as the prisoners scattered around the roads surrounding the goal, which is eight miles south-west of Belfast.

Cars were hijacked and according to reports up to ten prisoners escaped in one vehicle. Several of those recaptured were seized on Ulster's M1 motorway, which runs along- side the southern side of the prison.

The escapers broke up into several parties and one group was seen to make for the banks of the nearby river Lagan, where they were seen to change from their civilian style prison clothing into genuine civvies which were apparently hidden for them in plastic bags on the river bank. Some reports spoke of prisoners dressed only in their underpants when they broke out. Four of the men recaptured were caught as the swam across the Lagan.

Last night road blocks were in place around a wide radius from the prison and a manhunt, employing thousands of police and soldiers was under way.

The escapers came from cells in a section of the goal, which contains the H blocks where 10 Republican hunger strikers fasted to death in 1981.

A search of Block H7 after the break-out found 20 rounds of ammunition.

One woman who was out walking past the Maze at the time of the escape, said: "There were men running around the fields. After about half an hour I saw a policeman holding a gun and shouting to prisoners to halt. One was taken back to the Maze and then three more. They were marched down the road and held against a wall."

One escaper was chased by a soldier near the prison. After pursuing him for a short distance the soldier fired a single shot, at which the man stopped and surrendered. As he was led back to the prison by his captor he called out to bystanders, "Oh well, it was worth a try."

James Prior, the Northern Ireland Secretary, was duty minister at Stormont over the weekend. Last night he ordered an "immediate and searching inquiry at the highest level into all aspects of the escape."

The Northern Ireland Office said that Mr. Prior had satisfied himself that all the necessary resources of the security forces had been and would be deployed in order to recapture the escaped prisoners.

The reference by the Northern Ireland Office to a "segregated Republican block" is the first official admission that segregation of prisoners, strongly demanded by many Loyalist politicians, has been reintroduced in Northern Ireland prisons. Until now the official line has been that all prisoners would be treated equally as common criminals and that segregation would not be introduced.

The escape will certainly be hailed by the Provisional IRA as a major feat and will do much to restore its morale and that of the Irish National Liberation Army after the reverses they have suffered in recent months particularly from the effects of the "supergrass" trials.

The escape may cloud the political future of the Northern Ireland Office Minister of State, Mr. Nicholas Scott. After the general election he had extra responsibility placed on him, including the control of Ulster's prisons.

Mr. Colin Steel, the Chairman of the Prison Officers' Association in England and Wales, said last night that he had been in close touch with the POA in Northern Ireland. He was "extremely concerned" that guns had been smuggled into the Maze.

There are now thought to be 87 Irish Republican prisoners serving goal sentences in England and Wales.

Yesterday's break-out is the third spectacular prison escape pulled off by the Provo's in recent years. In meticulously planned operation eight suspected IRA terrorists broke out of the Crumlin Road goal in Belfast in June 1981.

Seven months earlier Gerrad Tuite, an IRA man on the Scotland Yard bomb squad's "most wanted" list, was the key man in planning his escape from Brixton with two other prisoners.

Tuite made his break when he and two fellow inmates tunneled through walls of their cells in Brixton's top security remand wing, dropped into a yard and used builders' planks and scaffolding piled up for repairs to scale the 15ft perimeter wall.

In 1973 three prisoners including Seamus Twomey, then chief of staff of the Provisional IRA, escaped from Mountjoy Prison, in Dublin in a helicopter.

In 1975 another IRA prisoner escaped from the Maze when he forced a Canadian priest to strip and, wearing his clothes, bluffed his way past the guards."

The young recruit found himself thrust into this security and political maelstrom as he arrived at the camp which was shared with the Ulster Defence Regiment (UDR). When he found his billet in the barracks he discovered he was completely alone, the rest of the battalion were out searching for the escaped prisoners. For his first few days it was as if he had been transported back in time off the Azores in the Atlantic Ocean to December 1872 and boarded the American merchant brigantine 'Mary Celeste' to find everything in place and no- one there. The first soldier he met in barracks was scruffy, dirty and unshaven after days on patrol. Nickname Bin-Man, he was a short ugly soldier with a large flattened nose and a nasal accent, David was speedily put in his place-as he discovered he had inadvertently bedded down in the senior NCO's and Corporals Quarters.

Adjusting to life in Northern Ireland during 'The Troubles' was a far cry from 'civvy street' at home. David explains "The first job I ever did as a fully pledged soldier was to escort a transit van full of weapons to Belfast. Issued with a 9mm Browning pistol with ten rounds of ammunition which the Army deemed sufficient, as unfortunately the weapon was liable to jam if fully loaded with thirteen rounds. Travelling to Belfast pistols were kept out of sight while passing through Royal Ulster Constabulary road blocks. Not unnaturally the RUC could be trigger happy is they spotted men with weapons. The Ambush Drill when travelling was if attacked to get out of the vehicle and run as hard as you can, firing in the general direction of the ambush and pray you can make it to the nearest ditch. But that was unlikely, in a good, well drilled and executed ambush, you have no chance of survival. I felt like a fish out of water all the way there and all the way back!"

Live firing practice on the camp ranges familiarised the soldiers with all manner of different weapons. Firstly, the Belgian FN General Purpose Machine Gun (GPMG's) developed by Fabrique Nationale for automatic fire support. It could be carried by an individual operator via a shoulder strap while on patrol, set up in the fire support role on a folding bipod, used to protect positions by using a heavy- duty tripod or mounted on vehicles in a traditional way and used for the suppression of enemy fire.

Soldiers were trained to use the rifle as an extension of the arm to allow free movement. During training they often carried a Light Support Weapon, a converted Bren Gun firing 7.62 rounds. When in a city they carried DONK guns that fired rubber bullets. The DONK manufactured by Webley and Scott was a break action single shot gun with a fixed metal stock and a Webley and Scott handgrip.

David on patrol in Bandit Country

Another weapon used extensively by the Americans during the Vietnam War, the M79 a single shot shoulder fired shotgun shaped Grenade Launcher commonly called 'The Thumper' because of the distinctive sound of the recoil. It offers accurate maximum mortar firepower for an individual, can also fire buckshot, smoke and teargas and, is simple to use and easy to load making it an ideal Squad automated weapon.

David had no problem handling the range of weapons necessary, as a boy he had been interested in guns, then after leaving school he had spent six months work experience in the Armoury at RAF Chivenor in North Devon near his home. He had spent a lot of time scrubbing cannons, mainly the Aden belt-fed Cannon first produced in 1953 by the Royal Small Arms Factory in Enfield. Though integral as a built-in armament to a wide range of aircraft 30% of the cannons he worked on were for the Hawker Hunter.

Fresh from the quiet beauty of the West Country, the urban areas David patrolled in 1983 were horrible places, dark and grubby, in close proximity to the rural 'Bandit Country' of South Armagh. Off duty David rarely left camp, on or off patrol leaving the camp was nerve wracking, the moment of maximum danger, opening the gates with no idea whether there was likely to be an ambush or a sniper outside.

David remembers his first tour of Crossmaglen in October 1983. "We flew in

THROUGH FIRE, SHOT AND SHELL

by helicopter and had to spend a week in the small market town of Crossmaglen right on the edge of the border. Our job was only to patrol Crossmaglen and its surrounding areas from RUC station. My first patrol on the day after we arrived to familiarise ourselves with the area was an early start at 3am. I felt vulnerable as the big heavy metal gate of the RUC station clanked open to expose the outer barrier of security bollards. We were all wearing patrol gloves with padded knuckles and Enabia Vests, Kevlar jackets with plates back and front to protect the heart that would stop a 9mm round. We heard the odd dog barking but saw no-one as our platoon led by Lance Corporal Steve Taverner patrolled the town.

Our second patrol on 26th October was in daylight, it was made up of five X four-man teams called a brick, each brick commanded by a senior rank or a senior private. We left the RUC station at noon, cutting through the outskirts and approached the town centre. As we got into the square where the RUC station was I noticed a young lad in a green anorak, his fur lined hood obscuring his face, hurrying along the on the opposite side of the street. Going in the opposite direction I glimpsed blue Saab, it passed too quickly for me to see the driver.

The whole platoon passed a red Ford Escort parked in the square and the rest of the teams went inside the station. There were four of us covering them from the rear. Steve Taverner was ahead of us with Nigs (Jeremy Richards), my mate Smudge (Brian Smith} and I were further back. Steve must have noticed something, or perhaps he was just curious, so he approached the car, suddenly there was a huge explosion, glass shattered, there was a plume of smoke and fragments of metal everywhere. I saw bits of the chassis heading towards us, I grabbed Smudge and pulled him behind cover. In the immediate aftermath of the explosion time stood still. Around the corner was a butcher's shop, as I looked to one side I saw the window was smashed, two young girls, one about twelve, the other nine or so, crying! The older girl was pulling the younger, I will never forget her expression as she looked at me, it was a mixture of fear and hatred!

Smudge ran towards Steve who was laying on his stomach on the ground with his boots on fire. I followed and was relieved to see he appeared to be intact, that he had both arms and legs, then I noticed his legs were bare, his trousers were gone. Unlike the rest of us who had been wearing thicker combat trousers he had been wearing light jungle trousers which offered no protection.

Then I saw he was badly burned, he had horrendous injuries to his face and head. His combat jacket was on fire and we had no water. Because Steve had told me we were going to 'hard target' (moving fast) I had not taken much water on patrol as it was an additional weight. I took off my jacket to smother the flames, checked on Nigs who had a huge chunk of metal embedded in one leg and was hobbling around. We waited for help to appear from the station which was only about 50 -100 metres away. We realised that we were on our own, that help would only come after it had been ascertained the danger was over. I have never felt so alone in my life!

We tried to comfort the injured men, Steve was in shock, he was trying to talk but having difficulty breathing, we knew that burns caused swelling, his neck looked puffy and we were afraid that his throat would close, we had a tube with a U bend mouthpiece and tried to get him to open his mouth so we could open his airway. His teeth were clenched and despite our best efforts we were unable to get the tube into his mouth.

Eventually, after what seemed ages, but was probably about fifteen minutes help arrived in the form of an armoured Pig painted white with a red cross on it and someone ran to get water. The Medical sergeant too one look at Steve and promptly threw up. His medical orderly, a private in the Guards attended to Steve, Smudge assisted the orderly in attempting to give morphine and with the tracheostomy to help Steve breathe. While this was happening, I was covering the road where we had just come from for possible threats, as the rest of the team came across the square to help. Steve was helicoptered from the RUC station to the hospital.

A Catholic Priest came across the road and asked if anyone needed Last Rites. He was only interested in civilian casualties, when he saw it was injured soldiers he didn't want to know.

For many years I had been racked with guilt that I did not have a full water bottle, it wasn't until a chance reunion with Smudge that we talked at length about the whole incident that he told me that it would not have made a difference, another half a bottle of water would not have saved Steve."

Lance Corporal Stephen William Taverner   24463879 Devon and Dorset Regiment suffered 86% burns. He died of wounds aged twenty-four on 5th November 1983.

This was a reality check for Private David North who had been on his first daylight patrol. He could never again cross the square without reliving the events of that afternoon in October. Even today- thirty -five years later he is traumatised by what happened in Crossmaglen. The only person he has ever really talked about it until now is to Smudge, who was there.

Nigs was awarded The Queen's Gallantry Medal (for gallantry " not in the face of the enemy") for his actions that afternoon.

David has been haunted not only by what happened but puzzled to why the bomb had not gone off earlier? A three-quarters of the patrol had passed the car with two guys walking side by side. Why wait to detonate the Improvised Explosive Device when there were so few soldiers in harm's way. As well as the Devonshire and Dorset Regiment there was a Coldstream Guard platoon billeted there as well. Was the IED meant for them and but for a sharp-eyed Lance Corporal who stopped to check, the car bomb would have been remotely detonated when it could claim more lives.

David recalled that three weeks before he was killed Steve had been on a Gunner Orientation exercise with a four-man team. One of the soldiers, Jimmy J had been unsuccessfully attempting to get through a hedgerow with is General Purpose Machine Gun because his sling was improperly positioned. When told to adjust it the Jimmy J. completely lost plot. He screamed at Steve "Fuck you and fuck the army" throwing down his weapon and pulling off his jacket he took off down the field with Steve in hot pursuit. David vividly remembers how he and Smudge looked at each other when before Steve set off he said "If he goes for that GPMG shoot him." Jimmy J was dismissed from the army. David North never forgot how weird it was to watch a man totally lose control.

BERLIN 1985 – 1987

In March 1985 the regiment was posted to Berlin. Even during the Cold War, it must have been a great relief to escape the tension of Northern Ireland. They flew into RAF Gatow, constructed for the Luftwaffe as a Staff and technical college in the mid 1930's. In April 1945 the airfield was occupied by the advancing Red Army who turned it over to the British after the Potsdam Conference when Berlin was divided into four sectors. In June 1945, 284 Field Squadron, RAF Regiment arrived through Magdeburg to a hostile reception from the Soviet troops. RAF Getow played a key role in the Berlin Airlift of 1948, it was the only known operational base for flying boats in central Europe during the Berlin Blockade.

West Berlin made a very different impression on David that Ireland had. It was an immaculately clean city, without graffiti or rubbish. There were four men to a room in Brook Barracks accommodation, the place was and spacious, with double glazed windows.

"My first Christmas in Berlin to my delight it snowed, to me this was the icing on the cake, it really felt like Christmas! I was selected to do guard duty which meant a twenty-four-hour guard of the camp and its surrounding perimeter, my duty started at 1800 and finished at 1800 the following day. I was selected to guard the front gate, during the night the gates were closed. When I entered the guard room where the guard commander sat I noticed a set of red mittens, a red hat and a white beard on his desk, this was going to be the new gate guard uniform. After much ridicule from my fellow comrades I stood guard.

About an hour into my two-hour duty I noticed out of the corner of my eye, cruising at a slower pace than a normal car, a large olive-green saloon with a big red star on its bonnet and on the driver's door, with four bored Russian soldiers inside. Under the 1947 agreement with the Soviet Union, SMLM (Soviet Military Liaison Mission) were allowed to travel anywhere in West Germany including West Berlin, except for areas specifically marked as being off limits. This was also the case for the other three Occupying Powers. As they drew level with the gate, I stood close to it in my Santa Claus outfit, grinning like a Cheshire Cat waving merrily at the bewildered Russian foe as they stared in stone faced puzzlement. The car never returned but I hope they managed to get a quick photo of me, but I don't think so! At least I brightened up someone's rather dull day and it must have caused amusement when they wrote up their report!"

David loves history and he felt that Berlin oozed culture. One of his most memorable experiences was to walk up the steps to the Zoological gardens at 9pm in the darkness and look at the lights and the people. The two years he spent there were the best two years of his army life. In his first week he was able to go through Checkpoint Charlie into East Berlin, pulling into a Soviet camp for his first sight of Russian soldiers in uniform.

He was able to take trips into the Eastern Sector when off duty. Groups of six to eight young soldiers wearing their dress uniform (No.2's) would cross the border, always with a sense of being followed! 1 West German Mark was worth 5 East German Marks so their money went a long way. In East Berlin restaurants they could have a four- course meal the menu consisted of boiled egg topped off with caviar, steak, champagne, and cigars, all for the equivalent of £3.50. As they walked back into the Western Sector they would throw their remaining East German Marks into the air!

From a high point at the far end of Spandau it was possible to see a hill outside the city made up of rubble from, WW2. When it snowed over Christmas the soldiers would queue with wooden sledges to go up and down the hill. From the vantage point at the top they had a good view into East Germany, to the watchtowers, mine fields, barbed wire fences and dogs.

One of the duties of the British Army of the Rhine (BOAR) was to take over the responsibility for guarding Spandau Prison every four months. By 1985 only one solitary prisoner was in the building, Rudolph Hess who had been incarcerated after the Nuremburg trials of Nazi War criminals thirty- eight years before. Hess had been fifty-three when he entered the prison with six other prominent Nazi's, all to serve sentences from between ten years to life. Erich Raeder, Walther Funk and Rudolph Hess Had all received maximum sentences, but both other men had been released early, Raeder in 1955 and Funk in 1957. Albert Speer and Baldur von Schirach who were serving twenty years were released in September 1966, Raeder in 1955 and Funk in 1957. For the next twenty-one years Hess was alone except for staff and guards. He died 17th August 1987 aged ninety-one.

David describes Spandau as he first saw it in 1985 as a mostly derelict prison made of bright red brick. The only habitable part housed Hess. The British changed with the Americans, providing a platoon strength guard housed in very basic accommodation, with a bed and their own a small cookhouse.

From a door in the building there was an edged gravel path leading into a large garden with a scattering of derelict buildings. Each day Hess would come out for a period exercise wearing a camel coloured Naval duffel coat and shuffled very slowly on two sticks. He had his own chef and his own doctor whether they changed in rotation or they were a constant is uncertain.

When Hess was taken ill with a suspected heart problem he was rushed to the secure British Military Hospital. David was one of the British soldiers who surrounded the hospital while Hess was a patient. He had the whole floor of the hospital which was secured for the two weeks was there. A guard checked everyone's identity cards irrespective of rank. High ranking officers from Russia, France and Britain all came to visit. When a Russian General arrived, he was offended when David required identification while the British General stood outside the door yelling to be let in!

THROUGH FIRE, SHOT AND SHELL

On patrol in Northern Ireland

With Trabant in Berlin

Spandau had six watch towers with tower number three overlooking the portacabin where Hess committed suicide by hanging himself with an electrical extension cord 17th August 1987. David remembers that that the portacabin was like a sun house and the guards on the watchtower had a good view into the interior. Having read through the comprehensive Military Special Investigation Branch Reports available on the web there seems no doubt that despite age and infirmity Hess had succeeded at his 3rd suicide attempt. On 26th November 1959 and 22nd February 1977, he had attempted suicide by cutting his left wrist.

When exercising some of his guards would allow Hess some time alone in the summerhouse, to read or rest, never leaving him alone for long periods. The extension lead was used for a pair of standard lamps, it had been fastened to a rear window. The Post Mortem Report performed by a Professor of Forensic Medicine from University of London concludes from his examination of the body that the linear mark on the left side of the neck is consistent with ligature and that Hess died from Asphyxia. External marks on the body were evidence of energetic cardiac resuscitation.

THE FALKLANDS - 1987

After Berlin the Battalion were posted back to the UK to Bulford before spending four months in the Falklands arriving in June 1987. It was early autumn in the South Atlantic, David had flown from Britain in a Tristar to the barren, lava rock that was Ascension Island, before landing at the huge air base that was Mount Pleasant, better known as 'concrete city.' For the only time in his army career David enjoyed the luxury of a single man's room, small with just a bed, a cabinet and a window but blissfully private and warm. It was only the mobile section (David was a driver) who were allocated single rooms during this tour.

The barracks were made of concrete, dingy with a long main corridor, a NAAFI, a Gym and a Cookhouse, the latter a long way from the main building. When not on patrol the soldiers were bored, there was radio and videos but no television as there was no signal. When off duty the men would meet in the Gym to play football or cricket, and maybe have a couple of beers. There were no bars, no entertainment and no eligible girls.

To go on patrol the soldiers were helicoptered to a remote location- (everywhere was remote,) land to patrol for a short period in a treeless landscape and hope to find a barn to shelter from the strong wind. The terrain was difficult to walk on, full of 'elephants' feet' large clumps of grass that grew close together so it was easy to catch your ankle between the clumps.

THROUGH FIRE, SHOT AND SHELL

With penguins in the Falklands

On one patrol they were left for three days on an island with just one farm and a two to three story barn that was used for sheep. The farmer allowed the platoon to sleep in the building which smelt of the sheep. To alleviate their boredom the patrol devised a game of off the ground tig, the idea for one person to move in the pitch black and to catch the others who would escape by clinging to posts and rails to stay elevated.

When they were in a settlement, normally just a small cluster of houses, one of the houses would usually have a bar either in their house or barn, where the neighbours would visit for a drink or a party. David recalls that there were hardly any women, and those there were were either old or middle-aged. The settlers had weird accents that sounded Australian. He got the impression that while the Islanders were grateful to get their country back they had become irritated by the presence of the military and would be glad to see them go.

KENYA - 1989

By the end 1988 David's six- year period of enlistment was coming to an end. In mid-January 1989 after the Christmas leave the Battalion would be leaving for a six-week short term training tour of Kenya. David, together with about ten other soldiers who were due to leave the army would be segregated, left behind as the rear party for a period of continuous guard duty while the rest of the Battalion were away. In conversation with his father David expressed his frustration that he would be missing out on the opportunity to travel to Africa, his father advised him to request to go along. David approached his Sgt Major who promised to speak to the Commanding Officer, Major H. who had been his OC in Northern Ireland. The Major needed a driver so when the Battalion flew to Nairobi David was the only one of his group to go along. From the airport the Battalion boarded coaches to the residential army base for a few days to get acclimatised before each of the three companies began the period of rotation, living in the field, alternating in three different areas for live firing exercises.

David was stationed at HQ, driving the OC along "bloody awful hot, dusty roads full of huge potholes. The local drivers had no sense of road safety, they drove all over the place, I hated driving at night because they drove without lights and walked in the middle of the road. One day we were on a dirt road when we passed a young girl carrying a jerry can full of water on her shoulder strapped across her back. We stopped to give her a lift, I couldn't lift the jerrycan off her shoulder- it was so heavy!

Another day driving along a dirt road we hit tarmac, a little further on I saw the

Presidential Palace with black Mercedes Benz vehicles in the drive. I learned that two miles on either side of the Palace there were made-up roads. Just beyond the tarmac there was a shanty town and people living in extreme poverty- they had nothing.

One day the Sgt Major sent me off with a Kenyan soldier to take rations out as a goodwill gesture. We pulled up in the middle of nowhere where a man, his wife and two children, one a babe in arms, lived in two mud huts. The huts were surrounded by a boma, a prickly enclosure which also acted as a stockade for his livestock. I went into one of the huts, all the family had was a rug, a stool, a spoon and a bowl, yet the man was happy. It made me even more aware of how privileged I was.

I did do three days of jungle training while I was in country. We were taken to a dense forest where the SAS trained us. They warned us about the huge rats- as big as cats. Food was stored in large tin cans; the rats would carry the cans away and gnaw through them with their strong teeth. Our first night was sleepless as we stayed awake in our bivouacs armed with stout sticks.

There were about 20 curious young squaddies, on one of the odd times we had off while in Kenya the Company was asked if we would like to visit a snake farm, run by an English couple. It was a small ram-shackled place with a couple of buildings and covered areas. Most interesting to us were the glass cases around a covered area with about 30 or so venomous snakes, most fascinating was the spiting cobra where most of us annoyed It by tapping at the glass and watching it rear up and spit at the glass. The lady owner was quite pleased to see us, giving us a quick tour of the place and began with telling us what they did (collecting venom for anti-venom vaccines for snake bites) I felt she was waffling a little when she mentioned she had been bitten by all the venomous snakes in Africa and still alive to tell the tail. At this point she showed us two class tanks which held two (more or less) identical snakes, one being poisonous the other not. In that instant she dipped her hand into a tank and proceeded to extract a two-foot-long snake by its tail. Now I'm no snake expert but common sense tells me you should never pick a snake up by its tail. And why this lady did I shall never know, but the snake did not take too kindly to being picked up, and to show his appreciation he bit her between the thumb and index finger. She dropped the snake, and before the snake had even touched the ground we all had made a 'tactical retreat' (in other words, ran for our lives/) The snake was promptly caught by the woman and placed back into its glass case and with that, we gingerly returned to the scene. Before our eyes the woman began to shake quite visibly, we quickly got her a chair and an assistant was called to fetch her husband.

257

The concerned husband turned up and their Land Rover was called for, we presumed to take her to hospital but NO, jump leads were quickly fitted to the battery and the husband began to give the woman electric shocks to the hand. Forty pairs of fascinated eyes looked on as the Land Rover delivered the treatment. At this point we were ushered away never to see the woman again. We later found out she was fine, it was the none-poisonous snake, but it was quite odd that the 'experienced' snake woman picked the snake up from the wrong end. So, there's a valuable lesson to be learnt here and that is 'Don't pick an arsey snake up by its rear end'.

I had a period of R & R, visiting Mombasa then staying in a hut by the beach for five days. The camp was guarded and was supposed to be secure, we were told it was safe to leave things in the huts. On the second or third night there was a break in and wallets, money, ID cards and passports were stolen. Luckily, I had my passport with me but I lost my wallet with my ID card in it. If you lost your ID card you were always in a lot of trouble. When I got back to England I explained the situation, the security guards had told us the camp was secure but I still got fined £50! A fitting end to an army career!

Kenya was an amazing place, to drive through plains teeming with wild life, to see giraffes and zebras in the wild was mind boggling. When I was at a holiday resort used by the army, a Lodge surrounded by a low wall with a helicopter pad in the grounds I actually came upon a crocodile. How many people can say that!"

Northern Ireland proved a baptism of fire, it also shaped a raw recruit into a capable soldier who can look back on his six years in the Army as the most influential and positive time of his life. It helped his confidence and encouraged his resourcefulness and it allowed him to live in foreign countries at the Governments expense and to experience places he would never have had the opportunity to visit.

NOTES:
    CO   **Commanding Officer** *of a Battalion*
    OC   **Officer Commanding** *Company Commander*

SPANDAU PRISON
Was constructed initially as a military detention centre in 1876. From 1919 it was also used for civilian inmates holding up to 600 prisoners at a time. In 1933 the prison held opponents of Hitler who were tortured and abused by the Gestapo while in 'protective custody.'. At the end of that year when the first Nazi concentration camps were built all

prisoners held in state prisons in so called 'protective custody' were transferred to the camps.

At the end of WWII, it was operated by the Four Allied Powers to house Nazi war criminals sentenced after the Nuremberg trials. On 18th July 1947 seven men were imprisoned there.

Karl Donitz *convicted of crimes against peace and war crimes sentenced to 10 years released early September 1956*

Konstantin von Neurath *convicted of war crimes sentenced 15 years released early November 1954*

Albert Speer *found guilty of crimes against humanity and war crimes sentenced, 20 years released early September 1966*

Baldur von Schirach *found guilty of against peace, war crimes and waging a war of aggression sentenced 20 years, released September 1966*

Erich Raeder *found guilty of waging aggressive war sentenced Life, released early September 1955*

Walther Funk *charged and found guilty of crimes against peace, crimes against humanity and war crimes sentenced Life   released early May 1957*

Rudolph Hess *conspiracy to wage a war of aggression and crimes against peace, convicted of sentenced Life died in prison 17th August 1987 aged 93.*

Only four fully served their sentences, Neurath, Raeder and Funk were released early on grounds of ill health. Hess was the only prisoner in Spandau between 1966 and his death in 1987. The prison was demolished that year to prevent it becoming a Nazi shrine.

All four powers had to agree to release Hess and close Spandau. America, Britain and France had petitioned to release the lone prisoner in the latter years on humanitarian grounds. The Soviets insisted he serve out his sentence until his death.

BY THE SAME AUTHOR

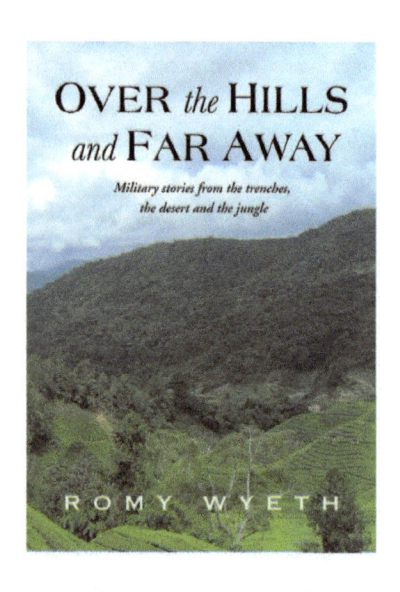

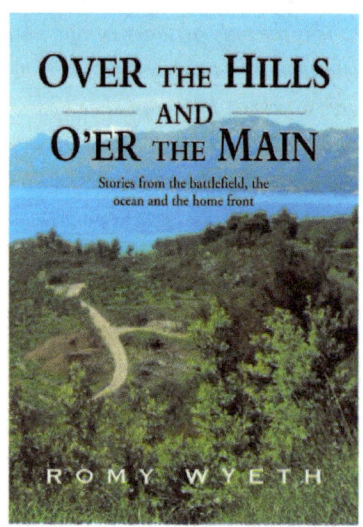

OVER *the* HILLS and FAR AWAY

Military stories from the trenches, the desert and the jungle

ROMY WYETH

OVER THE HILLS AND O'ER THE MAIN

Stories from the battlefield, the ocean and the home front

ROMY WYETH

2007

2002

THE MEN OF ST MARY'S
&
THE ANZAC WAR GRAVES

The Parish Church of St Mary
Codford, Wiltshire

2013

The Parish Church of St Peter
Codford, Wiltshire

War Memorials

2012

2005

1997

1995

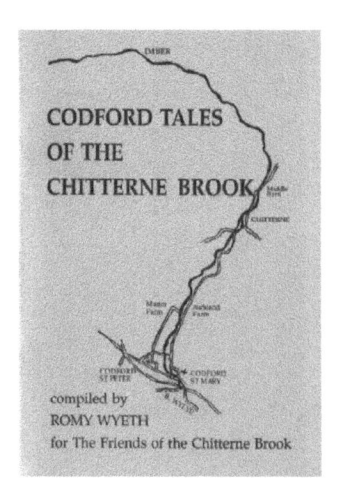

1994